William Ross Wallace

Patriotic and heroic eloquence

A book for the patriot, statesman and student

William Ross Wallace

Patriotic and heroic eloquence
A book for the patriot, statesman and student

ISBN/EAN: 9783337196516

Printed in Europe, USA, Canada, Australia, Japan

Cover: Foto ©Andreas Hilbeck / pixelio.de

More available books at **www.hansebooks.com**

PATRIOTIC AND HEROIC

ELOQUENCE:

A BOOK FOR THE

PATRIOT, STATESMAN, AND STUDENT.

"I speak to you as American citizens having a voice—and that a potential one—in deciding the destinies of our common country, and as men acknowledging your final responsibility to God."
Hon. Salmon P. Chase.

"America! Home of the free!
'Tis thy dear starry emblem that holds
The enchantment that binds us to thee—
All our fortunes with thine in its folds!
On the wretch who its honor or glory would pall,
Shall the lightning-winged vengeance of patriots fall."

NEW YORK
JAMES G. GREGORY,
(SUCCESSOR TO W. A. TOWNSEND & CO.,)
46 WALKER STREET.
1861.

Entered according to Act of Congress, in the year 1861,

By JAMES G. GREGORY,

In the Clerk's Office of the District Court of the United States, for the Southern District of New York.

C. A. ALVORD, STEREOTYPER AND PRINTER.

CONTENTS.

	PAGE.
PRELUDE.................... .... *John Savage.*	7
PERPETUITY OF THE AMERICAN UNION................ *Webster.*	11
THE UNITED STATES FLAG, 1861.................... *Wallace.*	13
SPEECH AT THE GREAT UNION MEETING IN UNION SQUARE, N. Y. CITY, 1861. ....*Shaffer.*	14
THE NEW YEAR AND THE UNION....................*Prentice.*	21
DUTIES OF AMERICAN CITIZENS.................... *Chandler.*	22
ON LAYING THE CORNER STONE OF THE BUNKER HILL MONUMENT. *Webster.*	24
THE SWORD OF BUNKER HILL....................... *Wallace.*	26
SPEECH ON PRESENTING A UNITED STATES FLAG...... *Waterbury.*	27
PERPETUITY OF THE UNION........................ *Rosseau.*	28
DEEDS, NOT WORDS................................ *Field.*	29
SOLDIER'S DIRGE................................ *O'Hara.*	31
THROUGH FOEMEN SURROUNDING,........................	32
NO SECESSION FROM THE UNION..................... *Motley.*	32
EULOGY ON GENERAL ANDREW JACKSON........... *B. F. Butler.*	35
THE GLORY OF THE HERO AND PATRIOT............... *Moore.*	37
CHARACTER OF WARREN........................... *Magoon.*	38
WARREN'S ADDRESS .... *Pierpont.*	39
THE BATTLE OF LEXINGTON........................ *Holmes.*	40
MORAL AND REPUBLICAN PRINCIPLES NOT TO BE ABANDONED. *Everett.*	42
THE FALCON..................................... *Lowell.*	43
CHARACTER OF DANIEL WEBSTER...... .... *Seward.*	43
ODE FOR THE METROPOLITAN OBSEQUIES OF WEBSTER.... *Wallace.*	45
AMERICA.. .... *Phillips.*	48
WAR QUESTIONS TO COL. C. M. CLAY................ *Wallace.*	49
DEATH OF J. Q. ADAMS.......................... *Seward.*	50

CONTENTS.

	PAGE
RIENZI TO THE ROMANS............................*Moore.*	51
SPEECH OF MACBRIAR TO THE SCOTCH INSURGENTS.........*Scott.*	53
REBELLION TO BE PUT DOWN—THE NATION TO BE SAVED....*Holt.*	54
MARTIAL ELEGY.........................*Tyrtæus.*	57
SPEECH AT THE GREAT AMERICAN UNION MEETING, MAY, 1861, IN PARIS, FRANCE....................*C. M. Clay.*	58
SPEECH AT THE SAME MEETING....................*Fremont.*	61
EXTRACT FROM A SPEECH AT THE UNION MEETING IN UNION SQUARE, NEW YORK, 1861.........................*Dix.*	63
WORDS FOR THE HOUR...........................*Ottarson.*	64
PATRIOTIC DUTY OF THE PRESENT GENERATION..........*Evarts.*	65
CALL TO ARMS.......................*Lyon.*	66
THE REVOLUTIONARY BATTLE OF EUTAW..............*Simms.*	67
WASHINGTON TO BE DEFENDED—SECESSION TO BE CRUSHED. *Raymond.*	70
IT IS GREAT FOR OUR COUNTRY TO DIE................*Percival.*	72
THE UNITED STATES SUPERIOR TO A SINGLE STATE ......*Mitchell.*	72
THE MOTHERS OF OUR FOREST LAND...............*Gallagher.*	75
ADDRESS TO THE GRADUATING CLASS OF COLUMBIA COLLEGE. *President King.*	77
COMMODORE PERRY AFTER THE BATTLE OF LAKE ERIE...*Bancroft.*	79
CRIMINALITY OF TREASON..................*N. Y. Evening Post.*	82
THE AMERICAN STATESMAN AND LITERATURE..................	85
CHARACTER OF WILLIAM PENN...................*Duponceau.*	86
COLUMBIA.........................*Elliott.*	88
THE PRESIDENT OF THE UNITED STATES—WHAT HE OUGHT TO BE. *McLane.*	89
TRUE DIGNITY..........................*Owen Jones.*	91
CHARACTER OF GENERAL WINFIELD SCOTT............*Headley.*	92
THE PATRIOT'S BATTLE PRAYER......................*Prince.*	94
ADDRESS TO THE U. S. HOUSE OF REPRESENTATIVES.......*Grow.*	96
THE MYRTLE AND STEEL...........................*Hoffman.*	100
THE FUGITIVE LIEUTENANT ....*N. Y. Ledger.*	100
DECISIVE INTEGRITY............................*Wirt.*	108
EULOGIUM ON THE CAPTORS OF MAJOR ANDRE.........*Raymond.*	110
THE NATIONAL FLAG.......................*N. Y. Ledger.*	112

CONTENTS.

		PAGE.
UPWARD! ONWARD!	John H. Bryant.	114
OUR COUNTRY	Webster.	115
NEW ENGLAND AND THE UNION (1846)	Hamlin.	117
THE CHARTER OAK	Prentice.	118
CHARACTER OF THE DISUNIONISTS (1861)	Holt.	119
PROPHECY OF FREEDOM	Prentice.	123
KENTUCKY AND THE DISUNIONISTS (1861)	Holt.	124
THE SAME SUBJECT CONTINUED	Holt.	129
ITALY	Bryant.	131
EXTRACTS FROM AN ADDRESS, JULY 4TH, 1861	Jay.	133
ON THE DEATH OF LIEUTENANT CHARLES G. HUNTER, U. S. N.	Tuel.	138
REPUBLICAN GOVERNMENT	N. Y. Ledger.	140
RECITATIVE AND SONG OF THE UNION	Bourne.	142
CHARACTER OF WASHINGTON	Ames.	145
SWORD CHANT	Motherwell.	148
NATIONAL RECOLLECTIONS THE FOUNDATION OF NATIONAL CHARACTER	Everett.	150
NOT YET	Bryant.	153
TOMB OF WASHINGTON	Joseph W. Savage.	154
O LAND OF HAPPY HEARTS AND HOMES	W. A. Butler.	157
ADAMS AND JEFFERSON	Webster.	158
THE TIDES	Bryant.	160
EULOGIUM ON A DECEASED PATRIOT	Meagher.	161
GEORGE WASHINGTON	Upham.	163
DEATH OF GERTRUDE AND THE LAMENT OF OUTALISSI	Campbell.	166
EFFECTS OF A DISSOLUTION OF THE FEDERAL UNION	Hamilton.	168
FREEDOM'S BIRTH	Moses.	172
REFLECTIONS ON THE BATTLE OF LEXINGTON	Everett.	173
APPEAL IN FAVOR OF THE UNION	Madison.	175
IN MEMORY OF THE HEROIC CAPTAIN HERNDON		177
CHARACTER OF HAMILTON	Ames.	179
THE CRUEL CASE OF COL. PEGRAM	N. Y. Tribune.	182
EXTRACT FROM A SPEECH DELIVERED IN THE U. S. SENATE, JULY 27TH, 1861	Johnson.	186
FREEDOM OF THE ANCIENT ISRAELITES	Croly.	189

CONTENTS.

		PAGE
RESISTANCE TO TYRANNY	*Henry.*	191
THE LIBERTY BELL	*Wallace.*	194
THE SOLEMN DUTY OF THE U. S. GOVERNMENT	*Louisville Journal.*	196
WHO IS RESPONSIBLE FOR THE SLAVERY AGITATION?		201
TRUTH AND FREEDOM	*Gallagher.*	203
GEORGE WILKES'S DESCRIPTION OF THE BATTLE OF BULL RUN,	*N. Y. Ledger.*	205
THE PIONEERS	*C. A. Jones.*	207
THE MEN TO MAKE A STATE: THEIR MAKING AND THEIR MARKS.	*Doane.*	209
THE GREEK REVOLUTION	*Henry Clay.*	214
EULOGY ON HENRY CLAY	*John B. Fry.*	218
WHAT IS LIFE	*Drake.*	220
A SEA FIGHT	*Cooper.*	222
GOD BLESS OUR STARS	*B. F. Taylor.*	232
GENERAL LYON		234
BURNING OF A SHIP	*Cooper.*	235
HEROIC SPEECH, 1861	*General B. F. Butler.*	248
WAR POEM	*Croly.*	251
THE CONSTITUTION	*Bunce.*	252
SANGUINARIA CANADENSIS	*Benton.*	255
EXTRACT FROM A SPEECH ON THE EXTENSION OF SLAVERY.	*W. H. Fry.*	256
REVOLUTIONARY STORY	*Alice Cary.*	257
VOICE OF THE NORTHERN WOMEN	*Phebe Cary.*	260
INJUSTICE OF SECESSION	*President Lincoln.*	261
L'ENVOI—A PSALM OF THE UNION	*Wallace.*	263

PRELUDE.

WASHINGTON.*—*John Savage.*

ART in its mighty privilege receives
   Painter and painted in its bonds forever;
A girl by Raphael in his glory lives—
A Washington unto his limner gives
   The Ages' love to crown his best endeavor.

The German Emperor, with whose counterpart
   The gorgeous Titian made the world acquainted,
Boasted himself immortal by the art:
But he who on *thy* features cast his heart
   Was made immortal by the head he painted!

For thou before whose tinted shade I bow,
   Wert sent to show the wise of every nation
How a young world might leave the axe and plough
To die for Truth! So great, so loved wert thou,
   That he who touched thee won a reputation.

* Written upon contemplating Stuart's portrait in the Boston Athenæum.

The steady fire that battled in thy breast,
   Lit up our gloom with radiance, good though gory;
Like some red sun which the dull earth caressed
Into a wealthy adoration, blest
   To be its glory's great reflected glory.

Thou—when the earthly heaven of man's soul—
   The heaven of home, of liberty, of honor—
Shuddered with darkness—didst the clouds uproll
And burst such light upon the nation's dole
   That every state still feels thy breath upon her.

Could I have seen thee in the council—bland,
   Firm as a rock, but as deep stream thy manner;
Or when at trembling Liberty's command,
Facing grim havoc like a flag-staff, stand,
   And squadrons rolling round thee like a banner!

Could I have been with thee on Princeton's morn!
   Or swelled with silence in the midnight muster;
Beheld thee ever, every fate adorn—
Or on retreat, or winged victory borne—
   The warrior throbbing with the sage's lustre:

Could I have shouted in the wild acclaim
   That rent the sky o'er Germantown asunder;
Or when, like cataract, 'gainst the sheeted flame
You dashed, and chilled the victor-shout to shame
   On Monmouth's day of palsy-giving thunder:

PRELUDE.

Could I have followed thee through town and camp!
    Fought where you led, and heard the same drums rattle;
Charged with a wild, but passion-steadied tramp,
And witnessed, rising o'er death's ghastly damp,
    The stars of empire through the clouds of battle!—

Oh! to have died thus 'neath thy hero-gaze,
    And won a smile, my bursting youth would rather,
Than to have lived with every other praise,
Saving the blessing of those epic days
    When you blest all, and were the nation's father.

The autumn sun caresses Vernon's tomb,
    Whose presence doth the country's honor leaven:
Two suns they are, that dissipate man's gloom;
For one's the index to Earth's freeborn bloom,
    The other to our burning hope in Heaven!

Thy dust may moulder in the hollow rock;
    But every day thy soul makes some new capture!
Nations unborn will swell thy thankful flock,
And Fancy tremble that she cannot mock
    Thy history's Truth that will enchant with rapture.

How vain the daring to compute in words
    The height of homage that the heart would render!
And yet how proud—to feel no speech affords
Harmonious measure to the subtle chords
    That fill the soul beneath thy placid splendor!

PATRIOTIC AND HEROIC ELOQUENCE.

Perpetuity of the American Union.—*Hon. Daniel Webster.*

I PROFESS, sir, in my career hitherto, to have kept steadily in view the prosperity and honor of the whole country, and the preservation of our federal Union. It is to that Union we owe our safety at home, and our consideration and dignity abroad. It is to that Union that we are chiefly indebted for whatever makes us most proud of our country. That Union we reached only by the discipline of our virtues in the severe school of adversity. It had its origin in the necessities of disordered finance, prostrate commerce, and ruined credit. Under its benign influences these great interests awoke, as if from the dead, and sprang forth with newness of life. Every year of its duration has teemed with fresh proofs of its utility and its blessings; and although our territory has stretched out wider and wider, and our population spread farther and farther, they have not outrun its protection, or its benefits. It has been to us all a copious fountain of national, social and personal happiness.

I have not allowed myself, sir, to look beyond the Union, to see what might lie hidden in the dark recess behind. I have not coolly weighed the chances of preserving liberty, when the bonds that unite us together shall be broken asunder. I have not accustomed myself to hang over the precipice of disunion, to see whether with my short sight I can fathom the depth of the abyss below; nor could I regard him as a safe counsellor in the affairs of this government, whose thoughts should be mainly bent on considering not how the Union should be best preserved, but how tolerable might be the condition of the people when it shall be broken up and destroyed.

While the Union lasts, we have high, exciting, gratifying prospects spread out before us for us and our children. Beyond that I seek not to penetrate the veil. God grant that in my day, at least, that curtain may not rise. God grant that on my vision may be never opened what lies behind. When my eyes shall be turned to behold, for the last time, the sun in heaven, may I not see him shining on the broken and dishonored fragments of a once glorious Union; on states dissevered, discordant, belligerent; on a land rent with civil feuds, or drenched, it may be, in fraternal blood! Let their last feeble and lingering glance, rather, behold the gorgeous ensign of the republic, now known and honored throughout the earth, still full high advanced, its arms and trophies streaming in their original lustre, not a stripe erased or polluted, nor a single star obscured—bearing for its motto no such miserable interrogatory as, *What is all this worth?* nor those other words of delusion and folly, *Liberty first, and Union afterward;* but everywhere, spread all over in characters of living light, blazing on all its ample folds, as they float over the sea and over the land, and in every wind under the whole heavens, that other sentiment, dear to every true American heart, LIBERTY AND UNION, NOW AND FOREVER, ONE AND INSEPARABLE!

The United States Flag—1861.—*William Ross Wallace.*

It shall not sever! No! as soon
  The sister-stars by tempest-wrack
Shall be divided in their sky,
  And darkle into chaos back.
Flag of the valiant and the tried,
Where Marion fought and Warren died!
Flag of the mountain and the lake!
  Of rivers rolling to the sea
In that broad grandeur fit to make
  The symbols of eternity!
O fairest flag! O dearest land!
  Who shall your banded children sever?
God of our fathers! here we stand,
A true, a free, a fearless band,
Heart pressed to heart, hand linked in hand,
  And swear that flag shall float forever!

Still, radiant banner of the free!
The nations turn with hope to thee:
And when thy mighty shadow falls
Along the armory's trophied walls,
The ancient trumpets long for breath;
  The dinted sabres fiercely start
To vengeance from each clanging sheath,
  As if they sought some traitor's heart!

O sacred banner of the brave!
  O standard of ten thousand ships!
O guardian of Mount Vernon's grave!
  Come, let us press thee to our lips!—
There is a heaving of the rocks—
New England feels the patriot-shocks;
There is a heaving of the lakes—
New York, with all the West, awakes;
And, lo! on high the glorious shade
  Of Washington smites back the gloom,
And points unto these words arrayed
  In fire around his tomb:

"*Americans!* YOUR FATHERS *shed*
　　THEIR BLOOD *to rear the Union's* *fane;*
For this that fearless banner spread
　　On many a gory plain!
Americans! let no one dare,
　　On mountain, valley, prairie, flood,
By hurling down that temple there,
　　To desecrate that blood!
The right shall live, while faction dies;
　　All traitors draw a fleeting breath!
But patriots drink from God's own eyes,
　　Truth's light that conquers death!"

Then, dearest flag, and dearest land!
　　Who shall your banded children sever?
God of our fathers! here we stand,
A true, a free, a fearless band,
Heart pressed to heart, hand linked in hand,
　　AND SWEAR THAT FLAG SHALL FLOAT FOREVER!

SPEECH AT THE GREAT UNION MEETING IN UNION SQUARE, NEW YORK CITY, 1861.—*Hon. Chauncey Shaffer.*

'TIS done—the climax of delusion has been attained, and "madness rules the hour."

In a time of profound peace and unwonted prosperity, when from the coasts of Maine athwart a continent to the placid waters of old Pacific, the open hand of the benevolent God has filled the nation with profusion; while the choicest treasures of ocean and of earth are seeking our shores, when our peace-propagating commerce has met a welcome reception in ports for ages closed against the ingress of civilization and Christianity; and when ambassadors from afar, and even those sprung from the loins of kings, and whose nursing-

---

* *How pure the spirit in that form enshrined.*—GOV. CHASE.

mothers queens are, cross oceans to pay their willing devotion to the wisdom of our institutions and the grandeur of our youthful proportions; in this young republic, this asylum of the oppressed and home of the enterprising, this "land of the free," this "home of the brave," where liberty herself sits enthroned—at a time too when the genius of "American liberty," civil and religious, is permeating all lands, founding in the seats of ancient empire republics modelled after our own "model republic;" when the Turk is becoming Christian, when Chinese walls are crumbling before the shock of an on-marching civilization, when serfdom is blossoming into manhood, when liberty, having crossed mountains and oceans hand in hand with Christianity, is making the circuit of the globe, and with the trump of jubilee seems about to usher in the millennial morn—here in this our own republic, not yet having made the circle of a century, what sights do we see? What sounds do we hear? Why, the highest tribunal of the republic, in emulation of the infidelity that ushered in "the French revolution," have adjudged and decreed "that God hath *not* made of one blood all nations of men for to dwell on all the face of the earth." And further, that "God hath *not* determined the times before appointed and the bounds of their habitation;" and by just deduction, that Africa is not one of the "four quarters of the globe," and that the African is not *a man* entitled to "life, liberty and the pursuit of happiness;" while, as a legitimate consequence of this decree, we hear the vice-president of the rebellious Confederacy proclaiming that "in forming the old constitution our fathers were in a great error. They believed slavery wrong, and of course intended it should not last, and *framed the old constitution* wrong to suit their wrong creed. The South [meaning the oligarchs] believe slavery right and to be perpetuated. Our new constitution is based on African slavery *as right*, and is therefore the best constitution on earth." Hear this, O Africa, and, as you "stretch your hands to God," pray for the freedom of the Arab of the desert rather than the liberty of "the Confederate Republic."

We see time-honored covenants repealed, lovers of the Union expiating their crime on the scaffold, women imprisoned for teaching the Bible, Christ's ambassadors slain with their hands upon the altar, vowing eternal fidelity to God, "the constitution, and the laws," while others (of whom the Southern Confederacy is not worthy) are wandering in exile, destitute, afflicted, tormented, while others still "have trial of cruel mockings and scourgings, yea, moreover, of bond and imprisonment." We behold the "merciless Indian savages," whose known rule of warfare is an undistinguished destruction of all ages, sexes, and conditions, summoned to a co-operation with the rebellious sons of treason; yet let us hope that they will modify the *chivalrous* mode of warfare practised by "the Confederate chivalry."

We see and hear the decree of treason proclaimed in seven confederate states, that our beneficent constitution is to be destroyed, our capital sacked, while treason, sitting enthroned amidst the ruins of a nation's temple, surrounded by the sentinel furies of rebellion, shall decree the destruction of liberty and law, of commerce and science, of the freedom of the press and of speech, the hopeless bondage of the African and the serfdom of the "poor unfortunate white man" (for think not that the lust of tyrants is satiated by the color of a skin), and the eternal "setting up of the abomination of desolation" in the holy place where Washington and Jefferson, the Adamses and a Jackson stood!

We hear the thunders of artillery proclaiming to the Spartan band within Sumter's walls that the decrees of treason are being enforced by the last argument of kings; while all around the Gulf of Mexico, the once golden bowl of a world's commerce, martial sounds are heard, blended with the warwhoop of the savage, and upon the bosom of that gulf the pirate illustrates the maxim that "dead men tell no tales." Sepoys of India, send your ambassadors to "the Confederate States of America," that they may perfectly acquire the art of Sepoy warfare! Send them not to "the aboriginal American."

It is unnecessary to declare "the causes of these things." The cause of causes is known. The fathers are gone, and their children have held the truth in unrighteousness. The fathers knew their duty, and did it as far as they could. The sons have not done their duty. The fathers decreed human slavery a curse, a cause of war against which all the attributes of Jehovah proclaimed unceasing hostility. The sons say: "Human bondage is the chief corner-stone of our republic." The fathers were filled with the Anglo-Saxon idea of liberty. The sons with the Norman idea of feudalism.

Having held the truth in unrighteousness, they have become vain in their imaginations, their foolish heart is darkened, and they are given over to a reprobate mind, and are filled with a vile ambition, wickedness, covetousness, maliciousness, deceitfulness, and malignity, together with the whole hell-brood of passions essential to make up that most hated word, "treason."

Without assuming to sit in judgment upon my fellow man, I cannot help asking, have not the authors of this great rebellion already proved themselves "despiteful, proud, boasters, inventors of evil things, without understanding, covenant-breakers, without fraternal affection [else why do they daily put to death their "kith and kin" for no other crime than fidelity to the constitution and the Union], implacable, unmerciful?"

The necessity of the case requires a remedy. The

many, who in these treasonable states have not bent the knee at the hateful shrine of discord, demand a remedy speedy and thorough; they who flee from the land of their birth and the home of their childhood demand the application of a remedy. Commerce and science, law and religion, those who in distant lands look with longing eyes to the Canaan of their hopes beyond the ocean flood, demand the speedy application of that remedy. The dignity of human nature, the voice that speaks from many a revolutionary battlefield, from Massachusetts to Georgia, voices from Mount Vernon, from Monticello, from Ashland, and the Hermitage, demand in the great name of "the Eternal" that the remedy be applied so that "the Union shall be preserved," and her banner proudly float, as in former days, "by sea and by land, not a single stripe erased, nor a star obscured," while the claims of eternal justice, as well as the voice of Him who gave us this goodly land to inherit, unite in the same demand, even though in the application of that remedy war should promulgate the Lord's fast, "even the breaking of bonds and letting the oppressed go free."

Ordinarily, the remedy is to be determined by reference to the cause of the disease. Not so here; for the cause dates far backward, beyond merely the sowing of tares by a Calhoun and his disciples. It strikes back to the darkness of the strictly feudal ages. But, admitting that the cause dates no farther backward than the gloomy year of 1832, the question still arises, "How can the evil be removed?"

When we reflect that we are now reaping the harvest of false principles sown by "the great architect of ruin;" that human slavery is right and not wrong, a blessing and not a curse; that states at their option have the right to sever the bands that bind them in fidelity to the Union, and "shoot madly from their spheres," and that in still later times, the doctrine has been promulgated and urged upon our brethren of the Confederate States (I speak of the masses, and not of the instigators), until they believe that their brethren of "the North" are no longer brethren, but enemies intent upon their political and social extinction; and when I further reflect that peace and truth have no power to invade that soil to correct that error, and prevent "the immortality of the lie," I am compelled to declare it as my firm conviction that force, physical force, the force of war, and *that alone*, is the only remedy; and, terrible as is the thought in this case, that "without the shedding of blood there can be no remission," it is nevertheless true; for treason is an awful word, as well as an awful crime.

The war, then, inaugurated by the enemies of our government must go on; the slumbers of Mount Vernon must be disturbed by the thunders of artillery. The soil of "the mother of states and of statesmen" must be drenched with fraternal blood; the head of the serpent infolded in Sumpter's flag must be bruised; and that city which was first to break the peace of the nation, by the first overt act of treason, must return to her allegiance, or from her smoking ruins the column must rise, bearing the inscription, "Charleston was," and, if need be, the fate of Charleston must be the fate of all other cities in like manner offending against our government. And that fate must be speedy—unnecessary delay in this emergency is *almost treason itself*. Think not that I say this thoughtlessly, or without due consideration. War, and most of all, civil war, is naught but horrors on horror's head accumulating. Ordinarily war arrests the wheels of civilization and hurls earth backward toward the gloom of the dark ages.

This is eminently true of unjust wars. But this law is not universal. Wars have urged onward civilization, liberty and Christianity. War has advanced the purposes of "Him who maketh the wrath of man to praise

Him." The battles of Marathon, Platæa and Salamis, not only rolled back the tide of Asiatic barbarism, but developed the heroic qualities of the republican Greek.

Leonidas and his three hundred fell at Thermopylæ, but how much benefit have law and government derived from the inscription, " Go, stranger, and declare to the Lacedæmonians that we died here in obedience to their divine laws ?" The wars of Napoleon the First filled Europe with more liberal ideas; while " the late Crimean war," which turned the cheek of commerce pale, as Northern came in collision with the civilization of Western Europe, opened the door of an empire for the ingress of religious liberty. And Magenta and Solferino are followed by like results in the land once " peeled and torn."

And may we not derive benefit from even this fratricidal war? My faith dictates an affirmative response. This opening strife may open our eyes to a contemplation of the sublime destiny to which a benevolent God invites us; may correct our characteristic faults; may develop and expand our latent virtues; may teach us that ours is a higher destiny than to " go to, and put money in our purse ;" may teach us other lessons than those of exultation over the magnitude of that republic whose shores are laved by two oceans; may impart to us a purer patriotism; may arrest a tendency supposed to exist amongst us of dishonesty in legislation and partisanship in the administration of the law; may teach us the value of constitutional liberty, by the evils which flow from anarchy and rebellion; may teach all parties in our land the duty of justice and charity in judging each other; may imprimate the power of our government, for war as well as for peace, upon the minds of other nations; and may teach one and all, at home and abroad, the power of this government to punish crime as well as to protect virtue; and thus, like the mountain oak buffeted by the storm, whose roots take a firme-hold on "the old foundation," a love for our noble constitution, our equal and just laws, for all parts, sections and divisions of our Union, may take a more lasting hold upon the nation's heart.

Nor let it be considered as the least of these advantages, the national degradation from which the coming war will save us. I mean an independent Southern slave Confederacy, extending from ocean to ocean, from the heart of the temperate zone to the Isthmus of Darien, marching in the bloody track of aggressive war, devastating, conquering and swallowing up the islands of the seas; from collision with the other powers of Christendom; from further civil wars between "the United" and "the Confederate States;" from the revival of the African slave-trade in all its horrors, and from the loathing contempt of indignant civilization everywhere.

The New Year and the Union.—*George D. Prentice.*

God has made
A wilderness of worlds; His will and strong
Creative spirit shook ten thousand worlds,
Like golden dewdrops, from his waving wing,
To roll in beauty through abysmal space,
And chant the chorus of his love divine.
He made the milky-way to span the sky,
A pearly bow of promise, every drop
That sparkles there a singing, shining world!
He woke the music of the Northern Harp,
The wild weird chiming of the Pleiades—
And bade the arches of a southern sphere
Reverberate their hallelujahs high.

The mighty One
Who sweeps the lyre of ages, and commands
The praises of ten thousand singing worlds,
Creates the stars of Union, and attunes

The lofty heart of liberty! . . . shall we,
Proud children of the brave, the free,
Behold our banner, blazoned by the breath
Of glory, sullied by a slave?—our stars,
Of Union tossing wildly to and fro
Upon the wave of faction, as they were
But shining shadows, not eternal orbs,
Forever circling through the boundless heaven
Of everlasting purpose?—or shall we
Hear *dissolution* sounded, and forbear
To brand the traitor hearts that dare forget
The bond for which our fathers fought and bled?
Cursed be the traitors—doubly, trebly doomed—
The pit of Discord for her victims yawns,
Then, back recoiling, shudders to receive
Their hearts—a fouler and a fiercer hell!

God save the Union!—Give the dawning year
This proud baptismal anthem—let its last
Dissolving sigh be—Union undissolved!
New states, with starry emblems, one by one,
Come stealing through the future's twilight dim,
Like orbs of evening from its dusky sky,
To take their place at last with those that tread
Their high, unwearied and unwearying round
Before the golden gates and battlements
Of Paradise. The harp of Liberty
Shall sound amain, till Death himself expire;
Till God has made us free, immortally,
And Time is dust upon his broken lyre!
Thrice raptured moment!—if all-blessed like thee
Are heaven's bright centuries, how brief will be
Its countless ages of eternity!

Duties of American Citizens.—*P. W. Chandler*.

The motives to moral action press upon the American citizen with unusual force at the present time. Upon us the hopes of man are resting in every part of the world. Wherever humanity toils for a scanty subsistence; wherever the iron hand of oppression falls upon the people; wherever the last of liberty is dead—

> ———"From the burning plains
> Where Lybian monsters yell,
> From the most gloomy glens
> Of Greenland's sunless climes,
> To where the golden fields
> Of fertile England spread
> Their harvest to the sky"—

"the voices of the past and the future seem to blend in one sound of warning and entreaty, addressing itself not only to the general but to the individual ear, calling upon us, each and all, to be faithful to the trust which God has committed to our hands."

Let the American citizen feel the responsibilities of his position, with a determination that the hopes of the world shall not be disappointed. Nor let him mistake the nature of his duties. Many men acknowledge our evils and our dangers, but seek in vain for the remedy. They are ready for any sacrifice, but earnestly inquire when and where it is be made. We eagerly seize upon any excuse for the non-performance of duty. "Give me where to stand," cried the ancient philosopher, "and I will move the world." "Find where to stand!" shouts the modern reformer. "Stand where you are," is the voice of reason and religion. It is not upon some great and distant enterprise that our duty will call us. It is not in the tented field that our services will be needed. The battle-ground is in our own hearts; the enemy in our own bosoms. And when the passions of men are subdued; when selfishness is purged from humanity; when anger is entirely restrained; when jealousy, hatred, and revenge are unknown—then, and then only, is the victory won.

Let no man merge his identity in the masses, nor forget his individual responsibility to his country and his

God. Is his position lowly and obscure? Let him remember that every one exerts an influence, for good or for evil, and no one is so humble as not to need the protection of a good government. Is he called to places of responsibility and trust? Let him bear his honors meekly but firmly, yielding nothing to the blandishments of power or the acclamations of the multitude. He may be hurled from his station by those who placed him in it, and the voices of praise, which were once sweet music to his ears, may be changed to execrations. Let him lay down his power in dignity and silence; as he has filled a high place without pride, he may fill a low one without humiliation. And if, in the performance of duty, sterner trials await him; if misrule and lawless faction should select him as a victim; let him calmly die, remembering that the best and the bravest, earth's noblest children, have drunk the cup of degradation to the dregs, and better men than he have been sacrificed by popular violence. In whatever position he may be placed, wherever his lot may be cast, let him maintain the integrity of his soul.

> "This above all: to thine own self be true;
> And it must follow, as the night the day,
> Thou canst not then be false to any man."

On Laying the Corner-stone of the Bunker Hill Monument.—*Daniel Webster*.

Let it not be supposed that our object is to perpetuate national hostility, or even to cherish a mere military spirit. It is higher, purer, nobler. We consecrate our work to the spirit of national independence, and we wish that the light of peace may rest upon it forever. We rear a memorial of our conviction of that unmeasured benefit which has been conferred on our land, and of the happy influences which have been produced, by the same events, on the general interests of mankind. We come, as Americans, to mark a spot which must forever be dear to us and our posterity. We wish that whosoever, in all coming time, shall turn his eye hither, may behold that the place is not undistinguished where the first great battle of the revolution was fought. We wish that this structure may proclaim the magnitude and importance of that event to every class and every age. We wish that infancy may learn the purpose of its erection from maternal lips, and that weary and withered age may behold it, and be solaced by the recollections which it suggests. We wish that labor may look up here, and be proud, in the midst of its toil. We wish that, in those days of disaster, which, as they come on all nations, must be expected to come on us also, desponding patriotism may turn its eyes hitherward, and be assured that the foundations of our national power still stand strong. We wish that this column, rising toward heaven among the pointed spires of so many temples dedicated to God, may contribute also to produce, in all minds, a pious feeling of dependence and gratitude. We wish finally, that the last object on the sight of him who leaves his native shore, and the first to gladden his who revisits it, may be something which shall remind him of the liberty and glory of his country. Let it rise, till it meet the sun in his coming; let the earliest light of the morning gild it, and parting day linger and play on its summit.

The Sword of Bunker Hill. — *William Ross Wallace.*

"'76 IS FOREVER TO BE SUNG."—*Anon.*

He lay upon his dying bed,
  His eye was growing dim,
When with a feeble voice he called,
  His weeping son to him:
"Weep not, my boy," the veteran said,
  "I bow to heaven's high will,
But quickly from yon antlers bring,
  The sword of Bunker Hill."

The sword was brought; the soldier's eye
  Lit with a sudden flame;
And as he grasped the ancient blade,
  He murmured Warren's name;
Then said, "My boy, I leave you gold,
  But what is richer still,
I leave you, mark me, mark me, now,
  The sword of Bunker Hill.

"'Twas on that dread, immortal day,
  I dared the Briton's band,
A captain raised this blade on me,
  I tore it from his hand;
And while the glorious battle raged,
  It lightened Freedom's will;
For, boy, the God of Freedom's blessed
  The sword of Bunker Hill.

"Oh! keep the sword," his accents broke—
  A smile, and he was dead;
But his wrinkled hand still grasped the blade,
  Upon that dying bed.
The son remains, the sword remains,
  Its glory growing still,
And twenty millions bless the sire
  And sword of Bunker Hill.

SPEECH ON PRESENTING A UNITED STATES FLAG (*in New York*) TO THE THIRD REGIMENT OF MAINE VOLUNTEERS, JUNE 6TH, 1861.—*S. L. Waterbury, Esq.*

MEN of Maine—citizens of the Union! The time for discussion is past. Open rebellion has trampled upon our constitution. We have the issue, and in this state men's minds are one. We have laid aside our partisan wranglings and we have sworn, as the Lord liveth, that treason shall be crushed if the Carolinas be a forest of gibbets. My friends, the men of Maine resident in this city have desired to bid you welcome, and almost in the same breath, farewell. They wish to give you as they part, a token that shall speak of their brotherhood. Each mother has given to her boy in your ranks that fittest pledge of a mother's love, her Bible. Each dear one has given some pledge that speaks of softer and sweeter hours. Your brethren in this hour of battle would give you a strong man's gift—your country's flag. That flag shall be your guardian. Its starry eyes shall look upon you in watchful love; its blended stripes shall stream above you with protection. It is the flag of history. Those thirteen stripes tell the story of our colonial struggle, of the days of '76. They speak of the savage wilderness, of old Independence Hall, of Valley Forge and Yorktown. Those stars tell the story of our nation's growth, how it has come from weakness to strength, from thirteen states to thirty-four, until its gleam in the sunrise over the forests of Maine crimsons the sunset's dying beams on the golden sands of California. Let not the story of the flag be folded now and lost forever. Wherever your axe has rung, the school-house has been reared alongside the hut of the fisherman and the pioneer. Maine is the child of Massachusetts, and in your hearts flows the blood of the old Bay State. Soldiers! I know that every heart gives an eager response to those which the Massachusetts man uttered as he fell stricken by a Baltimore mob: "All hail to the stars and stripes!" We give this flag to you, and with it we give you our prayers, and not ours alone, for as the loved home circle gathers far in the Pine-Tree State, gray-haired fathers and loving mothers will speak in prayer the name of their boy. Sir, in behalf of the sons of Maine in this city, I give you this flag. Guard it as a woman guards her honor, as children guard the ashes of their father. That flag shall float in triumph. That flag shall hover with more than mother's love over your dead. We hear to-day, above the sound of conflict, the voice of the archangel crying: "Victory is on the side of liberty, victory is on the side of law." With unbroken ranks may your command march beneath its folds. God bless you! Farewell!

Perpetuity of the Union.—*Senator Rosseau, of Kentucky.*

Mr. Speaker, I am sick and tired of all this gabble about irritation over the exercise by others of their undoubted right, and I say once for all, to you secession gentlemen, that we Union men know our rights, and intend to maintain them; and if you intend to get irritated about it, why—get irritated. Snuff and snort yourselves into a rage; go into spasms if you will; die if you wish to. What right have you to get irritated because we claim equal rights and equality with you? We are for peace; we desire no war, and deprecate collision. All we ask is—peace. We do not wish to hurt you, and do not intend that you shall injure us if we can help it. We beg of you to let us live in peace under the good old government of our fathers. We only ask that. Why keep us ever on the alert watching you, to prevent you from enslaving us by a destruction of that government?

The gentleman says, "it is already destroyed." No, sir! The Union will never be dissolved. We may have much suffering; we may endure many calamities. War, pestilence and famine may befall us; our good old Kentucky may be drenched in blood, but the Union will never, *never* be dissolved.

Our government, constitutionally administered, is entitled to our support, no matter who administers it. If we will not support it, and yet enjoy its blessings, in Heaven's name let us not war against it. But who can look an honest man in the face while professing neutrality, yet secretly and traitorously warring against it? For one, sir, I will have none of it. Away with it! Let us be men, honest men, or pretend to be nothing but vagabonds.

May God in his mercy save our glorious republic!

DEEDS, NOT WORDS.*—*Hon. David Dudley Field.*

THIS is not a time for words but for deeds. Our Union is assailed; that Union which was created after so many years of patient labor, of common suffering and common glory. Our constitution is defied; that constitution which Washington, Franklin, Madison, Hamilton and their compatriots made, and which has served us so well in peace and war. Our liberties are menaced; those liberties which we inherited from our brave and suffering fathers, and which we received as an inheritance to be

* Delivered at the great Union meeting held in New York, 1861,

transmitted intact to our children. The symbol of our country's strength and honor—that flag which our countrymen have borne over so many lands and seas, has been insulted and trampled. Our fortresses, arsenals, mints, custom-houses, hospitals, have been seized. The roads to our national capital have been obstructed, and our own troops, marching to its succor, molested and stopped; every form of contumely and insult has been used toward us. The foundations of government and society are rocking around us. Truly, my fellow-citizens, this is no time for words—we must act, act now, act together, or we are lost. This is no occasion to inquire into the causes of this awful state of things. All hands, all hearts, all thoughts, should be concentrated upon the one great object of saving our country, our Union, our constitution —I had almost said, our civilization. If we fail in this great emergency, if we allow a single source of discord to intrude into our councils, if we do not give to our glorious land, in this hour of its peril, our substance, our labors, and our blood, we shall prove ourselves most degenerate children. A great conspiracy has been forming and extending for many years to overthrow this government; and people have only now believed its existence; it was something so monstrous as to be incredible, till an armed rebellion has overcome seven states, and seems to be spreading over more; a military despotism has obtained control of eight millions of people, and is knocking at the gates of the capital. Therefore arm yourselves, for this contest is to be decided by arms; let every man arm himself. None capable of bearing arms can be spared. It is not thirty thousand that this state must get ready, but three hundred thousand. Arm yourselves by land and sea; prepare for the worst; rally to the support of the government; give your counsel and your strength to the constituted authorities whom the votes of the people and the laws of the land have placed in power. Never give up. Never despair. Never shrink. And from this darkness and gloom, from the smoke and flame of battle, we shall, with God's blessing, come out purified as by fire, our love of justice increased, the foundations of our institutions more firmly cemented, and the blessings of liberty more certainly secured to ourselves and our posterity. Every motive that can influence men is present to us this day—love of honor and love of right, the history of the heroic past, the vast interests of the present, and the future of all the millions that for ages shall inhabit this continent.

SOLDIER'S DIRGE.*—*Colonel O'Hara.*

    THE muffled drum's sad roll has beat,
        The soldier's last tattoo;
    No more on life's parade shall meet,
        That brave and fallen few.
    On Fame's eternal camping-ground,
        Their silent tents are spread ;
    And glory guards with solemn round
        The bivouac of the dead.

    No rumor of the foe's advance
        Now swells upon the wind;
    No troubled thought at midnight haunts
        Of loved ones left behind;
    No vision of the morrow's strife
        The warrior's dream alarms—
    No braying horn, nor screaming fife,
        At dawn shall call to arms.

    Rest on, embalmed and sainted dead,
        Dear as the blood ye gave;
    No impious footstep here shall tread
        The herbage of your grave.

---

* On the reinterment in the cemetery of Frankfort, Ky., of the brave Kentuckians who fell at the battle of Buena Vista.

Nor shall your glory be forgot,
While Fame her record keeps,
Or Honor points the hallowed spot
Where Valor proudly sleeps.

Through Foemen Surrounding.

Through foemen surrounding,
Our war-steeds are bounding;
The trumpets are sounding
    That call to the fight:
Let Liberty's chorus
Rise grandly before us,
The God who rules o'er us,
    Will stand by the right!

Shall we meanly sever
From Liberty?—never!
Shall we suffer ever
    A tyrant's control?
No! truth o'er us stealing,
Is brightly revealing
In all but one feeling—
    In all but one soul!

No Secession from the Union.—*John Lothrop Motley, LL. D.*

THE men who had conducted the American people through a long and fearful revolution, were the founders of the new commonwealth which permanently superseded the subverted authority of the crown. They placed the foundations on the unbiased, untrammelled consent of the people. They were sick of leagues, of petty sovereignties, of governments which could not govern a single individual. The framers of the constitution, which has now endured three-quarters of a century, and under which the nation has made a material and intellectual progress never surpassed in history, were not such triflers as to be ignorant of the consequences of their own acts. The constitution which they offered, and which the people adopted as its own, talked not of sovereign states—spoke not the word confederacy. In the very preamble to the instrument are inserted the vital words which show its character: "We, *the people of the United States, to insure a more perfect union, and to secure the blessings of liberty for ourselves and our posterity, do ordain and establish this constitution.*" *Sic volo, sic jubeo.* It is the language of a sovereign solemnly speaking to the world. It is the promulgation of a great law, the *norma agendi* of a new commonwealth. It is no compact.

"A compact" says Blackstone, "is a promise proceeding from us. Law is a command directed to us. The language of a compact is, We will or will not do this; that of a law is, Thou shalt or shalt not do it."

And this is, throughout, the language of the constitution. Congress shall do this; the President shall do that; the states shall not exercise this or that power. Witness, for example, the important clauses by which the "sovereign" states are shorn of all the great attributes of sovereignty—no state shall coin money, nor emit bills of credit, nor pass *ex post facto* laws, nor laws impairing the obligation of contracts, nor maintain armies and navies, nor grant letters of marque, nor make compacts with other states, nor hold intercourse with foreign powers, nor grant titles of nobility; and that most significant phrase: "This constitution, and the laws made in pursuance thereof, *shall be the supreme law of the land.*"

Could language be more imperial? Could the claim to state "sovereignty" be more completely disposed of at a word? How can that be sovereign, acknowledging no superior, supreme, which has voluntarily accepted a supreme law from something which it acknowledges as superior?

The constitution is perpetual, not provisional or temporary. It is made for all time—"for ourselves and our posterity." It is absolute within its sphere. "This constitution shall be the supreme law of the land, any thing in the constitution or laws of a state to the contrary notwithstanding." Of what value, then, is a law of a state declaring its connection with the Union dissolved? The constitution remains supreme, and is bound to assert its supremacy till overpowered by force. The use of force —of armies and navies of whatever strength—in order to compel obedience to the civil and constitutional authority, *is not "wicked war," is not civil war, is not war at all.* So long as it exists the government is obliged to put forth its strength when assailed. The President, who has taken an oath before God and man to maintain the constitution and laws, is perjured if he yields the constitution and laws to armed rebellion without a struggle. He knows nothing of states. Within the sphere of the United States government he deals with individuals only, citizens of the great republic, in whatever portion of it they may happen to live. He has no choice but to enforce the laws of the republic wherever they may be resisted. When he is overpowered, the government ceases to exist. The Union is gone, and Massachusetts, Rhode Island and Ohio are as much separated from each other as they are from Georgia or Louisiana. Anarchy has returned upon us. The dismemberment of the commonwealth is complete. We are again in the chaos of 1785.

But it is sometimes asked why the constitution did not make a special provision against the right of secession. How could it do so? The people created a constitution over the whole land, with certain defined, accurately enumerated powers, and among these were all the chief attributes of sovereignty. It was forbidden to a state to coin money, to keep armies and navies, to make compacts with other states, to hold intercourse with foreign nations, to oppose the authority of the government. To do any one of these things is to secede, for it would be physically impossible to do any one of them without secession. It would have been puerile for the constitution to say formally to each state: "Thou shalt not secede." The constitution, being the supreme law, being perpetual, and having expressly forbidden to the states those acts without which secession is an impossibility, *would have been wanting in dignity had it used such superfluous phraseology.* This constitution is supreme, whatever laws a state may enact, says the organic law. Was it necessary to add, "and no state shall enact a law of secession." To add to a great statute, in which the sovereign authority of the land declares its will, a phrase such as "and be it further enacted that the said law shall not be violated," would scarcely seem to strengthen the statute.

It was accordingly enacted that new states might be admitted; but no permission was given for a state to secede.

Extracts from a Funeral Eulogy on General Andrew Jackson.—*Hon. Benjamin F. Butler.*[*]

Mournful but pleasant, friends and fellow-citizens, is the service in which we are engaged. Andrew Jackson,

[*] The editor of this volume would take this fitting occasion to express his affection and admiration, an affection and admiration felt by the people of the United States generally, for Mr. Butler. His death was indeed a national calamity, as he was a great lawyer, a profound statesman, an ardent patriot, a devoted friend and an *earnest Christian.*

upon whose bed of sickness and suffering have been so intensely fixed the filial and solicitous regards of the millions of America, is no more. His great soul has ascended to its Author; his venerable form has sunk into the grave. To that grave, with swelling hearts and tearful eyes, and sad funereal rites, a nation is repairing. We have come to it to-day. While we linger within its sacred precincts, the praises of the hero we reverenced, the magistrate we honored, and the man we loved, rise instinctively to our lips. To their free utterance nature prompts, duty enjoins, affection compels us. It is fitting, it is right, that such tributes should be paid to those who, in council or in camp, have advanced the glory of their country and the welfare of their kind. The homage thus bestowed is at least disinterested; for the dead who are its objects, insensible alike to praise and to blame, can make no return to the living who proffer it. It exerts a humanizing influence on the universal heart; it promotes the formation of a true nationality; it softens the asperities of party; it incites to a virtuous emulation. Next in purity and meekness to the thanksgivings which we owe to the God who gave, and guided, and sustained them, is the feeling of grateful reverence we should ever cherish toward those who are the instruments of his goodness. To the claims of our great men, of every age and time, of every sect and party, let us then be faithful. Let history transmit to other generations the story of their lives; let the canvas and the marble perpetuate the image of their forms; let poetry and music breathe forth their names in hymns and harmonies; let the united voice of their countrymen echo their praises to the remotest shores—so that wherever an American foot shall tread, or a lover of American liberty be found, there, too, the memory of their greatness shall abide—a beauty and an excellence, the joy of all the earth!

We are now to contemplate Andrew Jackson in the

new and conspicuous theatre in which he attracted the regards not only of America, but of the world. Rallying to his standard, at the first moment when the action of the government enabled him to do so, the gallant spirits of his division, he dedicates their persons and his own to the service of the nation. From November, 1812, to the cessation of hostilities, he is constantly employed in creating and leading the armies, fighting the battles, and vanquishing the enemies of his country. It is not my purpose to enter into the details of his military exploits. Of all and of each it may be said, that, in each and in all he acquitted himself as no other man but Andrew Jackson could have done. With his first touch of the marshal's truncheon, the hand of one born to command at will the energies of his troops, to infuse into them his own daring spirit, and successfully to cope in any and every field with the most skilful and courageous of his enemies, is evidently seen. Throughout his whole military career he exhibits, in felicitous combination, all the qualities of a great commander—comprehensiveness and accuracy of view, genius to devise, skill and courage to execute, coolness and decision in every emergency, perfect command of his resources, sagacity to discover and ability to defeat the plans of his antagonist.

The Glory of the Hero and Patriot.—*Thomas Moore.*

Remember the glories of Brian the brave,
  Though the days of the hero are o'er;
Though, lost to Mononia and cold in the grave,
  He returns to Kinkora no more!
That star of the field, which so often has poured
  Its beam on the battle, is set;

But enough of its glory remains on each sword
   To light us to victory yet!

Mononia! when nature embellished the tint
   On thy fields and thy mountains so fair,
Did she ever intend that a tyrant should print
   His footsteps of slavery there?
No, freedom, whose smile we shall never resign,
   Go, tell our invaders, the Danes,
That 'tis sweeter to bleed for an age at thy shrine,
   Than to sleep but a moment in chains!

Forget not our wounded companions who stood
   In the day of distress by our side;
While the moss of the valley grew red with their blood,
   They stirred not, but conquered and died!
The sun that now blesses our arms with his light,
   Saw them fall upon Ossory's plain—
Oh, let him not blush when he leaves us to-night,
   To find that they fell there in vain!

CHARACTER OF WARREN.—*Rev. E. L. Magoon.*

INDIGNANT at the efforts made to stifle free discussion, and to cheat the popular mind " of that liberty which rarifies and enlightens it like the influence of heaven," he proclaimed the rights of man, undismayed by menace, and cheered on his patriotic brethren, while he awed unprincipled sycophants into silence. His brave example and eloquent speech caused millions of hearts to beat with a common sentiment of resistance. Every rock and wild ravine was made a rampart to " the sons of liberty," and their banner was on every summit unfurled, inscribed in letters of fire, " *Resistance to tyrants is obedience to God!*"

Warren was eminently chivalrous and brave. Like Louis XII. at Aignadel, he would exclaim to the timid: " *Let those who have fear, secrete themselves behind me!*" Or, like the bold and generous Condé, he would animate his countrymen in the darkest hour with the cheerful cry: "Follow my white plume; *you shall recognize it always on the road to victory!*"

In speech, as in action, he was sagacious and energetic. His words teem with the sulphurous breath of war, and are lurid with patriotic indignation, as if coined at the cannon's mouth. He seized his victim as a vulture grasps a serpent in his talons, and bearing him aloft in triumph, tore him in fearless strength and scattered the fragments to the winds. But this was the rage produced by foreign aggression, and not the blind fury of ambition. Herein was Warren, like Washington, greater than Napoleon. Warren was a powerful orator, because he was a true man, and struggled for man's highest rights. Eloquence and liberty are the inseparable offspring of the same mother, nursed at the same breast; two beams from the same sun; two chords from the same harp; two arrows from the same quiver; two thunderbolts twin-born in heaven.

> " 'Tis Liberty alone that gives the flower
> Of fleeting life its lustre and perfume,
> And we are weeds without it."

Warren's Address.—*John Pierpont.*

Stand! the ground's your own, my braves!
Will ye give it up to slaves?
Will ye look for greener graves?
    Hope ye mercy still?
What's the mercy despots feel?
Hear it in that battle peal!
Read it on yon bristling steel!
    Ask it—ye who will!

Fear ye foes who kill for hire?
Will ye to your homes retire?
Look behind you!—they're afire,
    And before you see
Who have done it! From the vale
On they come! and will ye quail?
Leaden rain and iron hail
    Let their welcome be.

In the God of battles trust!
Die we may, and die we must:
But, oh! where can dust to dust
    Be consigned so well,
As where heaven its dews shall shed
On the martyred patriot's bed,
And the rocks shall raise their head,
    Of his deeds to tell?

The Battle of Lexington.—*Dr. O. Wendell Holmes.*

Slowly the mist o'er the meadow was creeping,
  Bright on the dewy buds glistened the sun,
When from his couch, while his children were sleeping,
  Rose the bold rebel and shouldered his gun.
      Waving her golden veil
      Over the silent dale,
Blithe looked the morning on cottage and spire;
      Hushed was his parting sigh,
      While from his noble eye
Flashed the last sparkle of liberty's fire.

On the smooth green where the fresh leaf is springing,
  Calmly the first-born of glory are met;
Hark, the death-volley around them is ringing!
  Look! with their life-blood the young grass is wet.
      Faint is the feeble breath,
      Murmuring low in death,
"Tell to our sons how their fathers have died;"
      Nerveless the iron hand,
      Raised for its native land,
Lies by the weapon that gleams by its side.

Over the hill-side the wild knell is tolling,
    From their far hamlets the yeomanry come,
As through the storm-clouds the thunder-burst rolling,
    Circles the beat of the mustering drum.
        Fast on the soldier's path
        Darken the waves of wrath,
Long have they gathered and loud shall they fall;
        Red glares the musket flash,
        Sharp rings the rifle's crash,
Blazing and clanging from thicket and wall.

Gayly the plume of the horseman was dancing,
    Never to shadow his cold brow again;
Proudly at morning the war-steed was prancing,
    Reeking and panting he droops on the rein;
        Pale is the lip of scorn,
        Voiceless the trumpet-horn,
Torn is the silken-fringed red cross on high:
        Many a belted breast
        Low on the turf shall rest,
Ere the dark hunters the herd have passed by.

Snow-girdled crags where the hoarse wind is raving,
    Rocks where the weary floods murmur and wail,
Wilds where the fern by the furrow is waving,
    Reeled with the echoes that rolled on the gale;
        Far as the tempest thrills
        Over the darkened hills,
Far as the sunshine streams over the plain.
        Roused by the tyrant band,
        Woke all the mighty land,
Girded for battle, from mountain and main.

Green be the graves where the martyrs are lying!
    Shroudless and tombless they sunk to their rest—
While o'er their ashes the starry fold flying,
    Wraps the proud eagle they roused from his nest—
        Borne on her northern pine,
        Long o'er the foaming brine,
Spread her broad banner to storm and to sun;
        Heaven keep her ever free,
        Wide as o'er land and sea
Floats the fair emblem her heroes have won.

MORAL AND REPUBLICAN PRINCIPLES NOT TO BE ABANDONED.—*Hon. Edward Everett.*

WAR may stride over the land with the crushing step of a giant. Pestilence may steal over it like an invisible curse, reaching its victims silently and unseen, unpeopling here a village and there a city, until every dwelling is a sepulchre. Famine may brood over it with a long and weary visitation, until the sky itself is brazen, and the beautiful greenness gives place to a parched desert—a wide waste of unproductive desolation. But these are only physical evils. The wild flower will bloom in peace on the field of battle and above the crushed skeleton. The destroying angel of the pestilence will retire when his errand is done, and the nation will again breathe freely. And the barrenness of famine will cease at last—the cloud will be prodigal of its hoarded rain, and the wilderness will blossom.

But for moral desolation there is no reviving spring. Let the *moral* and *republican* principles of our country be abandoned—let impudence, and corruption, and intrigue triumph over honesty and intellect, and our liberties and strength will depart forever. Of these there can be no resuscitation. The "abomination of desolation" will be fixed and perpetual; and as the mighty fabric of our glory totters into ruins, the nations of the earth will mock us in our overthrow, like the powers of darkness, when the throned one of Babylon became even as themselves—and the "glory of the Chaldees' excellency had gone down."

The Falcon.—*James Russell Lowell.*

I know a falcon swift and peerless
    As e'er was cradled in the pine;
No bird had ever eye so fearless,
    Or wing so strong as this of mine.

The winds not better love to pilot
    A cloud with molten gold o'errun,
Than him, a little burning islet,
    A star above the coming sun.

For with a lark's heart he doth tower,
    By a glorious upward instinct drawn;
No bee nestles deeper in the flower,
    Than he in the bursting rose of dawn.

No harmless dove, no bird that singeth,
    Shudders to see him overhead;
The rush of his fierce swooping bringeth,
    To innocent hearts no thrill of dread.

Let *fraud*, and *wrong*, and *baseness* shiver,
    For still between them and the sky
The falcon Truth hangs poised forever,
    And marks them with a vengeful eye.

Character of Daniel Webster.— *Wm. H. Seward.*

Who that was even confessedly provincial, was ever so indentified with any thing local as Daniel Webster was with the spindles of Lowell, and the quarries of Quincy; with Faneuil Hall, Bunker Hill, Forefathers' Day, Plymouth Rock, and whatever else belonged to Massachusetts? And yet, who that was most truly national has ever so sublimely celebrated, or so touchingly commended to our reverent affection, our broad and ever broadening continental home; its endless rivers, majestic mountains, and capacious lakes; its inimitable and indescribable constitution; its cherished and growing capital; its aptly conceived and expressive flag, and its triumphs by land and sea; and its immortal founders, heroes, and martyrs? How manifest it was, too, that, unlike those who are impatient of slow but sure progress, he loved his country, not for something greater or higher than he desired or hoped she might be, but just for what she was, and as she was already, regardless of future change.

No, sir; believe me, they err widely who say that Daniel Webster was cold and passionless. It is true that he had little enthusiasm; but he was, nevertheless, earnest and sincere, as well as calm; and therefore he was both discriminating and comprehensive in his affections. We recognize his likeness in the portrait drawn by a Roman pencil:

> ——" Who with nice discernment knows
> What to his country and his friend he owes;
> How various nature warms the human breast,
> To love the parent, brother, friend, or guest,
> What the great offices of judges are,
> Of senators, of generals sent to war."

Daniel Webster was cheerful, and, on becoming occasions joyous, and even mirthful; but he was habitually engaged in profound studies on great affairs. He was, moreover, constitutionally fearful of the dangers of popular passion and prejudice; and so, in public walk, conversation, and debate, he was grave and serious, even to solemnity; yet he never desponded in the darkest hours of personal or political trial; and melancholy, never in health, nor even in sickness, spread a pall over his spirits.

It must have been very early that he acquired that just estimate of his powers which was the basis of a self-reliance which all the world saw and approved, and which, while it betrayed no feature of vanity, none but a superficial observer could have mistaken for pride or arrogance.

Daniel Webster was no sophist. With a talent for didactic instruction which might have excused dogmatism, he never lectured on the questions of morals that are agitated in the schools. But he seemed, nevertheless, to have acquired a philosophy of his own, and to have made it the rule and guide of his life. That philosophy consisted in improving his powers and his tastes, so that he might appreciate whatever was good and beautiful in nature and art, and attain to whatever was excellent in conduct. He had accurate perceptions of the nature and qualities of things. He overvalued nothing that was common, and undervalued nothing that was useful, or even ornamental. His lands, his cattle, and equipage, his dwelling, library, and apparel, his letters, arguments, and orations—every thing that he had, every thing that he made, every thing that he did, was, as far as possible, fit, complete, perfect. He thought decorous forms necessary for preserving whatever was substantial in politics and morals, and even in religion. In his regard, order was the first law, and peace the chief blessing on earth, as they are in heaven. Therefore, while he desired justice and loved liberty, he reverenced law as the first divinity of states and of society.

ODE FOR THE METROPOLITAN OBSEQUIES OF DANIEL WEBSTER.— *William Ross Wallace.*

I.

Not in the capitol's high halls,
Nor by the solemnly-sounding main,
Nor where the mountains lift their grand old walls,
Shall he be seen again.

The voice is hushed that made the nations bow,
   And that majestic form forever gone,
As though an Alp with thunder-daring brow,
     Should suddenly disappear,
     When all the sky is clear,
And leave where tall crags towered an unregarded lawn.

II.

   Yet doth the earth no token give
That he, the wondrous one, hath ceased to live;
    No forests wave the music of their woe;
    No great winds melancholy blow;
    No streams with slower motion flow;
      No ocean folds his psalms,
      And stills his stormy palms;
No cloud in funeral drapery is furled,
   Though he lies low in death;
And not an orb can feel our sister-world
   Move on with fainter breath:
But calm and beautiful as in her prime,
Earth rolls around her mighty dome of Time
    A joy is in her glowing heart—
     A joy too deep for any sign
     Or human or divine:
    For she hath done her part;
    And therefore with an inward smile,
      She saw her Titan-son—
His glorious mission done, his massive laurels won—
   From this her interstellar isle
      Set free,
And crowned to wander through Eternity.

So, tearless, she can mark the summons still
   From Death's dim, melancholy deeps,
And hear the thunders of Almighty will
   Go sounding down the everlasting steeps.

III.

    Be we! Ah, we!
Ours is a lesser life and thought than hers,
    And even our smiles
Are but the prophets of a realm of tears.

Then bid the nation's burial banners sweep
A darkness o'er the Titan's sleep;
And for remembrance of the mighty dead,
With funeral garlands bind each mountain's head;
And let the North come up with oaken bough
To hold above his large pale brow;
And let the sad West from her prairies bring
   The grandest flowers that image sorrow's gloom,
To wave beneath the Southern pine, when Spring
   Leans gently o'er the patriot's hallowed tomb;
And bid the great winds give their organs breath
   In clouds of sound o'er states that weep below—
When shadowed thus by such majestic death,
   No common deed can speak uncommon woe.

IV.

Yet in our darkest grief
   Before that pale but cherished form,
Come radiant thoughts that bring to us relief,
   Like rainbows brought by storm.
Lo! smiling Memory proudly points us back
   To his stupendous track:
But speak his name and in the Senate hall
   The banners, bearing many a battle-scar,
   Yet beautiful with each rejoicing star,
Lift every fold and rustle on the wall:
But speak his words, there is a brighter beam
On Plymouth's rock and far Missouri's stream;
And over Ossa stride victorious Greeks,
   To freedom dedicate each daring soul,
While round the enchanted white Olympian peaks
   Exulting thunders roll.

Oh joy! for thus we hold his glories still
On every storied wave and hill:
The god departs, yet Delphos is divine;
   The Samian dies, but lingering, sound his strains;
The prophet fades, still Zion reads her shrine;
   The builder sinks, his pyramid remains.

V.

Then fold the glorious slumberer's hands,
   And let his nation, reverent, spread his pall;

Now, rising, proudly tell the listening lands,
  Our Titan sleeps in death's selectest hall;
And, in the light of his own glory shrined,
  A king of thought, here takes his place at last,
With all the mighty monarchs of the mind
    Who royally trod the mountains of the past.
      Nor this the nation speaks alone,
      But lifts a loftier tone—
The cloud cannot destroy the climbing star,
But only hides the orb that seeks afar,
    Beyond all mortal pains,
    A larger place on the eternal plains.
      Thus, freed from mortal ill,
      We know, we know he liveth still!
And, though far off from his ethereal clime,
  The finer sense can hear his massive tread
Beneath the immortal dome that curves sublime
  Above the solemn cities of the dead.

So, in despite of mountains reared between
  Our homes and some vast ocean's distant shore,
We, with hushed breath, a moment, listening, lean,
And know the great waves are, though still unseen—
  The billows waft their murmurs evermore.

America.—*Charles Phillips.*

I APPEAL to history! Tell me, thou reverend chronicler of the grave, can all the illusions of ambition realized, can all the wealth of a universal commerce, can all the achievements of successful heroism, or all the establishments of this world's wisdom, secure to empire the permanency of its possessions? Alas! Troy thought so once; yet the land of Priam lives only in song! Thebes thought so once; yet her hundred gates have crumbled, and her very tombs are but as the dust they were vainly intended to commemorate! So thought Palmyra—where is she? So thought the countries of Demosthenes and the Spartan; yet Leonidas is trampled by the timid slave, and Athens insulted by the servile, mindless, and enervate Ottoman! In his hurried march, time has but looked at their imagined immortality; and all its vanities, from the palace to the tomb, have, with their ruins, erased the very impression of his footsteps! The days of their glory are as if they had never been; and the island that was then a speck, rude and neglected in the barren ocean, now rivals the ubiquity of their commerce, the glory of their arms, the fame of their philosophy, the eloquence of their senate, and the inspiration of their bards! Who shall say, then, contemplating the past, that England, proud and potent as she appears, may not, one day, be what Athens is, and the young America yet soar to be what Athens was! Who shall say that, when the European column shall have mouldered, and the night of barbarism obscured its very ruins, that mighty continent may not emerge from the horizon, to rule for its time, sovereign of the ascendant!

WAR QUESTIONS—To COLONEL C. M. CLAY—1861.— *William Ross Wallace.*

DEDICATED TO J. FRANK HOWE.

"The battle is for the entity of the nation."—DR. CHAPIN.

O SOLDIER! O soldier! why thus is your hand
With such eagerness clasped on your sharp battle-brand?
Has your flag been insulted? its eagle betrayed?
For revenge flash the flames of that blood-drinking blade?
"Not revenge, not revenge, that is arming me now,
But as white as a dove's is the plume on my brow,
Though the flag was insulted—the star-flag that rolled
Like a storm for the right o'er my fathers of old!"

O soldier! O soldier! Is't glory you seek
Where the war demon shouts, and the death-vultures shriek?

Does your manly brow yearn for the laurels that wave
On the tree that is nursed by the blood of the brave?
"O no! 'tis not glory that calls on my soul,
Where the black cannons roar and the red banners roll,
Though 'tis there that the bold, gallant hand may entwine
Greenest wreaths for his name on a world-worshipped shrine."

O soldier! O soldier! then *why* is your hand
With such eagerness clasped on that sharp battle-brand?
While the flush on your brow, and the flash in your eye,
Show that storms of deep passion are thundering by?
"'Tis the right! 'Tis the right! God's own high holy right,
That has called me, and armed for the terrible fight!
O ye shades of my fathers! O ye, to whose hand
We have owed the great Union that blesses our land,
Lo, the traitors have struck! They would rend the star-fold
That for freedom, and honor, and truth ye unrolled!
How your grand eyes look on me!—I rush to the strife
Not for fame or revenge—but *the national life!*"

Death of John Quincy Adams.—*Hon. William H. Seward.*

The distinguished characteristics of his life were beneficent labor and personal contentment. He never sought wealth, but devoted himself to the service of mankind. Yet, by the practice of frugality and method, he secured the enjoyment of dealing forth continually no stinted charities, and died in affluence. He never solicited place or preferment, and had no partisan combination or even connections; yet he received honors which eluded the covetous grasp of those who formed parties, rewarded friends, and proscribed enemies; and he filled a longer period of varied and distinguished service than ever fell to the lot of any other citizen. In every stage of this progress he was content. He was content to be president, minister, representative or citizen.

Stricken in the very midst of this service, in the very act of rising to debate, he fell into the arms of conscript fathers of the republic. A long lethargy supervened and oppressed his senses. Nature rallied the wasting powers, on the verge of the grave, for a brief period. But it was long enough for him. The rekindled eye showed that the recollected mind was clear, calm and vigorous. His weeping family and his sorrowing companions were there. He surveyed the scene and knew at once its fatal import. He had left no duty unperformed; he had no wish unsatisfied; no ambition unattained; no regret, no sorrow, no fear, no remorse. He could not shake off the dews that gathered on his brow, he could not pierce the thick shades that rose up before him. But he knew that eternity lay close by the shores of time. He knew that his Redeemer lived. Eloquence, even in that hour, inspired him with his ancient sublimity of utterance. "This," said the dying man, "this is the last of earth." He paused for a moment, and then added, "I am content." Angels might well have drawn aside the curtains of the sky to look down on such a scene—a scene that approximated even to that scene of unapproachable sublimity, not to be recalled without reverence, when, in mortal agony, One who spake as never man spake, said, "It is finished."

RIENZI TO THE ROMANS.—*Thomas Moore.*

ROMANS! look round you—on this sacred place
  There once stood shrines, and gods, and godlike men—
What see you now? what solitary trace
  Of all that made Rome's glory then?
The shrines are sunk, the sacred mount bereft
  Even of its name—and nothing now remains

But the deep memory of that glory, left
   To whet our pangs and aggravate our chains!
But *shall* this be?—our sun and sky the same,
   Treading the very soil our fathers trod—
What withering curse has fallen on soul and frame?
   What visitation has there come from God,
To blast our strength and rot us into slaves,
Here on our great forefathers' glorious graves?
It cannot be! Rise up, ye mighty dead,
   If we, the living, are too weak to crush
These tyrant priests, that o'er your empire tread
   Till all but Romans at Rome's tameness blush!

Happy Palmyra! in thy desert domes
   Where only date-trees sigh and serpents hiss;
And thou whose pillars are but silent homes
   For the stork's brood, superb Persepolis!
Thrice happy both, that your extinguished race
Has left no embers, no half-living trace,
No slaves to crawl around the once proud spot,
Till past renown in present shame's forgot;
While Rome, the queen of all, whose very wrecks,
   If lone and lifeless through a desert hurled,
Would wear more true magnificence than decks
   The assembled thrones of all the assembled world—
Rome, Rome alone is haunted, stained and cursed,
   Through every spot her princely Tiber laves,
By living human things, the deadliest, worst
   That earth engenders—tyrants and their slaves!

And we—oh, shame!—we, who have pondered o'er
   The patriot's lesson and the poet's lay;
Have mounted up the streams of ancient lore,
   Tracking our country's glories all the way—
Even *we* have tamely, basely kissed the ground
   Before that regal power, that ghost of her,
The world's imperial mistress—sitting crowned
   And ghastly on her mouldering sepulchre!

But this is past—too long have lordly priests
   And priestly lords led us, with all our pride
Withering about us—like devoted beasts
   Dragged to the shrine, with faded garlands tied.

'Tis o'er !—the dawn of our deliverance breaks!
Up from his sleep of centuries awakes
The genius of the old republic, free
As first he stood in chainless majesty,
And sends his voice through ages yet to come,
Proclaiming ROME, ROME, ROME, ETERNAL ROME!

SPEECH OF MACBRIAR TO THE SCOTCH INSURGENTS.—
Walter Scott.

YOUR garments are dyed, but not with the juice of the wine-press ; your swords are filled with blood, but not with the blood of goats or lambs ; the dust of the desert on which ye stand is made fat with gore, but not with the blood of bullocks, for the Lord hath a sacrifice in Bozrah and a great slaughter in the land of Idumea. These were not the firstlings of the flock ; this is not the savor of myrrh, of frankincense, or of sweet herbs, that is steaming in your nostrils ; but these bloody trunks are the carcasses of those that held the bow and the lance, who were cruel and would show no mercy, whose voice roared like the sea, who rode upon horses, every man in array as if to battle.

Leave not, therefore, the plough in the furrow ; turn not back from the path on which you have entered ; like the famous worthies of old, whom God raised up for the glorification of his name, and the deliverance of his afflicted people, halt not in the race you are running, lest the latter end should be worse than the beginning. Wherefore set up a standard in the land ; blow a trumpet upon the mountains ; let not the shepherd tarry by his sheepfold, nor the seedsman continue in the ploughed field, but make the watch strong, sharpen the arrows, burnish the shields, name ye the captains of thousands, and captains of hundreds, of fifties, and of tens ; call the footmen like the rushing of winds, and cause the horsemen to come up like the rushing of many waters, for the passages of the destroyers are stopped, their rods are burned, and the face of their men of battle hath been turned to flight.

Up, then, and be doing; the blood of martyrs, reeking upon scaffolds, is crying for vengeance; the bones of saints, which lie whitening in the highways, are pleading for retribution; the graves of innocent captives, from desolate isles of the sea, and from the dungeons of the tyrants' high places, cry for deliverance; the prayers of persecuted Christians, sheltering themselves in deserts from the sword of their persecutors, famished with hunger, starving with cold, lacking fire, food, shelter, and clothing, because they serve God rather than man—all are with you, pleading, watching, knocking, storming the gates of heaven in your behalf.

Rebellion to be Put Down—the Nation to be Saved—1861.—*Hon. Joseph Holt.*

It is true that before this deliverance of the popular mind of the South from the threatenings and alarm which have subdued it, can be accomplished, the remorseless agitators who have made this revolution, and now hold its reins, must be discarded alike from the public confidence and the public service. The country in its agony is feeling their power, and we well understand how difficult will be the task of overthrowing the ascendency they have secured. But the Union men of the South—believed to be in the majority in every seceded state, except perhaps South Carolina—aided by the presence of the government, will be fully equal to the emergency. Let these agitators perish, politically, if need be, by the score:

"A breath can unmake them what a breath has made,"

but destroy this republic and—

"Where is that Promethean heat
That can its light relume?"

Once entombed, when will the angel of the resurrection descend to the portals of its sepulchre? There is not a voice which comes to us from the cemetery of nations that does not answer: "Never, never!" Amid the torments of perturbed existence, we may have glimpses of rest and of freedom, as the maniac has glimpses of reason between the paroxysms of his madness, but we shall attain to neither national dignity nor national repose. We shall be a mass of jarring, warring, fragmentary states, enfeebled and demoralized, without power at home or respectability abroad, and, like the republics of Mexico and South America, we shall drift away on a shoreless and ensanguined sea of civil commotion, from which, if the teachings of history are to be trusted, we shall be finally rescued by the iron hand of some military wrecker, who will coin the shattered elements of our greatness and of our strength into a diadem and a throne. Said M. Fould, the great French statesman, to an American citizen, a few weeks since: "Your republic is dead, and it is probably the last the world will ever see. You will have a reign of terrorism, and after that two or three monarchies." All this may be verified, should this revolution succeed.

Let us, then, twine each thread of the glorious tissue of our country's flag about our heart-strings, and looking upon our homes, and catching the spirit that breathes upon us from the battle-fields of our fathers, let us resolve that, come weal or woe, we will, in life and in death, now and forever, stand by the stars and stripes. They have floated over our cradles, let it be our prayer and our struggle that they shall float over our graves. They have been unfurled from the snows of Canada to the plains of New Orleans, and to the halls of the Montezumas, and amid the solitudes of every sea; and everywhere, as the luminous symbol of resistless and beneficent power, they have led the brave and the free to victory and to glory. It has been my fortune to look upon this flag in foreign lands and amid the gloom of an oriental despotism, and right well do I know, by contrast, how bright are its stars, and how sublime are its inspirations! If this banner, the emblem for us of all that is grand in human history, and of all that is transporting in human hope, is to be sacrificed on the altars of a Satanic ambition, and thus disappear forever amid the night and tempest of revolution, then will I feel—and who shall estimate the desolation of that feeling?—that the sun has indeed been stricken from the sky of our lives, and that henceforth we shall be but wanderers and outcasts, with naught but the bread of sorrow and of penury for our lips, and with hands ever outstretched in feebleness and supplication, on which, in any hour, a military tyrant may rivet the fetters of a despairing bondage. May God in his infinite mercy save you and me, and the land we so much love, from the doom of such a degradation.

No contest so momentous as this has arisen in human history, for, amid all the conflicts of men and of nations, the life of no such government as ours has ever been at stake. Our fathers won our independence by the blood and sacrifices of a seven years' war, and we have maintained it against the assault of the greatest power upon the earth; and the question now is, whether we are to perish by our own hands, and have the epitaph of suicide written upon our tomb. The ordeal through which we are passing must involve immense suffering and losses for us all; but the expenditure of not merely hundreds of millions, but of billions of treasure, will be well made, if the result shall be the preservation of our institutions.

Could my voice reach every dwelling in Kentucky, I would implore its inmates—if they would not have the rivers of their prosperity shrink away, as do unfed streams beneath the summer heats—to rouse themselves from their lethargy, and fly to the rescue of their country before it is everlastingly too late. Man should appeal to man, and neighborhood to neighborhood, until the electric fires of patriotism shall flash from heart to heart in one unbroken current throughout the land. It is a time in which the workshop, the office, the counting-house, and the field, may well be abandoned for the solemn duty that is upon us, for all these toils will but bring treasure, not for ourselves, but for the spoiler, if this revolution is not arrested. We are all, with our every earthly interest, embarked in mid-ocean on the same common deck. The howl of the storm is in our ears, "the lightning's red glare is painting hell on the sky," and while the noble ship pitches and rolls under the lashings of the waves, the cry is heard that she has sprung a leak at many points, and that the rushing waters are mounting rapidly in the hold. The man who, in such an hour, will not work at the pumps, is either a maniac or a monster.

Martial Elegy.—*Tyrtæus*.

How glorious fall the valiant, sword in hand,
In front of battle, for their native land!
But, oh! what ills await the wretch that yields,
A recreant outcast from his native fields!

The mother whom he loves shall quit her home,
An aged father at his side shall roam;

His little ones shall weeping with him go,
And a young wife participate his woe.

But we will combat for our native land;
And we will drain the life-blood where we stand,
To save our children:—fight ye side by side,
And serried close, ye men of youthful pride!

The hero youth that dies in blooming years,
In man's regret he lives, in woman's tears;
More sacred than in life, and lovelier far
For having perished in the front of war!

Speech at the Great American Union Meeting, May, 1861, in Paris, France.—*Hon. C. M. Clay.*

Gentlemen: I had desired to go where my government had ordered me without entering upon political questions. It was with no ordinary feelings that, landing at Calais, I first set foot upon this land of our ancient ally and steadfast friend, who so gallantly aided us in the achieving our independence and founding a great nation. As an agriculturist I was interested in the thorough culture of the soil, and as a lover of nature I was enchanted with the large vista over green fields, hill and dale, intercepted by occasional dense forests, which more than realized all I had imagined of "La Belle France." But what shall I say of Paris?—her spacious and elegant streets, her grand old classic structures, her beautiful works, her galleries of arts—the fine and the useful—her monuments of dramatic history, and above all, her development of progress and civilization? For I must say that I have not seen a beggar, a ragged man or a drunkard in France. A manly sympathy with the cause of liberty in '76 has not, by the eternal laws, been lost upon her people. Does any man venture to say that the French of to-day have paid too much in treasure and blood for the liberties they now enjoy, which this great people and the great chief of their choice equally recognize? The political empyric only is impatient; waiting upon nature, and following upon the fading footprints of the ages, the world-wide statesman and philanthropist withholds the hand of rash propagandism. With hopeful aspirations for the future, with all my heart, I say, "*Vive la France, vive l'Amérique!*" Yes, gentlemen, my country shall live. She sacrifices property, and life, and kindred to justice. She suffers all things for the whole race; not forgetting the language of Lafayette and all the martyrs of '76, she draws her sword once more in "defence of the rights of human nature." Yes, our Union, our constitution, and our liberties shall live. That is why I have said elsewhere, this rebellion shall go down. "Cotton is king!" No; "Grass is king;" for the United States produce more dollars' worth of grass than of cotton. Let the South send $400,000,000 worth of cotton to the nations—if she pays it out, all out, for clothes and food, and mules and cotton-gins, and farming utensils—what does it matter? She finds herself at the end of the year indebted in advance of her income. Her banks are exhausted of their coin to pay for food; her notes are not redeemed; her currency ceases to circulate; her stocks are nothing; her credit is gone. Does *The Times* understand me? Therefore I say, of course, we can conquer her. I am accused of threatening England. I am not in the habit of casting about me to see how I may make truth most palatable. Let those who stand in the way of truth look out. If England, after all she has said against slavery, shall draw her sword in its defence, then I say, great as she is, she shall "perish by the sword." For then not only France, but all the world shall cry, "*Perfide Albion!*" When she mingles the red crosses of the union-jack with the piratical black flag of the "Confederate States of America"—will not just as certainly the tricolor and the stars and stripes float once more in fraternal fold. Can France forget who has doggedly hedged in all the fields of her glory? Can Napoleon forget St. Helena? Will he at her bidding turn his back upon the East? Shall "*Partant pour la Syrie*" be heard no more in France forever? Russia strengthens herself by giving up slave labor for the omnipotent powers of nature—which by steam, and electricity, and water, and the mechanical forces, share with man the creative omnipotence. Shall England cross half the globe to check the Eastern march of her new-born civilization? I have spoken to England not as an enemy but as a friend. For her own sake, I would have her be true to herself. If England would preserve cotton for her millions of operatives, let her join in putting down the rebellion. Her interference in defence of the rebels of the South will force us to do that which would be a calamity to us as well as to them— at a blow to destroy slavery forever. The interests of England and France lie in the same direction—in the preservation of the Union, and the making of successful rebellion impossible. Especially does France find safety in our unity and prosperity—for between us there is no antagonism whatever. We want her silks, her brandies, her wines, her porcelains, her cloths, her finer cottons; her thousand articles of unequalled taste. She wants our tobacco, our meats, our grains, and all that; while she will not envy us the prosperity of our ruder manufactures, which put money in our purse, and make us able to purchase all she has to sell us. Let England, and France, and Russia, and Spain, and Mexico, and all the nations join with us. The Union—it shall be preserved. Planting myself upon the broad principles of natural law, which it was the glory of Lord Chatham to introduce into modern diplomacy, I most heartily respond to your resolutions; I join the old Romans in the purity of my patriotism; of our nationality my undying aspiration is, "*Esto perpetua ;*" of slavery, "*Delenda est Carthago!*"

SPEECH AT THE SAME MEETING.—*Major-General John C. Fremont.*

MR. PRESIDENT, LADIES AND GENTLEMEN: I am deeply sensible to the warm and flattering expressions of confidence and regard with which I have just been honored, and still more deeply sensible to your kind approval of them. They are very grateful to me, and I thank you very sincerely. But you will be very sure that I do not receive them as due to myself; I am conscious that I owe them to the partiality of friendship and to that sort of attachment which a soldier always feels for the banner under which he has fought. To Mr. Burlingame and the other friends around me who have spoken to-day, I represent the standard on which old watchwords were inscribed. It is themselves who were the leaders, themselves who bore with you the heat of the day, and who have won their battle gloriously. And they have come among us here, with their habitual eloquence, to convey to our true-hearted countrymen at home the assurance of our unalterable devotedness to the country, and our unbounded admiration of the generous loyalty with which they rallied to its calls. A few days back our honored flag was trailing in the dust at the foot of an insolent foe; at present its stars are refulgent from a thousand heights, swarming with brave hearts and strong arms in its defence. We drink to them to-day, our brave and loyal countrymen. Faithfully, too, have our scattered people responded to them, from Italy, from England, and from France. Well have they shown that they, too, can cross the seas and change their skies, and never change their hearts. I am glad that a happy chance has brought me to participate with you here on this occasion. Here is this splendid capital of a great nation, where near by us the same tombstone records the blended names of Washington and Lafayette. I feel that I breathe a sympathetic air. France is progress, and I am happy to believe that here we shall not see a people false to their traditional policy. From here we shall see no strong hand stretched out to arrest the march of civilization, and aid in throwing back a continent into barbarism. We expect nowhere active co-operation, but we look for the sympathy which the world gives to a good cause. We are willing to work out our own destiny, and make our own history. Before this struggle closes, the world will recognize that enlightened liberty is self-sustaining, and that a people who have once fully enjoyed its blessings will never consent to part with them. We have deprecated this war as fratricidal and abominable; most gladly would we welcome back our people if they would return to their allegiance. We would bury, deep as the ocean, the hasty anger which their patricidal conduct provoked. But they must return at once to their allegiance. We shall not permit them to dishonor our flag, and desecrate our sacred graves. They cannot be permitted to dismember our country and destroy our nationality. We shall maintain these in their fullest integrity, in the face of every evil and at every hazard. Above every consideration is our country, as we have learned to love it—one and indivisible, now and forever, and so we will maintain it; we will do our duty loyally, and we will make no compromise with treason, and no surrender to rebellion.

Extract from a Speech made at the Union Meeting, in Union Square, New York, 1861.—*Hon. John A. Dix.*

I am for supporting the government. I do not ask who administers it. It is the government of my country, and as such I shall give it in this extremity all the support in my power. I regard the pending contest with the secessionists as a death-struggle for constitutional liberty and law—a contest which, if successful on their part, could only end in the establishment of a despotic government, and blot out, wherever they were in the ascendant, every vestige of national freedom. You know, fellow-citizens, that I have always been in favor of adjusting controversies between the states by conciliation, by compromise, by mutual concession—in a word, in the spirit in which the constitution was formed. Whenever the times shall be propitious for calm consultation, they will find me so still. But until then, let us remember that nothing could be so disastrous, so humiliating, and so disreputable to us all, as to see the common government overthrown, or its legitimate authority successfully resisted. Let us, then, rally with one heart to its support. I believe it will act with all the moderation and forbearance consistent with the preservation of the great interests confided to it. There is no choice left but to acquiesce in its surrender to revolutionary leaders, or to give it the means it needs for defence, for self-preservation, and for the assertion of its authority, holding it responsible for their legitimate use. Fellow-citizens, we stand before the statue of the father of his country. The flag of the Union which floats over it hung above him when he presided over the convention by which the constitution was framed. The great work of his life has been rejected, and the banner by which his labors were consecrated has been trampled in the dust. If the inanimate bronze in which the sculptor has shaped his image could be changed to the living form which led the armies of the revolution to victory, he would command us, in the name of the hosts of patriots and political martyrs who have gone before, to strike for the defence of the Union and the constitution.

WORDS FOR THE HOUR.—*Franklin J. Ottarson.*

I.

THE only free flag under heaven
   Is trampled by a traitor brood,
Its stars are dimmed, its stripes are riven;
   Up, freemen! justice calls for blood!
Up, from your indolent repose;
   Arm for the fratricidal strife—
Unnatural brothers are your foes;
   Up, then, for freedom, law, and life!

II.

That flag, on every sea and shore,
   Has nobly won a noble name;
Alas, that those who should adore,
   Would blast it with eternal shame!
The mightiest king that holds a throne,
   Respects the banner of the free,
Gives it a rank beside his own,
   And bows before its majesty.

III.

Not all the earth could yield a foe
   That dared defy the stripes and stars;
Treason alone hath struck the blow,
   And challenged to the field of wars.
Up, then, to give the rebel band
   The lesson never yet unheard,
And write it in a freeman's hand,
   With bullet, bayonet and sword!

IV.

    Up with the banner of the free!
        And forward, to the battle-field!
    On, for your nationality,
        Till every treacherous foe shall yield;
    Till over Sumter's shattered wall,
        The stars and stripes again shall rise,
    Though every rebel's head shall fall,
        To just revenge a sacrifice!

V.

    On, till you reassert the right
        Of freemen to their native land;
    Till vindicated in the sight
        Of all the world our flag shall stand;
    Till spotted Treason, crushed in blood,
        Sinks to the hell from which it rose,
    And Freedom, in the name of God,
        Shall triumph over all her foes!

Patriotic Duty of the Present Generation[*]—
Hon. W. M. Evarts.

Mr. Chairman and Gentlemen: I regard this as a business meeting commencing the greatest transaction that this generation of men have seen. We stand here the second generation from the men who declared our independence, fought the battles of the revolution, and framed our constitution. The question for us to decide is, whether we are worthy children of such men—whether our descendants shall curse us as we bless our fathers. Gentlemen, you have got something more to do than you have done hitherto—something more than merely to read the glorious history of the past; you have got to write a history for the future that your children will either glory

[*] Delivered at the great Union meeting in New York, 1861.

in or blush for. When Providence puts together the 19th of April, 1776, when the first blood was shed at Lexington, and the 19th of April, 1861, when the first blood was shed at Baltimore, I tell you it means something. What that statue of Washington sustains in its firm hands, the flagstaff of Fort Sumter—I tell you it means something. There is but one question left, and that is, whether you mean something, too. If you mean something, do you mean enough? Do you mean enough of time, of labor, of money, of men, of blood, to seal and sanction the glories of the future of America? Your ancestors fought for and secured independence, liberty and equal rights. Every enemy of liberty, independence and equal rights, has told you that those ideas are inconsistent with government. It is for you to show that government of the people means that the people shall obey the government. Having shown what the world never saw till the Declaration of Independence was made —what a people which governs itself can do in peace, you are to show what a people which governs truly means to accomplish, when it wages war against traitors and rebels. Each man here is fighting his own quarrel and protecting the future of his children. With these sentiments, you need no argument and no suggestion to carry you through the conflict. You are to remember your fathers and care for your children.

Call to Arms.*—*Hon. Caleb Lyon.*

Fellow countrymen, and men of the empire state! Before me I see the stalworth arms of those who are ready and willing to lay their lives down in behalf of the honor and dignity of your country. Yes, you are willing

---

* Delivered at the great Union meeting in New York, 1861.

to sacrifice your lives on the altar of your country for your country's cause. Many years ago there went forth a great apostle, who preached a crusade to the people. He endeavored to raise followers to his banner, but after two years' preaching he did not raise one-third of the men he required to vindicate the Holy Sepulchre. Peter the Hermit, preached for two years, and in preaching he at last succeeded in raising an army for the rescue and defence of the sepulchre of Christ; and now it devolves upon us, in our turn, to take our part in this great struggle to save the sepulchre of Washington from desecration. You are called on to stop the parricidal hands, and rise in your herculean might to save that sepulchre and your country. Men of New York, this is a proud day for you. Your cheers will strike terror to the dwellers of the South, and tell them that you are determined to support that Union which your forefathers built on so lasting a basis. The men of Massachusetts, from Boston, were fired at by the infuriated mob, incited by men who had boasted for the last ten years that they would rather "rule in hell than serve in heaven." General Jackson, in his day, regretted that he did not hang Calhoun, and was sorry that he was not the man to serve the process to arrest him. We are now called upon to teach the people of the South a lesson, and I hope it will be a salutary one—one which they will not soon forget, but that they will remember as long as the stars burn in the sky.

THE REVOLUTIONARY BATTLE OF EUTAW.— *W. Gilmore Simms.*

> HARK! 'tis the voice of the mountain,
>   And it speaks to our heart in its pride,
> As it tells of the bearing of heroes
>   Who compassed its summits and died!

How they gathered to strife as the eagles,
    When the foeman had clambered the height?
How, with scent keen and eager as beagles,
    They hunted him down for the fight!
                  Hurrah!

Hark! through the gorge of the valley,
    'Tis the bugle that tells of the foe;
Our own quickly sounds for the rally,
    And we snatch down the rifle and go.
As the hunter who hears of the panther,
    Each arms him and leaps to his steed,
Rides forth through the desolate antre,
    With his knife and his rifle at need.

From a thousand deep gorges they gather,
    From the cot lowly perched by the rill,
The cabin half hid in the heather,
    'Neath the crag where the eagle keeps still;
Each lonely at first in his roaming,
    Till the vale to the sight opens fair,
And he sees the low cot through the gloaming,
    When his bugle gives tongue to the air.

Thus a thousand brave hunters assemble
    For the hunt of the insolent foe,
And soon shall his myrmidons tremble
    'Neath the shock of the thunder-bolt's blow,
Down the lone heights now wind they together,
    As the mountain-brooks flow to the vale,
And, now, as they group on the heather,
    The keen scout delivers his tale.

" The British—the tories are on us,
    And now is the moment to prove
To the women whose virtues have won us,
    That our virtues are worthy their love!
They have swept the vast valleys below us,
    With fire, to the hills from the sea;
And here would they seek to o'erthrow us
    In a realm which our eagle makes free!"

No war-council suffered to trifle
　With the hours devote to the deed;
Swift followed the grasp of the rifle,
　Swift followed the bound to the steed;
And soon, to the eyes of our yeomen,
　All panting with rage at the sight,
Gleamed the long wavy tents of the foeman,
　As he lay in his camp on the height.

Grim dashed they away as they bounded,
　The hunters to hem in the prey,
And with Deckard's long rifles surrounded,
　Then the British rose fast to the fray;
And never, with arms of more vigor,
　Did their bayonets press through the strife,
Where, with every swift pull of the trigger,
　The sharp-shooters dashed out a life!

'Twas the meeting of eagles and lions,
　'Twas the rushing of tempests and waves,
Insolent triumph 'gainst patriot defiance,
　Born freemen 'gainst sycophant slaves;
Scotch Ferguson sounding his whistle,
　As from danger to danger he flies,
Feels the moral that lies in Scotch thistle,
　With its "touch me who dare!" and he dies!

An hour, and the battle is over,
　The eagles are rending the prey;
The serpents seek flight into cover,
　But the terror still stands in the way;
More dreadful the doom that on treason
　Avenges the wrongs of the state;
And the oak-tree for many a season
　Bears its fruit for the vultures of fate!
　　　　　　　　　　Hurrah!

Washington to be Defended—Secession to be Crushed.*—*Hon. H. J. Raymond.*

Thousands will rise and rush to the rescue of the capital, and to keep it from the possession of the rebels who have made piracy their watchword, and who commenced their present work with plunder, and who have adopted as a basis of their action and of their power, plunder and arson, and with the weapons stolen from the government have aimed an assassin blow at the heart of the republic. What we want is, that a terrible blow be struck, and that it will be felt by those who have strongly provoked it. They have already ascertained that they cannot longer trust to one great hope they had in their enterprise. They had counted confidently on the divisions of the North. They believed that they would be perfectly safe in marching an army to Washington, and that in doing so, they would receive support from this city. This reliance of theirs only shows them now how little they understood what the American heart is made of, whether that heart beats in the city of New York or in the western prairies. It shows they know nothing of liberty, or the impulses of liberty. It shows that they know nothing of the attachment of the people to the government—to that government under which we have grown great, and mighty, and prosperous, a government which gave to the South itself its only title to consideration among the nations of the earth. I have nothing further to say, but what I have already announced, that the Baltic sails to-morrow; and I trust that you will all rush to the rescue, and preserve the capital, and prevent its falling into the hands of the barbarians who threaten to destroy it. The South may rest

---

* Delivered at the great Union meeting in New York, 1861.

assured that the enterprise undertaken by her cannot succeed, and cannot long run on. They will learn that it is one thing to take a people and a government by surprise, but that it is quite another thing to wage a war of despotism over thirty millions of people. What have the secessionists done toward human liberty? What sort of a government have they established? A government of force, a government of despotism. Jefferson Davis is to-day as pure and as unmitigated and complete a despot over those he rules as any who sits upon any throne of Europe. If he gets possession of Washington, if he is allowed to form a government, it will be such a government as the people will have as little to do with as possible. No; but if he gets possession of the capital, one hundred thousand men will rush to the rescue and sweep rebellion from the head-quarters of the government. He will find that the heart of the American people is irrevocably fixed upon preserving the republic. I heard an anecdote to-day from Major Anderson, which may interest you, and at the same time illustrate this position. During the attack on Fort Sumter a report came here that the flag on the morning of the fight was half-mast. I asked him if that was true, and he said there was not a word of truth in the report. He said that during the firing one of the halyards was shot away, and the flag, in consequence, dropped down a few feet. The rope caught in the staff, and could not be reached, so that the flag could not be either lowered or hoisted, and, said the major: "God Almighty nailed that flag to the flag-mast, and I could not have lowered it if I tried." Yes, fellow-citizens, God Almighty has nailed that resplendent flag to its mast, and if the South dares to march upon Washington, they will find that it cannot be taken down. No, not by all the powers they can collect. No! they will find that that sacred sword which defends and strikes for human rights—that sword which

Cromwell wielded, and which our fathers brought into the contest, and which made us a nation—will be taken once more from its scabbard to fight the battle of liberty against rebellion and treason.

It is Great for our Country to Die.—*J. G. Percival.*

Oh! it is great for our country to die where ranks are contending:
 Bright is the wreath of our fame; glory awaits us for ages—
Glory that never is dim, shining on with light never ending—
 Glory that never shall fade, never, oh never, away.

Oh! it is sweet for our country to die: how fondly reposes
 Warrior youth on his bier, wet by the tears of his love;
Wet by a mother's warm tears: they crown him with garlands of roses:
 Weep, and then joyously turn, bright where he triumphs above.

Oh! then how great for our country to die, in the front rank to perish;
 Firm with one breast to the foe, victory's shout in our ear;
Long they our statues shall crown; in songs our memories cherish:
 We shall look forth from our heaven, pleased the sweet music to hear.

The United States Superior to a Single State.*—*Professor Mitchell.*

I am infinitely indebted to you for this evidence of your kindness. I know I am a stranger among you. I have been in your state but a little while; but I am with you, heart and soul, and mind and strength, and all that I have and am belongs to you and our common country, and to nothing else. I have been announced to you as a

---

* Delivered at the great Union meeting in New York, 1861.

citizen of Kentucky. Once I was, because I was born there. I love my native state, as you love your native state. I love my adopted state of Ohio, as you love your adopted state, if such you have; but, my friends, I am not a citizen now of any state. I owe allegiance to no state, and never did, and, God helping me, I never will. I owe allegiance to the government of the United States. A poor boy, working my way with my own hands, at the age of twelve turned out to take care of myself as best I could, and beginning by earning four dollars per month, I worked my way onward until this glorious government gave me a chance at the military academy at West Point. There I landed with a knapsack on my back, and, I tell you God's truth, just a quarter of a dollar in my pocket. There I swore allegiance to the government of the United States. I did not abjure the love of my own state, nor of my adopted state, but all over that rose proudly triumphant and predominant my love for our common country. And now to-day that common country is assailed, and, alas! alas! that I am compelled to say it, it is assailed in some sense by my own countrymen. My father and my mother were from old Virginia, and my brothers and sisters from old Kentucky. I love them all; I love them dearly. I have my brothers and friends down in the South now, united to me by the fondest ties of love and affection. I would take them in my arms to-day with all the love that God has put into this heart. But if I found them in arms I would be compelled to smite them down. You have found officers of the army who have been educated by the government, who have drawn their support from the government for long years, who, when called upon by their country to stand for the constitution and for the right, have basely, ignominiously, and traitorously either resigned their commissions, or deserted to traitors, and rebels, and enemies. What means all this? How can it be possible that men should act in this way? There is no question but one. If we ever had a government and constitution, or if we ever lived under such, have we ever recognized the supremacy of right? I say, in God's name why not recognize it now? Why not to-day? Why not forever? Suppose those friends of ours from old Ireland, suppose he who has made himself one of us, when a war should break out against his own country should say: "I cannot fight against my own countrymen." Is he a citizen of the United States? They are no countrymen longer when war breaks out. The rebels and the traitors in the South we must set aside; they are not our friends. When they come to their senses we will receive them with open arms; but till that time, while they are trailing our glorious banner in the dust, when they scorn it, condemn it, curse it, and trample it underfoot, then I must smite. In God's name I will smite, and as long as I have strength I will do it. Oh, listen to me, listen to me! I know these men; I know their courage; I have been among them; I have been with them; I have been reared with them; they have courage, and do not you pretend to think they have not. I tell you what it is, it is no child's play you are entering upon. They will fight, and with a determination and a power which is irresistible. Make up your mind to it. Let every man put his life in his hand and say: "There is the altar of my country; there I will sacrifice my life." I for one will lay my life down. It is not mine any longer. Lead me to the conflict. Place me where I can do my duty. There I am ready to go, I care not where it leads me. My friends, that is the spirit that was in this city on yesterday. I am told of an incident that occurred which drew the tears to my eyes, and yet I am not much used to the melting mood. I am told of a man in your city who has a beloved wife and two children, depending upon his personal labor day by day for their support. He went home and said:

"Wife, I feel it is my duty to enlist and fight for my country." "That's just what I've been thinking of, too," said she; "God bless you, and may you come back without harm; but if you die in defence of the country, the God of the widow and the fatherless will take care of me and my children." That same wife came to your city. She knew precisely where her husband was to pass as he marched away. She took her position on the pavement, and finding a flag she begged leave just to stand beneath those sacred folds and take a last fond look on him whom she, by possibility, might never see again. The husband marched down the street; their eyes met; a sympathetic flash went from heart to heart; she gave one shout and fell senseless upon the pavement, and there she lay for not less than thirty minutes in a swoon. It seemed to be the departing of her life. But all the sensibility was sealed up. It was all sacrifice. She was ready to meet this tremendous sacrifice upon which we have entered, and I trust you are all ready. I am ready. God help me to do my duty. I am ready to fight in the ranks or out of the ranks. Having been educated in the academy, having been in the army seven years, having served as commander of a volunteer company for ten years, and having served as an adjutant-general, I feel I am ready for something. I only ask to be permitted to act; and in God's name give me something to do.

The Mothers of our Forest-Land.— *William D. Gallagher.*

The mothers of our forest-land!
Stout-hearted dames were they
With nerve to wield the battle-brand,
And join the border-fray.

Our rough land had no braver,
  In its days of blood and strife—
Aye ready for severest toil,
  Aye free to peril life.

The mothers of our forest-land!
  On old Kentucky's soil
How shared they, with each dauntless band,
  War's tempest and life's toil!
They shrank not from the foemen—
  They quailed not in the fight—
But cheered their husbands through the day,
  And soothed them through the night.

The mothers of our forest-land!
  Their bosoms pillowed men!
And proud were they by such to stand
  In hammock, fort, or glen,
To load the sure old rifle—
  To run the leaden ball—
To watch a battling husband's place,
  And fill it should he fall.

ADDRESS TO THE GRADUATING CLASS OF COLUMBIA COLLEGE—1861.—*President King.*

YOUNG GENTLEMEN: I salute you as trained *athletes*, just entering upon the strifes of life. If we have at all succeeded with you in our efforts at education, you have learned how to use your faculties. It will now devolve upon you to make their use subservient to the highest aims and the largest good. So only shall you prove yourselves worthy of your *alma mater*—worthy of your glorious country.

Life is real—life is earnest, to all and at all times; but at the particular juncture at which it is your fortune to be called to act, it is more than usually real and earnest

—and it is this exceptional condition of affairs that seems to demand from me at this time and on this, our most solemn academic exercises, a plain and frank expression of opinion, as to matters concerning which it is criminal not to have an opinion, and cowardly not to express it when fitting occasion offers.

You put on the garment of manhood, and assume its obligations in the midst of the most wanton, wicked, unprovoked and unpardonable rebellion that has been witnessed in the annals of the human race. It has no parallel but in the rebellion of the fallen angels; and it has the same source, disappointed ambition and malignant hate. Against the most beneficial government, the most equal laws, and a system carrying within itself a recognized and peaceful mode of adjusting every real or imaginary wrong or hardship, a portion of the people of the United States—the least civilized, the least educated, the least industrious, without a single wrong specified on the part of the national government—have risen in rebellion against it, robbing its treasuries, and even its hospitals; firing upon and treading underfoot the flag of our country; menacing its capital with armed hordes, led by the double-dyed traitors who, educated at the cost of the nation, and sworn to defend its laws, have deserted in the hour of need, and turned their arms against their nursing mother; and appealing to all the scoundrels of the world to come and take service under the rebel flag, against the commerce of the United States.

Honor, loyalty, truth, stood aghast for a while incredulously in the presence of this enormous crime; but when Sumter fell the free people of this nation rose—yes! rose as no like uprising has been witnessed before—and now who shall stay the avenging arm? Who, with traitor lips shall talk of compromise, or with shaking knees clamor for peace? Compromise with what?—peace with whom?

It is no question of this or that system of policy—of

free-trade or tariff, of slavery or anti-slavery—it is a question of existence. To be or not to be—it is all there. There is no such thing as half being and half not being. Either we are a nation, or a band of anarchical outlaws. A grand continental Anglo-Saxon republic, such as our fathers made, one and indivisible, *e pluribus unum*, under a constitution equal for all and supreme over all— or an accidental assemblage of petty, jealous, barbarous, warring tribes, who acknowledge no law but the sword, and from among whom the sword will not depart.

My young friends, you enter upon life at the very moment this great question is under the issue of war. Shrink not back from it. We must be decided now and forever. The baleful doctrine of secession must be finally and absolutely renounced. The poor quibble of double allegiance must be disavowed. An American—and not a New Yorker, nor a Virginian—is the noble title by which we are to live, and which you, my young friends, must, in your respective spheres, contribute to make live, however it may cost in blood and money.

Go forth, then, my young friends—go forth as citizens of the great continental American republic—to which your first, your constant, your latest hopes in life should attach—and abating no jot of obedience to municipal or state authority within the respective limits of each— bear yourselves always, and everywhere, as Americans— as fellow-countrymen of Adams, and Ellsworth, and Jay, and Paterson, and Carroll, and Washington, and Pinckney—as heirs of the glories of Bunker Hill and Saratoga, and Monmouth and Yorktown, and Eutaw Springs and New Orleans, and suffer no traitor hordes to despoil you of such rich inheritance, or of so grand and glorious a country.

Commodore Perry after the Battle of Lake Erie.
—*Hon. George Bancroft.*

As the cannon ceased, an awful stillness set in; nothing was heard but the feeble groans of the wounded, or the dash of oars as boats glided from one vessel to another.

Possession having been taken of the conquered fleet, at four o'clock Perry sent an express to Harrison with these words:

"DEAR GENERAL: We have met the enemy, and they are ours; two ships, two brigs, one schooner, and one sloop."

As he wrote to the secretary of the navy, a religious awe seemed to come over him, at his wonderful preservation in the midst of great and long-continued danger; and he attributed his signal victory to the pleasure of the Almighty.

It was on board the Lawrence that Perry then received the submission of the captives. This was due to the sufferings of her crew, to the self-sacrificing courage of the unnamed martyrs who still lay unburied on her deck, to the crowd of wounded, who thought their trials well rewarded by the issue. The witnesses to the act of the British officers in tendering their swords were chiefly the dead and the wounded, and the scene of sorrow tempered and subdued the exultation of triumph.

The conqueror bade his captives retain their side-arms; and added every just and unaffected expression of courtesy, mercy, and solicitude for their wounded.

When twilight fell, the mariners who had fallen on board the Lawrence, and had lain in heaps on the side of the ship opposite to the British, were sewn up in their hammocks, and, with a cannon-ball at their feet, were dropped one by one into the lake.

At last, but not till his day's work was done, exhausted

nature claimed rest, and Perry, turning into his cot, slept as sweetly and quietly as a child.

The dawn of morning revealed the deadly fierceness of the combat. Spectators from the island found the sides of the Lawrence completely riddled by shot from the long guns of the British; her deck was thickly covered with clots of blood; fragments of those who had been struck—hair, brains, broken pieces of bones—were still sticking to the rigging and sides. The sides of the Detroit and Queen Charlotte were shattered from bow to stern; on their larboard side there was hardly a hand's breadth free from the dent of a shot. Balls, cannister, and grape were found lodged in their bulwarks; their masts were so much injured that they rolled out in the first high wind.

The loss of the British, as reported by Barclay, amounted to forty-one killed, of whom three were officers; and ninety-four wounded, of whom nine were officers. Of the Americans, twenty-seven were killed and ninety-six wounded. Of these, twenty-one were killed and sixty-one wounded in the Lawrence, and about twenty more were wounded in the Niagara after she received Perry on board.

An opening on the margin of Put-in-Bay was selected for the burial-place of the officers who had fallen. The day was serene, the breezes hushed, the waters unruffled by a wavelet. The men of both fleets mourned together; as the boats moved slowly in procession, the music played dirges to which the oars kept time; the flags showed the sign of sorrow; solemn minute guns were heard from the ships. The spot where the funeral train went on shore was a wild solitude; the Americans and British walked in alternate couples to the graves, like men who, in the presence of eternity, renewed the relation of brothers and members of one human family, and the bodies of the dead were likewise borne along and buried alternately, English and American side by side, and undistinguished.

The wounded of both fleets, meeting with equal assiduous care, were sent to Erie, where Barclay was seen, with tottering steps, supported between Harrison and Perry, as he walked from the landing-place to his quarters.

Perry crowned his victory by his modesty, forbearing to place his own services in their full light, and more than just to others. When, in the following year, he was rewarded by promotion to the rank of captain, he who had never murmured at promotion made over his own head, hesitated about accepting a preferment which might wound his seniors.

The personal conduct of Perry throughout the tenth of September was perfect. His keenly sensitive nature never interfered with his sweetness of manner, his fortitude, the soundness of his judgment, the promptitude of his decision. In a state of impassioned activity, his plans were wisely framed, were instantly modified as circumstances changed, and were executed with entire coolness and self-possession. The mastery of the lakes, the recovery of Detroit and the far west, the capture of the British army in the peninsula of upper Canada, were the immediate fruits of his success. The imagination of the American people was taken captive by the singular incidents of a battle in which every thing seemed to have flowed from the personal prowess of one man; and wherever he came the multitude went out to bid him welcome. Washington Irving, the chosen organ, as it were, of his country, predicted his ever-increasing fame. Rhode Island cherishes his glory as her own; Erie keeps the tradition that its harbor was his ship-yard, its forests the storehouse for the frames of his chief vessels, its houses the hospitable shelter of the wounded among his crews; Cleveland graces her public square with a statue of the

4*

hero, wrought of purest marble, and looking out upon the scene of his glory; the tale follows the emigrant all the way up the straits, and to the head of Lake Superior. Perry's career was short and troubled; he lives in the memory of his countrymen, clothed in perpetual youth, just as he stood when he first saw that his efforts were crowned with success, and could say in his heart: "WE HAVE MET THE ENEMY AND THEY ARE OURS."

CRIMINALITY OF TREASON.—*New York Evening Post.*

MANY people apprehend that some of our authorities, both military and civil, entertain a wholly inadequate conception of the real nature and hideous wickedness of the crime of treason. But the truth is, we are so unused to the offence in this country, that we do not any of us readily estimate its atrocity. Like children that have never seen a serpent or a wolf, and who are not aware how poisonous the fangs of the one or how murderous the teeth of the other, we require actual experience to teach us all the danger and evil of the deed.

The ancient nations, whose peace was often attacked in this manner, gave it a bad pre-eminence over all other crimes. They regarded it not only as the gravest of offences in its own nature, but as displaying the vilest personal qualities on the part of the offender. It was for this reason that it was punished—first, by inflicting the severest penalties upon the criminal himself, and secondly, by branding his posterity forever. A person so corrupt as to be a traitor, they said, must transmit his qualities to his descendants. Besides, he who plots to disturb a nation's tranquillity, and to overthrow its constitution, commits a crime against posterity, and ought to suffer in his offspring. While humanity shudders at the severity of the argument, it is still useful to recall it, in order to show the sense of those nations who have actually suffered from this kind of malice.

The common law punishment of treason, so terrible and apparently barbarous—a punishment originating in the middle ages and continuing in substance upon the English statute-book to the present time—marks the abhorrence with which this crime was viewed. Its penalties may sleep, it is true, at the will of the monarch, but they exist, and can at any moment be applied. "Traitors," says Coke, citing Scriptural authority, "are to be drawn to the place of execution; so was Joab. They are to be hung; so was Bigthana, as stated in the book of Esther. They are to be disembowelled; so was Judas. Their hearts are to be pierced while living; so with Absalom. They are to be beheaded; so was Sheba, the son of Bichri. The blood of their posterity is corrupted so that they cannot inherit. So it is written in the one hundred and ninth Psalm, Let his children be fatherless and his wife a widow; let them be vagabonds and beg; and, in the next generation let his name be blotted out."

The penalties for this crime, like those of most other crimes, are not, under the mollifying influences of Christianity and civilization, so aggravated as they were. Yet the enormity of the offence would seem to have increased with the progress of society. In rude and barbarous ages, when nearly every man, if not a warrior, went armed; when the state was either an oppressive, or at best an unstable and impotent institution; when social relations were few and simple; when there was little accumulated property to be lost; little or no commerce to be destroyed, and when domestic life possessed none of that sanctity which now cleaves to the home and the hearth-stone—an assault upon the public order and peace was a matter of comparatively little importance.

All society was so insecure that an invasion of it produced none of the terrible consequences which the same deed would now do. Not only are our communities more numerous, but they are less prepared for defence against internal treachery; they embody vast amounts of wealth, which a breath of sedition may dissipate; their relations of man to man are more complicated and more vital, and a rupture of them consequently more destructive; and to excite a serious alarm now for their tranquillity is far more pernicious than open war upon them would have been some centuries ago. Treason produces ten thousand times the ruin, the unhappiness, the terror, in England or the United States, that it would in Egypt, or Turkey, or even Russia. Of what millions upon millions of wealth have not the Southern traitors occasioned the loss; but who shall estimate the degree of their iniquity, when the precious lives spent by war and disease, when the breaking of fraternal ties, and when the ill-feelings engendered in once friendly communities, shall be taken into the account? The villain who demands your purse or fires your house commits a dreadful individual wrong, but he is infinitely less to be dreaded than the grander criminal who overturns all the securities of social order, and assails the very life of the state.

We cannot, nor is it desirable that we should, visit this offence, the mischiefs of which are so greatly aggravated, with the ferocity of punishment formerly in vogue. We cannot, in this age, revive the old barbarous methods of capital executions. They have passed away with their day. But it is none the less important to mark our sense of the awful nature of the crime, and of our utter detestation of the criminals. They should not be treated as mere political offenders, to be dismissed with a gentle reprimand. They have made needless and wanton war on the best of governments; they have arrested the prosperity of the most peaceful of societies; they have caused the sacrifice of thousands of harmless and noble lives; and justice to the integrity of our laws, to the instincts of the human heart, to the future well-being of myriads of people, demands some signal exemplifications of our estimate of their malignity.

The American Statesman and Literature.

Above this crowd, and beyond them all, stands that character which I trust many of you will become—a real American Statesman. For the high and holy duty of serving his country, he begins by deep and solitary studies of its constitution and laws, and all its great interests. These studies are extended over the whole circumference of knowledge—all the depths and shoals of human passions are sounded to acquire the mastery over them. The solid structure is then strengthened and embellished by familiarity with ancient and modern languages—with history, which supplies the treasures of old experience—with eloquence, which gives them attraction—and with the whole of that wide miscellaneous literature, which spreads over them all a perpetual freshness and variety. These acquirements are sometimes reproached by the ignorant as being pedantry. They would be pedantic if they intruded into public affairs inappropriately; but in subordination to the settled habits of the individual, they add grace to the strength of his general character, as the foliage ornaments the fruit that ripens beneath it. They are again denounced as weakening the force of native talent, and contrasted disparagingly with what are called rough and strong-minded men. But roughness is no necessary attendant upon strength; the true steel is not weakened by the highest polish—just as the scimitar of

Damascus, more flexible in the hands of its master, inflicts a keener wound than the coarsest blade. So far from impairing the native strength of the mind, at every moment this knowledge is available. In the play of human interests and passions, the same causes ever influence the same results; what has been, will again be, and there is no contingency of affairs in which the history of the past may not shed its warning light on the future. The modern languages bring him into immediate contact with the living science and gifted minds of his remote contemporaries. All the forms of literature, which are but the varied modifications in which the human intellect develops itself, contribute to reveal to him its structure and its passions; and these endowments can be displayed in a statesman's career only by eloquence—itself a master power, attained only by cultivation. For an idle waste of words—at once a political evil and a social wrong—his only remedy is study. From study he learns that the last degree of refinement is simplicity; the highest eloquence the plainest; the most effective style—the pure, severe and vigorous manner, of which the great masters are the best teachers.

Character of William Penn.—*Duponceau.*

WILLIAM PENN stands the first among the lawgivers whose names and deeds are recorded in history. Shall we compare him with Lycurgus, Solon, Romulus, those founders of military commonwealths, who organized their citizens in dreadful array against the rest of their species, taught them to consider their fellow-men as barbarians, and themselves as alone worthy to rule over the earth? What benefit did mankind derive from their boasted institutions? Interrogate the shades of those who fell in the mighty contests between Athens and Lacedæmon, between Carthage and Rome, and between Rome and the rest of the universe.

But see William Penn, with weaponless hand, sitting down peaceably with his followers in the midst of savage nations, whose only occupation was shedding the blood of their fellow-men, disarming them by his justice, and teaching them, for the first time, to view a stranger without distrust. See them bury their tomahawks in his presence, so deep that man shall never be able to find them again. See them under the shade of the thick groves of Coaquannock extend the bright chain of friendship, and solemnly promise to preserve it as long as the sun and moon shall endure. See him then with his companions establishing his commonwealth on the sole basis of religion, morality and universal love, and adopting as the fundamental maxim of his government the rule handed down to us from heaven, Glory to God on high, and on earth peace, and good will to all men.

Here was a spectacle for the potentates of the earth to look upon, an example for them to imitate. But the potentates of the earth did not see, or if they saw, they turned away their eyes from the sight; they did not hear, or if they heard, they shut their ears against the voice, which called out to them from the wilderness,

Discere justitiam moniti et non temnere Divos.

The character of William Penn alone sheds a never-fading lustre on our history.

COLUMBIA.—*George W. Elliott.*

America! Home of the free!
　To the star of thy liberties bright,
Turn the eyes of the millions who flee,
　For a rescue, from Tyranny's night.
Though thy magical name and thy ensign unfurled
Now enkindle both envy and joy in the world,
Yet the Star Spangled Banner, the flag of the brave,
Where 'tis flung to the breeze, there it ever shall wave!
　　　　　Chorus:
Yet the Star Spangled Banner, the flag of the brave,
Where 'tis flung to the breeze, there it ever shall wave!

Columbia, queen of the land,
　From the heart of the nation, her throne,
Has proclaimed this benignant command—
　"Let the will of my people be known!
They are free from the scourge of oppression's fell rod;
They are free, evermore, in the worship of God!
And the Star Spangled Banner, the flag of the brave,
O'er the glorious Union forever shall wave!"
　　　　　Chorus:
And the Star Spangled Banner, the flag of the brave,
O'er the glorious Union forever shall wave!

America! Home of the free!
　'Tis thy dear starry emblem that holds
The enchantment that binds us to thee—
　All our fortunes with thine in its folds!
On the wretch who its honor or glory would pall,
Shall the lightning-winged vengeance of patriots fall!
Yes! the Star Spangled Banner, the flag of the brave,
Where 'tis flung to the breeze, there unsullied shall wave!
　　　　　Chorus:
Yes! the Star Spangled Banner, the flag of the brave,
Where 'tis flung to the breeze, there unsullied shall wave!

The President of the United States—What he ought to be.—*Hon. L. McLane.*

A CHIEF-MAGISTRATE of the Union should look to noble objects, and consider himself called to a high destiny. I would have him rouse his spirit and expand his mind to the elevation and grandeur of his important trust; I would have him to realize that he is the governor of a great, free, and prosperous people: various in their habits, opinions, and occupations, but all pursuing the general end of human action—the happiness of themselves and their posterity, and all equally entitled to the protection and favor of their government. I would have him to purify himself from all temptation to proscription or intolerance, and all vindictive or personal suggestions, and to maintain himself at a sightless distance above the low intrigues and bitterness of faction. I would have him thoroughly to understand the spirit and import of the constitution of our country; to consider all its functionaries entitled to equal respect with himself; to preserve sacred the just balance and apportionment of power among the various departments, and, in all cases of diversity of opinion—whether between the heads of departments or among the people at large—to maintain a wise moderation and forbearance, and to endeavor to lead the jarring parties to entertain respect for each other, and to co-operate for the common good. "I would have him to think of fame as well as of applause, and prefer that which to be enjoyed must be given, to that which may be bought; to consider his administration as a single day in the great year of government, but as a day that is affected by those which went before, and that must affect those which are to follow." I would have him to consider the constitution and the laws as the sole rule of his conduct, neither stretching nor warping them either to enlarge his own power or to abridge that of the co-ordinate departments, or of the people. To usurp no authority inconsistent with their spirit, nor to abuse that which they confer. I would have him diligently to inform himself of all the great and diversified interests of this vast and growing country, and so to succor the various branches of enterprise as to crown the whole with prosperity. I would have him to reflect that amidst the diversity of interests and multifarious concerns, both foreign and domestic, of the nation, questions will constantly arise necessarily eliciting various opinions among his countrymen. These I would have him to treat with respect and indulgence, even when they differ from his own, but by no means to make them objects of anger and punishment. I would have him not only to tolerate, but to encourage, all decent and respectful examination into his public policy and official conduct. I would have him to keep the offices of the government above the reach of the flatterer and the demagogue, and never to bestow them as rewards for mere party service; to bring to his aid in the other trusts of the government the soundest patriotism, the most elevated and various intellect, the most enlarged capacity that his country affords; and lest in seeking for such qualities his range of observation might be too circumscribed, I would have him to maintain such relations with all classes and portions of his countrymen, that the scope of his selection might have no other limit than the welfare of the commonwealth. Such is my idea of a virtuous, enlightened, and patriotic chief-magistrate, fit to administer the government of a free and united people. Such a one it may be difficult, perhaps impossible, to find, though it is presumed no one will deny that it is desirable and even a duty to approach as near as possible to a perfect government, and social happiness under it. The only question is, how near it may be practicable for us to come; and all must admit that we shall approach the nearer as the efforts of the people and the government shall concur for that object. Happily for our country we have one illustrious example, who, it would seem, had been given to us by Providence as an ever-living oracle, from whom we might, in all future times, refresh our minds with lessons of real wisdom and patriotism. Washington was the head of the nation, and not of a party; and amid all the trials of his situation, critical and complex as it certainly was, and amid the labors of organizing and conducting a new government, arduous as they were, beset also with the most dangerous of all jealousies, he made and preserved a united people, and finally retired from their service with greater character and more durable renown than he carried into it. This country has produced no second Washington; and it may be feared that it will be long before it will. Nevertheless, it ought to be the fervent prayer of every true patriot, that that event may yet happen, and that its advent may be hastened, and that until it shall please Providence to raise up such another, we may constantly meditate upon his pure example, and that some one may yet be found who has so studied the model of that matchless patriot, as to be able to preside over a united people.

TRUE DIGNITY.—*Owen Jones.*

GIVE me the man whose frontal tablet bold
  Bespeaks a lofty soul, with purpose firm;
Who would not bow before the idol gold,
  Nor basely tread upon the lowly worm;—

Who would not swerve from truth though hell should frown,
  And, threatening vengeance, open wide its jaws;
Who would not barter for an empire's crown
  The smallest particle in freedom's cause.

Give me the man who honors worth alone,
  True worth, though found mid humble toil or want;
Who would denounce the tyrant on his throne,
  And look with scorn upon the sycophant.

My soul is harrowed when I hear and see
  How traitors stand unscathed where patriots stood—
How Treason lurks beside fair Liberty,
  And frowns on blessings bought with nations' blood.

Oh! speed the time when men shall cease to be
  The wretched counterfeits of God's design—
When treason, plots, oppression, infamy,
  Shall cease, and man be noble, pure, divine!

Character of General Winfield Scott.—*Hon. J. T. Headley.*

The most striking points of General Scott's character stand out in bold relief. In so long and eventful a career, a man's character cannot be concealed. His actions reveal it. Probably a more fearless man never lived. Like Bonaparte, he may be irritated and disturbed by trifles, but danger always tranquilizes him. Those who have been with him most, say that in the moment of greatest peril, his lip wears its serenest expression. It is in the thunder-crash of battle, when the brave battalions are linked in deadliest conflict, that his heart beats calmest. It is a little singular that the greatest warriors (not merely desperate fighters, but men fit to be leaders of armies) have been distinguished for more than ordinary humanity and tenderness of feeling.

Murat, whose natural element seemed the smoke and carnage of battle, never drew his sword in combat, lest he should slay some one. Ney, who moved amid death like one above its power, was as simple and tender as a child. The same is true of Scott. The sick and distressed have not merely commanded his *sympathy*, but he has again and again risked his life to succor them. Stern, nay, almost tyrannical, as a disciplinarian, his heart as a man is filled with all generous emotions. He was in New York at the time of the Astor Place riot, and within hearing of the firing. As his practiced ear caught the regular volleys of the soldiers, he wrung his hands and walked the room in an agony of excitement, exclaiming: "*They are firing volleys, they are shooting down citizens!*" What an apparently strange contradiction! This man, whose nerves seemed made of iron in battle, and who had galloped with the joy of the warrior for hours, amid a hail-storm of bullets, could not control his feeling when he knew the blood of American citizens was flowing in the streets of New York. But in the one case he acted as a commander whose business it was to conquer; while here he was a man feeling for his fellowman. That burst of feeling did him more honor than the greatest victory he ever gained.

Scott is also distinguished for great tenacity of purpose. The desperate manner in which he clung to the height at Lundy's Lane—charging like fire, when but a quarter of his brigade was left, and crying out, as, mangled and bleeding, he was borne from the field: "*Charge again*"—reveals a strength and firmness of will that no earthly power can shake. Such a man is hard to beat. As a military chieftain, he probably has no superior, if equal, in the world. Place a hundred and fifty thousand American troops, drilled under his own supervision, in his hands, and the miracles of Napoleon will be wrought over again. He possesses all the qualities necessary to make a great commander. Courage, coolness in the hour of danger, fertility of resources, extensive yet rapid combination, the power of covering a vast field of operations, yet losing none of its details, perfect control over his troops, tireless energy and great humanity, combine in him as they are rarely found in any man. Success cannot intoxicate him, nor defeat enervate him. Tempted by no sudden stroke of good fortune into rashness, he cannot be made listless by disappointment. A less nicely balanced character would never have carried us safely through the difficulties on our northern frontier.

His life is singularly clear of moral blemishes. Noble and confiding, he has often been wronged, yet he never could be forced into low retaliation or soured into distrust of his fellow-man. While in Mexico, a friend warned him against an officer whom he suspected of being an enemy in disguise. "I cannot help it," said the general: "it has all my life been a positive luxury to me to confide in my fellow-man, and rather than give it up, I should prefer being stabbed under the fifth rib daily." The temptations which surround elevation to rank and power have never corrupted him; and he is, at this day, as firm a friend of religion, temperance, and all the moral virtues, as though his life had been devoted solely to their inculcation. It is rare to see a long and public career so unstained by any vice.

The Patriot's Battle Prayer.—*John Critchley Prince.*

PARAPHRASED FROM THE GERMAN OF SCHILLER.

Father of Life! to Thee, to Thee, I call—
  The cannon sends its thunders to the sky;
The winged fires of slaughter round me fall;
  Great God of battles! let Thy watchful eye
Look o'er and guard me in this perilous hour,
And if my cause be just, oh! arm me with Thy power.

Oh! lead me, Father, to a glorious end,
  To well-won freedom, or a martyr's death;
I bow submissive to Thy will, and send
  A soul-felt prayer to Thee in every breath:
Do with me as beseems Thy wisdom, Lord,
But let not guiltless blood defile my maiden sword!

God, I acknowledge Thee, and hear Thy tongue
  In the soft whisper of the falling leaves,
As well as in the tumult of the throng
  Arrayed for fight—this human mass that heaves
Like the vexed ocean. I adore Thy name,
Oh, bless me, God of grace, and lead me unto fame.

Oh! bless me, Father! in Thy mighty hand
  I place what Thou hast lent—my mortal life;
I know it will depart at thy command,
  Yet will I praise Thee, God, in peace or strife;
Living or dying, God, my voice shall raise
To Thee, Eternal Power, the words of prayer and
          praise!

I glorify Thee, God, I come not here
  To fight for false ambition, vainly brave;
I wield my patriot sword for things more dear,—
  Home and my fatherland; the name of slave
My sons shall not inherit. God of Heaven!
For Thee and Freedom's cause my sacred vow is given!

God, I am dedicate to Thee forever;
  Death, which is legion here, may hem me round;
Within my heart the invader's steel may quiver,
  And spill my life-blood on the crimson ground:
Still am I Thine, and unto Thee I call—
Father I seek the foe—forgive me if I fall!

Address to the United States House of Representatives—1861.—*Hon. G. A. Grow.*

Gentlemen of the House of Representatives of the United States of America: Words of thanks for the honor conferred by the vote just announced, would but feebly express the heart's gratitude.* While appreciating the distinguished mark of your confidence, I am not unmindful of the trying duties incident to the position to which you have assigned me. Surrounded at all times by grave responsibility, it is doubly so in this hour of national disaster, when every consideration of gratitude to the past and obligation to the future gathers around the present.

Fourscore years ago, fifty-six bold merchants, farmers, lawyers and mechanics, the representatives of a few feeble colonies scattered along the Atlantic seaboard, met in convention to found a new empire, based on the inalienable rights of man. Seven years of bloody conflict ensued, and the fourth of July, 1776, is canonized in the hearts of the great and good as the jubilee of oppressed nationalities, and in the calendar of heroic deeds it marks a new era in the history of the race. Three-quarters of a century have passed away, and the few feeble colonists, hemmed in by the ocean in front, the wilderness and the savage in the rear, have spanned a whole continent with a great empire of free states, rearing throughout its vast wilderness the temples of science and of civilization on the ruins of savage life. Happiness, seldom if ever equalled, has surrounded the domestic fireside, and prosperity unsurpassed has crowned the national energies; the liberties of the people have been secure at home and abroad, while the

---

* He had just been elected Speaker.

national standard floated, honored and respected, in every commercial mart of the world. On the return of this glorious anniversary, after a period but little exceeding the allotted lifetime of man, the people's representatives are convened in the council chambers of the republic, to deliberate on the means for preserving the government under whose benign influence these grand results have been achieved. A rebellion, the most causeless in the history of the race, has developed a conspiracy of long standing to destroy the constitution formed by the wisdom of our fathers, and the Union cemented by their blood. This conspiracy, nurtured for long years in secret councils, first develops itself openly in acts of spoliation and plunder of public property, with the connivance, or under the protection of treason, enthroned in all the high places of the government, and at last in armed rebellion for the overthrow of the best government ever devised by man. Without an effort in the mode prescribed in the organic law for a redress of all grievances, the malcontents appeal to the arbitrament of the sword, insult the nation's honor, trample upon its flag, and inaugurate a revolution, which, if successful, would end in establishing petty jarring confederacies, or anarchy, upon the ruins of the republic, and the destruction of its liberties.

The 19th of April, canonized in the first struggle for American nationality, has been reconsecrated in martyr blood. Warren has his counterpart in Ellsworth, and the heroic deeds and patriotic sacrifices of the struggle for the establishment of the republic are being reproduced upon the battle-field for its maintenance. Every race and tongue of men almost are represented in the grand legion of the Union, their standards proclaiming in a language more impressive than words, that here indeed is the home of the emigrant and the asylum of the exile, no matter where was his birth-place or in what clime his infancy was cradled. He devotes his life to the defence of his adopted land, the vindication of its honor, and the protection of its flag, with the same zeal with which he would guard his hearth-stone and fireside. All parties, sects and conditions of men, not corrupted by the institutions of human bondage, forgetting bygone rancors or prejudices, blend in one phalanx for the integrity of the Union and the perpetuity of the republic. Long years of peace in the pursuits of sordid gain, instead of blunting the patriotic devotion of loyal citizens, seem but to have intensified its development, when the existence of the government is assailed. The merchant, the banker and the tradesman, with an alacrity unparalleled, proffer their all at the altar of their country, while from the counter, the workshop and the plough, brave hearts and stout arms, leaving their tasks unfinished, rush to the tented field; the air vibrates with martial strains, and the earth shakes with armed men. In view of this grand demonstration for self-preservation in the history of nationalities, desponding patriotism may be assured that the foundations of our national greatness still stand strong, and the sentiment which beats to-day in every loyal heart, will for the future be realized. No flag alien to the sources of the Mississippi will ever float permanently over its mouth, till its waters are crimsoned with human gore, and not one foot of American soil can be wrenched from the jurisdiction of the constitution of the United States until it is baptized in fire and blood.

"In God is our trust,
And the star-spangled banner forever shall wave
O'er the land of the free and the home of the brave."

Those who regard it as mere cloth bunting, fail to appreciate its symbolical power. Wherever civilization dwells, or the name of Washington is known, it bears on its folds the concentrated power of armies and navies, and surrounds the votaries with a defence more impregnable than a battlement of wall or tower. Wherever on the earth's surface an American citizen may wander, called by pleasure, business, or caprice, it is a shield securing him against wrong and outrage, save on the soil of the land of his birth. As the guardians of the rights and liberties of the people, your paramount duty is to make it honored at home as it is respected abroad. A government that cannot command the loyalty of its own citizens is unworthy the respect of the world, and a government that will not protect its own loyal citizens deserves the contempt of the world. He who would tear down this grandest temple of constitutional liberty, thus blasting forever the hopes of crushed humanity, because its freemen, in the mode prescribed by the constitution, select a chief-magistrate not acceptable to him, is a parricide to his race, and should be regarded as a common enemy of mankind. The Union once destroyed, is a shattered vase that no human power can reconstruct in its original symmetry. Coarse stones, when they are broken, may be cemented again—precious ones, never. If the republic is to be dismembered, and the sun of its liberty must go out in endless night, let it set amid the roar of cannon and the din of battle, when there is no longer an arm to strike or heart to bleed in its cause, so that coming generations may not reproach the present with being too imbecile to preserve the priceless legacy bequeathed by our fathers, so as to transmit it unimpaired to future times. Again, gentlemen, thanking you for your confidence and kindness, and invoking guidance from that Divine Power that led our fathers through the Red Sea of the revolution, I enter upon the discharge of the duties to which you have assigned me, relying upon your forbearance and co-operation, and trusting that your labors will contribute not a little to the greatness and glory of the republic.

The Myrtle and Steel.—*Charles Fenno Hoffman.*

One bumper yet, gallants, at parting,
  One toast ere we arm for the fight;
Fill round, each to her he loves dearest—
  'Tis the last he may pledge her to-night.
Think of those who of old at the banquet
  Did their weapons in garlands conceal,
The patriot-heroes who hallowed
    The entwining of myrtle and steel!
    Then hey for the myrtle and steel!
    Then ho for the myrtle and steel!
Let every true blade who e'er loved a maid,
  Fill round to the myrtle and steel!

Now mount, for our bugle is ringing
  To marshal the host for the fray,
Where proudly our banner is flinging
  Its folds o'er the battle array;
Yet, gallants—one moment—remember,
  When your sabres the death-blow would deal,
That mercy wears *her* shape who's cherished
  By lads of the myrtle and steel.
    Then hey for the myrtle and steel!
    Then ho for the myrtle and steel!
Let every true blade who e'er loved a maid,
  Fill round to the myrtle and steel!

The Fugitive Lieutenant.—*New York Ledger.*

It was while the American army was freezing and starving at Valley Forge, and the British army was rioting and luxuriating in Philadelphia, that a lame, dirty, beggarly-looking fellow, walking with a crutch, approached the northern outpost of the royal forces, and, with a simple, idiotic laugh and leer, announced his intention of entering the city and taking the British general prisoner.

"Indeed?—then I shall be under the necessity of arresting you!" said a young subaltern, winking at some of his companions, and assuming a serious air.

"He! he! he!" laughed the idiot; "just you try it, that's all."

"Why, my good fellow, what would you do?"

"Do?" exclaimed the other, drawing himself up with an air of defiance; "why, I'd tell the great General Washington."

"Then I am afraid to venture on your arrest. So pass on—you will probably find General Howe prepared to receive you."

The idiot suddenly looked troubled, glancing about him warily and suspiciously, as if he feared he might meet the general he was so boldly going to capture, but finally hobbled off toward the city. With some such silly dialogue he got past the different sentries, who seemed to give him no thought beyond the amusement of the time. By night he was fairly within the town, and kept on his way, sometimes humming snatches of old songs, and in general not much noticed by any. Through one street after another he continued to hobble forward, till he came to one of no great length, containing a block of three-story, respectable-looking houses, which might be occupied by persons in middling circumstances. This street was not lighted, and appeared deserted, so that when he stopped before one of the dwellings he was not perceived. He knocked at the door, and a woman's head appeared at the second-story window.

"Won't you give me something to eat, ma'm? I'm nearly starved!" said the idiot.

"Yes, poor fellow!" replied the woman, in a kindly tone; "in a minute I will hand you something."

Soon after a lower shutter was pushed a little back, and a hand, containing some bread and meat, was thrust out.

"Mother!" said a low voice.

"Gracious heaven!" exclaimed the female within, in an agitated tone.

"Hush!" returned the beggar, in a guarded whisper. A moment after the door was thrown open.

"Yes, ma'm—thank you—I don't care if I do," said the beggar, as if in reply to an invitation to come in, at the same time crossing the threshold, with an appearance of deep humility.

The moment the door closed behind him, the man dropped his crutch and threw his arms around the other, fairly sobbing.

"Mother! dear, dear mother!"

"William!" exclaimed the other, pressing the ragged mendicant to her heart; "oh, my dear, dear William! what is the meaning of this? and how is it I find you here in this sad plight?"

"I have passed the British lines in this disguise, playing the fool to the sentries. But tell me how you are, dear mother, and how you fare in these troublous times?"

"Indifferently well, my son. The British are our masters here, but so far I have little to complain of in the way of personal treatment. Provisions are scarce and high, and only by the strictest economy shall I be able to live through, if they continue to retain possession of the city any considerable length of time. Your sister Mary is at your uncle's in Delaware, and will deeply regret that she has missed this opportunity of seeing you."

"And are you alone, mother?"

"No, two English gentleman are boarding with me."

"Do they belong to the army?" inquired the young man, quickly and uneasily; "and are they now in the house?"

"No; they appear to be private gentlemen of some means, and neither is within at present. But you look troubled—have you any thing to fear, my son?"

"If detected, I may be hung as a spy."

"Good heavens!" exclaimed the mother, in alarm; "you terrify me! Are you here without permission? without a pass?"

"Yes—did I not say I played the fool to the sentries, and so got past them?"

"But I thought that was for your own amusement. Oh, William, if you should be discovered! Why did you venture in this desperate manner?"

"I could not get a pass, and I was so anxious to see you and Mary that I resolved to risk all."

"Quick, then, come up stairs, and let us fix upon a hiding-place at once, before any thing happens! Oh, William, I am so alarmed!"

Both hastened up stairs to the third story, and, after considering several places, decided that the loft close under the roof might be the best for concealment, as the trap-door leading to it could be fastened underneath, which would tend to blind a search; while the young man, if pressed, could escape to the roof, and, by means of a long rope, fastened to the chimney, could lower himself into either the yard or the street. This would not insure his escape, but it was the best plan the two could think of, and served to render both less fearful of detection and the serious consequences. Having provided the rope, the mother hastened to bring up a large quantity of food, which her son began to devour with a ravenousness that showed he had told no untruth, when, in the character of a beggar, he had declared himself in a state bordering on starvation.

While he was eating, his mother plied him with questions concerning the army at Valley Forge, in which he held a lieutenant's commission, and which he had left on a furlough; and the answers of the young soldier depicted a state of destitution and suffering that caused his hearer to weep for very sympathy. Three thousand soldiers had been down on the sick list at one time, and, without the common necessaries of life, had perished by hundreds; while of those capable of doing duty, scarcely one had a blanket to cover him at night, or food enough to keep soul and body together. Pale, emaciated, ragged and dirty, many with bare feet upon the frozen earth, they walked shivering through the camp by day, and crowded themselves together at night, to get what little warmth they could from each other's bodies, the most forlorn and wretched set of beings that ever a nation called to arms.

"God help us all!" ejaculated the mother, in a dejected tone. "I suppose, after all our hardships, we shall be compelled to succumb to our tyrannical foes."

"Never," cried the young officer, "while there are a thousand men left in our country to make a last desperate stand. We can only be conquered by annihilation; and if it is God's will that a tyrant shall rule over this broad continent, not a single true heart will live to feel the oppression and degradation. Ere that time, dear mother, I for one shall be beyond the reach of earthly monarch."

"God bless you, William!" cried the mother, enthusiastically grasping his hand; "your father's spirit speaks in you. He died on the battle-field with those sentiments in his heart; and I freely give you—my only son and hope—to the glorious cause which his blood and that of thousands of others has hallowed."

For several days the intrepid young officer remained concealed beneath his mother's roof, his presence supposed to be known only to themselves. But one evening, near the end of his furlough, when he was beginning to think about preparing for his secret departure, an officer with six men appeared at the door, and said he had orders to arrest one William Ruggles, supposed to be somewhere in the dwelling.

"Why, that is my son!" said the widow, in great trepidation.

"So much the more likely that he should be here, then," was the unfeeling reply.

"And for what would you arrest him? and what will be done with him if found?"

"We shall take him for a spy, and, if found guilty, he will be hung of course, as every cursed rebel should be. Here, Badger and Wilcot, guard the back-door; you, Bent and Walters, begin the search; and you, Jones and Johnson, remain where you are. Sharp now, all of you! Let the fellow be taken alive if possible—but, alive or dead, let him be taken. Now, good woman, if he is in the house, of which we are very strongly assured, let him appear, and save yourself much trouble, otherwise the consequences be on your own head."

"If you think my son is in the house, search to your heart's content!" returned the mother, externally calm, internally suffering.

And forthwith the search began.

Meantime the young lieutenant, who had heard enough to comprehend his danger, had set about effecting his escape, but not altogether in the manner first intended. He went out on the roof, it is true, and tied the long rope to the chimney, casting one end down toward the street, but this only for a blind. He had seen that the bricks of the dividing wall between the house occupied by his mother and one of the two adjoining buildings, had been loosely put up under the ridge-pole, and his present design was to remove a few of these, crowd through into the loft of the other house, and then replace them. This purpose he effected before the soldiers searching for him came up near enough to hear the little noise he was compelled to make. The open trap-door of the roof, and the rope around the chimney, served to mislead them, as he had hoped; and it was with a feeling of intense satisfaction that he heard

5*

them announce the manner of his escape. Immediately after, the whole party left in haste, first threatening Mrs. Ruggles with subsequent vengeance, for harboring, concealing, and conniving at the escape of a rebel spy, even though the man was her son.

When fully satisfied that all the soldiers had gone, young Ruggles attempted to return into his mother's dwelling by the way he had left, but in again displacing the bricks for this purpose, one of them slipped and went down through an open trap-door upon the floor below, making a loud noise. Immediately after a light flashed up through the opening, and a timid female voice demanded who was there.

Here was a dilemma. Should the young soldier reply, he would be exposed; and should he keep silence, a search would probably be made, which might prove even more serious in its consequences. What was to be done? A sudden inspiration seized him. It was a woman's voice, and women are seldom steeled to pity. He would make himself known, appeal to her sympathies, and throw himself upon her mercy.

"Lady," he began, in a gentle tone, calculated to reassure his fair hearer, "be not alarmed. I am a friend in distress, the son of your next-door neighbor. I am hunted as a spy by British soldiers, and, if found, my life will be forfeited. If you cannot pity me, for God's sake pity my poor mother, and assist me for her sake!"

He presented himself at the opening to the loft, and boldly descended the steps leading down from it, directly before the lady, a sweet, beautiful girl of eighteen, who stood with a light in her hand, and seemed dumb and motionless with a commingling of fear, surprise and curiosity. The young man continued to speak as he descended, and hurriedly went on to narrate all that had occurred, concluding with the search of the soldiers, and his escape into the loft above.

"Thank God, it is in my power to aid you, sir!" were the first words of the girl, spoken with a look and feeling of sympathy that made the heart of the soldier bound with strange emotions.

She then went on to tell him that a cousin from New Jersey, about his size and build, and looking not unlike him, was then on a visit to the family, having a pass from General Howe. This pass she had that evening been looking at, and by accident it was now in her possession, the cousin having gone out with the rest of the family, and forgotten it.

"Take it and fly, and may God preserve you!" she said. "I can arrange it with my kinsman," she continued; "I can have lost it, and he can easily procure another."

She hurried him down stairs, throwing a cloak over his shoulders on the way, which she insisted upon his wearing, saying it had belonged to a deceased brother, and he could return it at any future time. She then hastened to get the pass, which she placed in his hand, and urged him to go at once.

"If I could but see my mother for a moment!" he said.

"No, no—leave all to me—I will explain all to her—go while you can, before it is too late."

"God in heaven bless you, sweet lady!" he said, impulsively seizing her hand and touching it with his lips. "I will never forget you."

The next minute he was gone. He escaped. And, true to his declaration, he never did forget the sweet girl who befriended him in his hour of peril. Years after, the honored wife of General Ruggles was many a time heard to tell of her first romantic meeting with him she loved, then a hunted fugitive from the Continental army.

Decisive Integrity.—*Hon. William Wirt.*

The man who is so conscious of the rectitude of his intentions, as to be willing to open his bosom to the inspection of the world, is in possession of one of the strongest pillars of a decided character. The course of such a man will be firm and steady, because he has nothing to fear from the world, and is sure of the approbation and support of heaven, while he who is conscious of secret and dark designs which, if known, would blast him, is perpetually shrinking and dodging from public observation, and is afraid of all around, and much more of all above him.

Such a man may indeed pursue his iniquitous plans steadily; he may waste himself to a skeleton in the guilty pursuit; but it is impossible that he can pursue them with the same health-inspiring confidence and exulting alacrity, with him who feels, at every step, that he is in the pursuit of honest ends by honest means. The clear, unclouded brow, the open countenance, the brilliant eye which can look an honest man steadfastly yet courteously in the face, the healthfully beating heart, and the firm elastic step, belong to him whose bosom is free from guile, and who knows that all his motives and purposes are pure and right. Why should such a man falter in his course? He may be slandered; he may be deserted by the world; but he has that within which will keep him erect, and enable him to move onward in his course with his eyes fixed on heaven, which he knows will not desert him.

Let your first step, then, in that discipline which is to give you decision of character, be the heroic determination to be honest men, and to preserve this character through every vicissitude of fortune, and in every relation which connects you with society. I do not use this phrase, " honest men," in the narrow sense, merely, of meeting your pecuniary engagements, and paying your debts; for this the common pride of gentlemen will constrain you to do. I use it in its larger sense of discharging all your duties, both public and private, both open and secret, with the most scrupulous, heaven-attesting integrity; in that sense, further, which drives from the bosom all little, dark, crooked, sordid, debasing considerations of self, and substitutes in their place a bolder, loftier and nobler spirit; one that will dispose you to consider yourselves as born, not so much for yourselves, as for your country and your fellow-creatures, and which will lead you to act on every occasion sincerely, justly, generously, magnanimously.

There is a morality on a larger scale, perfectly consistent with a just attention to your own affairs, which it would be the height of folly to neglect: a generous expansion, a proud elevation, and conscious greatness of character, which is the best preparation for a decided course, in every situation into which you can be thrown; and it is to this high and noble tone of character that I would have you to aspire. I would not have you to resemble those weak and meagre streamlets, which lose their direction at every petty impediment that presents itself, and stop, and turn back, and creep around, and search out every little channel through which they may wind their feeble and sickly course. Nor yet would I have you to resemble the headlong torrent that carries havoc in its mad career. But I would have you like the ocean, that noblest emblem of majestic decision, which, in the calmest hour, still heaves its resistless might of waters to the shore, filling the heavens, day and night, with the echoes of its sublime declaration of independence, and tossing and sporting, on its bed, with an imperial consciousness of strength that laughs at opposition. It is this depth, and weight, and power, and purity of character, that I would have you to resemble; and I would have you, like the waters of the ocean, to become the purer by your own action.

Eulogium on the Captors of Major André.—*Hon. H. J. Raymond.*

Nothing is easier—nothing, I may add, is more unjust—than to disparage the worth and excellence of useful acts, by throwing distrust upon the motives of the men by whom they have been performed. There is no name so lofty that it cannot be thus assailed—no character so clear that it may not thus be stained. But if motives are to be judged by facts, by attendant circumstances, and by character—and I know no other test so decisive and so just—I can recall none of the actors in our revolutionary history who may defy the utmost scrutiny of such an inquisition, more fearlessly or more safely, than the captors of Major André. Their past lives, their labors, and their sufferings, attest their devotion to their country's cause. At the moment of their meeting André, they were engaged in the performance of a legalized and a useful service. Not a fact has ever been cited to disprove the averment that their search of his person, and their conversation with him, were for the sole purpose of deciding his character, and thus upon the course it would be proper for them to take; and they returned him to the American camp, in spite of the most tempting offers which the peril of his position could prompt; in ignorance of the real importance of his rank and mission; without any ground for expecting any great reward; and, so far as an unprejudiced judgment can decide, from the sole motive of guarding the country and the cause they served from the unknown peril which his presence seemed to threaten. If the bare opinion, unsupported by a single fact, of their chagrined and baffled captive—pronounced, with unmanly resentment, on his way to that scaffold which their detection of his crime had erected for him—is to outweigh all these considerations, and reverse the verdict of fifty years, then, indeed, is an honorable name among men one of the most precarious and unsubstantial of earthly possessions.

But I am conscious of giving more notice to this matter than it deserves. If I were in some distant land, a vindication of the captors of André might be needed: but here in Westchester; amid the descendants of those who knew them well; in presence of this large multitude assembled to do them honor; on the very spot made sacred by their heroic and undying act; and in shadow of the monument you have erected to perpetuate the remembrance of it through all coming time, I know it cannot be required: I only hope it may be excused.

And now, friends and fellow-citizens, your work of patriotism and of duty has been performed. This monument—simple, substantial, unpretending—fit emblem of the men it honors, stands complete. It commemorates no brilliant or renowned exploit; but it signalizes an honest and a manly act, which turned the adverse tide of a nation's struggle for independence, and produced results of vast beneficence in that nation's history. Richly have the men by whom it was performed, deserved this mark of your patriotic and grateful recollection. Their memory will be cherished, and the story of their virtue will be rehearsed, when generations to come shall vainly seek to trace their names on this crumbling stone; for what is this great nation, with its large and beneficent liberty, its growing grandeur, its advancing power, its uncounted blessings, and its bright example, but a mighty monument to the patriots who won its freedom, and laid the deep foundations of its fame? Loftier than the Pyramids, grander than the Pantheon, holier than that sacred temple where England garners up the immortal treasures of her heart, is the mausoleum where their ashes rest: for they repose in the soil redeemed by their blood; the heavens, that smiled on their toil, in benignity bend over their grave; the freedom and the happiness of the millions they blessed, sound unceasingly their anthem of praise; and,

> "So sepulchred, in such pomp they lie,
> That kings for such a tomb might wish to die."

The National Flag.—*New York Ledger.*

EIGHTY-FOUR years ago, on the fourteenth of the present month, it was resolved by Congress, "That the flag of the thirteen United States be thirteen stripes, alternate red and white, and that the *Union* be thirteen white stars on a blue field." Twenty-one new stars have since been added to the constellation of 1777, and the "blue field" is now spangled with thirty-four shining symbols of liberty and union. The progress of the republic during the period that has elapsed since the stars and stripes were adopted as the national ensign, has been little short of miraculous. Its population of scant three millions at the commencement of the war of independence, has increased to more than thirty millions, and although yet in its infancy, as we reckon the ages of nations, it ranks in political importance, in commercial power and influence, in material resources, and in all the elements of national glory, with the mightiest empires of the old world. Never was there such a bound from comparative insignificance to substantial greatness since time began. Our story is the very romance of history.

> The tree
> Whose drooping branches one by one take root

Until a forest hides the parent stem,
Symbols the rise of empires—yet for *ours*
Affords no parallel. *Its bursting seeds
Were scattered broadcast by the hand of God!*
Behold the increase!—where, on every side,
From the blue mountains to the bounding main.
Nestling in valleys, dotting fertile plains,
And on the hill-sides shining, crowned with spires,
Our cities rise; while down a hundred streams
Our inland fleets sweep laden to the sea!
Behold the lakes, where once the frail canoe
Timidly coasted! Lo, from port to port,
Trailing their smoky penuons through the sky,
The mighty steamers surging!
      In each zone
That belts the earth our star-lit banner shines,
And every gale sends forth to every shore,
Or home returns, our freighted argosies!

 The flag under which we have attained to such a pitch of prosperity and glory, was first displayed in battle on the 7th of October, 1777, at the memorable battle of Saratoga, which resulted in the surrender, a few days afterward, of more than six thousand British troops to the American arms. This was a glorious beginning, and the banner thus auspiciously launched upon its career, was borne on from victory to victory, until it floated over the heights of Yorktown, and the veterans of Cornwallis grounded their weapons under its triumphant folds. Thirty-four years later British valor again succumbed before it at the decisive battle of New Orleans. Then Algiers and Tripoli and Tunis were compelled to do it homage, and still more recently, after a series of the most brilliant successes, uninterrupted by a single reverse, it was planted, an emblem of conquest, in the capital of Mexico. Through three wars it has passed without a stain. For more than four-fifths of a century it has fluttered over the only free country on the face of the globe. It has been respected in every land and on every sea. No government has ever outraged it with impunity. It has been borne further into the regions of eternal ice than any other flag in Christendom. The greatest statesmen and orators of modern times—aye, or of any times—have flourished in its shadow. Genius has wedded it to immortal song. It was the battle standard and the pall of Washington. It is the only legitimate emblem of true civil liberty that floats this day between earth and heaven. The despot-ridden peoples of Europe look up to it with eyes as full of trust and hope, as if the motto of the sacred banner of Constantine, "In hoc signo vinces," *Under this sign shall ye conquer*, was written in letters of light across its stripes and stars. It is the flag not merely of this Union, but of freedom—*she has no other!* To abandon or dishonor it would be base ingratitude to heaven, and foul treason to mankind! LONG MAY IT WAVE!

UPWARD! ONWARD!—*John H. Bryant.*

UPWARD, onward, are our watchwords;
  Though the winds blow good or ill,
Though the sky be fair or stormy,
  These shall be our watchwords still.

Upward, onward, in the battle
  Waged for freedom and the right,
Never resting, never weary,
  Till a victory crowns the fight.

Upward, onward, pressing forward,
  Till each bondman's chains shall fall,
Till the flag that floats above us,
  Liberty proclaims to all.

Waking every morn to duty—
  Ere its hours shall pass away,

Let some act of love or mercy
Crown the labors of the day.

Lo! a better day is coming,
Brighter prospects ope before;
Spread your banner to the breezes—
Upward, onward, evermore!

Our Country.—*Daniel Webster.*

This lovely land, this glorious liberty, these benign institutions, the dear purchase of our fathers, are ours; ours to enjoy, ours to preserve, ours to transmit. Generations past, and generations to come, hold us responsible for this sacred trust. Our fathers, from behind, admonish us with their anxious paternal voices; posterity calls out to us from the bosom of the future; the world turns hither its solicitous eyes;—all, all conjure us to act wisely and faithfully in the relation which we sustain. We can never, indeed, pay the debt which is upon us; but by virtue, by morality, by religion, by the cultivation of every good principle and every good habit, we may hope to enjoy the blessing through our day, and to leave it unimpaired to our children.

Let us feel deeply how much, of what we are and of what we possess, we owe to this liberty, and these institutions of government. Nature has, indeed, given us a soil which yields bounteously to the hands of industry; the mighty and fruitful ocean is before us, and the skies over our heads shed health and vigor. But what are lands, and seas, and skies, to civilized man, without society, without knowledge, without morals, without religious culture? and how can these be enjoyed, in all their extent, and all their excellence, but under the protection of wise institutions and a free government?

There is not one of us, there is not one of us here present, who does not at this moment, and at every moment, experience in his own condition, and in the condition of those most near and dear to him, the influence and the benefits of this liberty and these institutions. Let us, then, acknowledge the blessing; let us feel it deeply and powerfully; let us cherish a strong affection for it, and resolve to maintain and perpetuate it. The blood of our fathers—let it not have been shed in vain; the great hope of posterity—let it not be blasted.

The striking attitude, too, in which we stand to the world around us, cannot be altogether omitted here. Neither individuals nor nations can perform their part well, until they understand and feel its importance, and comprehend and justly appreciate all the duties belonging to it. It is not to inflate national vanity, nor to swell a light and empty feeling of self-importance; but it is that we may judge justly of our situation, and of our own duties, that I earnestly urge this consideration of our position and our character among the nations of the earth.

It cannot be denied, but by those who would dispute against the sun, that with America, and in America, a new era commences in human affairs. This era is distinguished by free representative governments, by entire religious liberty, by improved systems of national intercourse, by a newly-awakened and an unconquerable spirit of free inquiry, and by a diffusion of knowledge through the community, such as has been before altogether unknown and unheard of. America, America, our country, our own dear and native land, is inseparably connected, fast bound up, in fortune and by fate, with these great interests. If they fall, we fall with them; if they stand, it will be because we have upholden them.

New England and the Union—1846.—*Hon. Hannibal Hamlin.*

Too often within these walls,* in the discussion of various measures, have I heard taunts and reproaches, either directly or by implication, cast upon various sections of this Union; and when they were directed to that section where it is my pride and my pleasure to reside, I have felt them thrill along my nerves, like an electric shock, and the impulses of my heart have been upon my lips to hurl them back again. But time and reflection have chastened these feelings; and I pass them by in sorrow that they should come from the lips of any individual on this floor; and while it is my pride to be an inhabitant of that section whose motives were so questioned here, I have a word to say in behalf of that people. I have no objections to interpose here in defence of what may have been the errors or wickedness of her politicians, but in behalf of her citizens I have a word to say. I believe them to be as patriotic as any other class of citizens to be found in our Union. They have exhibited their patriotism and their valor on many a well-fought field. Their bones have bleached on many a northern hill, and the barren sands of the south have drunk in their best blood. Sir, I point with pride to the north, and invite you there to witness a system which has grown up with us, and which is our ornament. I point you to our system of free labor. I point you to our common schools—to our churches pointing their spires toward heaven—and I glory in them. They are the monuments that belong to a free people, who have the true spirit of citizens of a free government. These things are the glory of the north. They are the blood-

---

* Of the United States House of Representatives.

less moral monuments which mark the progress of a free people. But I stop not here: I ask you to go with me throughout this whole broad nation; and I point you to her—I point you to the whole Union—as a monument of political grandeur towering toward the heavens, upon which the friend of freedom, wherever upon our globe he may be, may gaze; around whose summit the sunlight of glory forever shines, and at whose base a free people reposes, and I trust, will forever repose. So much for New England, my *home;* so much for the Union, my *country!*

The Charter Oak.—*By George D. Prentice.*

(Written before the old monarch's fall.)

Tree of the olden time! A thousand storms
Have hurried through thy branches—centuries
Have set their signets on thy trunk, and gone
In silence o'er thee like the moonlight mists,
That move at evening o'er the battlements
Of the eternal mountains! and yet thou
Shakest thy naked banner in the heavens
As proudly still as when great Freedom first
Crowned thee with deathless glory!

       Monument
Of nations perished! since thy form first sprang
From its green throne of forest, many a deep
And burning tide of human tears has flowed
Down to the ocean of the past, until
Its every wave is bitterness—but thou
Art reckless still!—no heart has ever throbbed
Beneath thy silent breast, and, though thy sighs
Have mingled with the night-storm, they were not
The requiem of the nations that have gone
Down to the dust, like thy own withered leaves
Swept by the autumn tempest!

>   Aye—bloom on,
> Tree of the cloud and sun! Gird on thy strength!
> Yet there will come a time when thou shalt sleep
> Upon thy own hill-tomb! The marshalled storms
> Shall seek but find thee not—and the proud clime,
> That long has been the consecrated home
> Of Liberty and thee, shall lie as erst
> In silent desolation! Not a sound
> Shall rise from all its confines save the moan
> Of passing winds, the cloud's deep tone of fear,
> The noise of stormy waters, and the wild
> And fearful murmuring of the earthquake's voice.

Character of the Disunionists—1861.—*Hon. Joseph Holt.*

COULD one an entire stranger to our history, now look down upon the South, and see there a hundred or a hundred and fifty thousand men marching in hostile array, threatening the capture of the capital and the dismemberment of the territory of the republic; and could he look again and see that this army is marshalled and directed by officers recently occupying distinguished places in the civil and military service of the country; and further, that the states from which this army has been drawn appear to be one vast seething cauldron of ferocious passion, he would very naturally conclude that the government of the United States had committed some great crime against its people, and that this uprising was in resistance to wrong and outrages which had been borne until endurance was no longer possible. And yet no conclusion could be further from the truth than this. The government of the United States has been faithful to all its constitutional obligations. For eighty years it has maintained the national honor at home and abroad, and by its prowess, its wisdom, and its justice, has given to the title of an American citizen an elevation among the nations of the earth which the citizens of no republic have enjoyed since Rome was mistress of the world. Under its administration the national domain has stretched away to the Pacific, and that constellation which announced our birth as a people, has expanded from thirteen to thirty-four stars, all, until recently, moving undisturbed and undimmed in their orbs of light and grandeur. The rights of no states have been invaded; no man's property has been despoiled, no man's liberty abridged, no man's life oppressively jeopardized by the action of this government. Under its benign influences the rills of public and private prosperity have swelled into rivulets, and from rivulets into rivers ever brimming in their fulness, and everywhere, and at all periods of its history, its ministrations have fallen as gently on the people of the United States as do the dews of a summer's night on the flowers and grass of the gardens and fields.

Whence, then, this revolutionary outbreak? Whence the secret spring of this gigantic conspiracy, which, like some huge boa, had completely coiled itself around the limbs and body of the republic, before a single hand was lifted to resist it? Strange, and indeed startling, as the announcement must appear when it falls on the ears of the next generation, the national tragedy, in whose shadow we stand to-night, has come upon us because, in November last, John C. Breckinridge was not elected president of the United States, and Abraham Lincoln was. This is the whole story. And I would pray now to know on what was John C. Breckinridge fed that he has grown so great, that a republic founded by Washington, and cemented by the best blood that has ever coursed in human veins, is to be overthrown, because, forsooth, he cannot be its president? Had he been chosen, we well know that we should not have heard of this rebellion, for the lever with which it is being moved would have been wanting to the hands of the conspirators. Even after his defeat, could it have been guaranteed, beyond all peradventure, that Jeff. Davis, or some other kindred spirit, would be the successor of Mr. Lincoln, I presume we hazard nothing in assuming that this atrocious movement against the government would not have been set on foot. So much for the principle involved in it. This great crime, then, with which we are grappling, sprang from that " sin by which the angels fell"— an unmastered and profligate ambition—an ambition that " would rather reign in hell than serve in heaven"—that would rather rule supremely over a shattered fragment of the republic than run the chances of sharing with others the honors of the whole.

The conspirators of the South read in the election of Mr. Lincoln a declaration that the democratic party had been prostrated, if not finally destroyed, by the selfish intrigues and corruptions of its leaders; they read, too, that the vicious, emaciated, and spavined hobby of the slavery agitation, on which they had so often rode into power, could no longer carry them beyond a given geographical line of our territory, and that in truth this factious and treasonable agitation, on which so many of them had grown great by debauching and denationalizing the mind of a people naturally generous and patriotic, had run its course, and hence, that from the national disgust for this demagogueing, and from the inexorable law of population, the time had come when all those who had no other political capital than this, would have to prepare for retirement to private life, so far at least as the highest offices of the country were concerned. Under the influence of these grim discouragements they resolved to consummate at once—what our political history shows to have been a long-cherished purpose—the dismemberment of the government. They said to themselves: " Since we can no longer monopolize the great offices of the republic as we have been accustomed to do, we will destroy it and build upon its ruins an empire that shall be all our own, and whose spoils neither the North nor the East nor the West shall share with us." Deplorable and humiliating as this certainly is, it is but a rehearsal of the sad, sad story of the past. We had, indeed, supposed that under our Christian civilization we had reached a point in human progress, when a republic could exist without having its life sought by its own offspring; but the Catilines of the South have proved that we were mistaken. Let no man imagine that because this rebellion has been made by men renowned in our civil and military history, that it is, therefore, the less guilty or the less courageously to be resisted. It is precisely this class of men who have subverted the best governments that have ever existed. The purest spirits that have lived in the tide of times, the noblest institutions that have arisen to bless our race, have found among those in whom they had most confided, and whom they had most honored, men wicked enough, either secretly to betray them unto death, or openly to seek their overthrow by lawless violence. The republic of England had its Monk; the republic of France had its Bonaparte; the republic of Rome had its Cæsar and its Catiline, and the Saviour of the world had his Judas Iscariot. It cannot be necessary that I should declare to you, for you know them well, who they are whose parricidal swords are now unsheathed against the republic of the United States. Their names are inscribed upon a scroll of infamy that can never perish. The most distinguished of them were educated by the charity of the government on which they are now making war. For long years they were fed from its table, and clothed from its wardrobe, and had their brows garlanded by its honors. They are the ungrateful sons of a fond mother, who dandled them upon her knee, who lavished upon them the gush-ing love of her noble and devoted nature, and who nurtured them from the very bosom of her life; and now, in the frenzied excesses of a licentious and baffled ambition, they are stabbing at that bosom with the ferocity with which the tiger springs upon his prey. The president of the United States is heroically and patriotically struggling to baffle the machinations of these most wicked men. I have unbounded gratification in knowing that he has the courage to look traitors in the face, and that, in discharging the duties of his great office, he takes no counsel of his fears. He is entitled to the zealous support of the whole country, and, may I not add without offence, that he will receive the support of all who justly appreciate the boundless blessings of our free institutions?

PROPHECY OF FREEDOM.—*George D. Prentice.**

WEEP not that Time
Is passing on—it will ere long reveal
A brighter era to the nations. Hark!
Along the vales and mountains of the earth
There is a deep, portentous murmuring,
Like the swift rush of subterranean streams,
Or like the mingled sounds of earth and air,
When the fierce tempest, with sonorous wing,
Heaves his deep folds upon the rushing winds,
And hurries onward with his night of clouds

---

* George D. Prentice, who at present wields such an unbounded influence in Kentucky, is sixty years old, but has lost none of the fire of youth. An attack of paralysis several years ago nearly deprived him of the use of his right hand, and he has since been compelled to employ an amanuensis. His face is fringed with dark hair, which begins to show the silver of age; but his eyes gleam out under their dark brows, while his conversation scintillates with that ready wit which has made him the most famous paragraphist in the world. His manner is exceedingly quiet and modest. He sits at his table more than twelve hours a day, and often writes two or three columns for a single morning issue of the Louisville *Journal*. His powerful pen has rendered nugatory traitorous attempts at correspondence, and, more than any other man, he is feared and hated by the secessionists.

Against the eternal mountains.   'Tis the voice
Of infant Freedom, and her stirring call
Is heard and answered in a thousand tones
From every hill-top of her western home—
And lo! it breaks across old Ocean's flood—
And "Freedom! Freedom!" is the answering shout
Of nations starting from the spell of years.
The day-spring!—see—'tis brightening in the heavens!
The watchmen of the night have caught the sign—
From tower to tower the signal-fires flash free—
And the deep watchword, like the rush of seas
That heralds the volcano's bursting flame,
Is sounding o'er the earth. Bright years of hope
Are on the wing! Yon glorious bow
Of Freedom bended by the hand of God,
Is spanning Time's dark surges. Its high arch,
A type of Love and Mercy on the cloud,
Tells that the many storms of human life
Will pass in silence, and the sinking waves,
Gathering the forms of glory and of peace,
Reflect the undimmed brightness of the heavens!

Kentucky and the Disunionists—1861.—*Hon. Joseph Holt.*

Before closing, I desire to say a few words on the relations of Kentucky to the pending rebellion; and as we are all Kentuckians here together to-night, and as this is purely a family matter, which concerns the honor of us all, I hope we may be permitted to speak to each other upon it with entire freedom. I shall not detain you with observations on the hostile and defiant position assumed by the governor of your state. In his reply to the requisition made upon him for volunteers under the proclamation of the president, he has, in my judgment, written and finished his own history, his epitaph included, and it is probable that in future the world will little concern itself as to what his excellency may propose to do, or as to what he may propose not to do. That response has made for Kentucky a record that has already brought a burning blush to the cheek of many of her sons, and is destined to bring it to the cheek of many more in the years which are to come. It is a shame, indeed a crying shame, that a state with so illustrious a past should have written for her, by her own chief-magistrate, a page of history so utterly humiliating as this. But your legislature have determined that during the present unhappy war the attitude of the state shall be that of strict neutrality, and it is upon this determination that I wish respectfully but frankly to comment. As the motives which governed the legislature were doubtless patriotic and conservative, the conclusion arrived at cannot be condemned as dishonorable; still, in view of the manifest duty of the state and of possible results, I cannot but regard it as mistaken and false, and one which may have fatal consequences. Strictly and legally speaking, Kentucky must go out of the Union before she can be neutral. Within it she is necessarily either faithful to the government of the United States, or she is disloyal to it. If this crutch of neutrality, upon which her well-meaning but ill-judging politicians are halting, can find any middle ground on which to rest, it has escaped my researches, though I have diligently sought it. Neutrality, in the sense of those who now use the term, however patriotically designed, is, in effect, but a snake in the grass of rebellion, and those who handle it will sooner or later feel its fangs. Said one who spake as never man spake, " He who is not with us is against us;" and of none of the conflicts which have arisen between men or between nations, could this be more truthfully said than of that in which we are now involved. Neutrality necessarily implies indifference. Is Kentucky indifferent to the issue of this contest? Has she, indeed, nothing at stake?

Has she no compact with her sister states to keep, no plighted faith to uphold, no renown to sustain, no glory to win? Has she no horror of that crime of crimes now being committed against us by that stupendous rebellion which has arisen like a tempest-cloud in the South? We rejoice to know that she is still a member of this Union, and as such she has the same interest in resisting this rebellion that each limb of the body has in resisting a poignard whose point is aimed at the heart. It is her house that is on fire; has she no interest in extinguishing the conflagration? Will she stand aloof and announce herself neutral between the raging flames and the brave men who are periling their lives to subdue them? Hundreds of thousands of citizens of other states —men of culture and character, of thought and of toil —men who have a deep stake in life, and an intense appreciation of its duties and responsibilities, who know the worth of this blessed government of ours, and do not prize even their own blood above it—I say, hundreds of thousands of such men have left their homes, their workshops, their offices, their counting-houses, and their fields, and are now rallying about our flag, freely offering their all to sustain it, and since the days that crusading Europe threw its hosts upon the embattled plains of Asia, no deeper, or more earnest, or grander spirit has stirred the souls of men than that which now sways those mighty masses whose gleaming banners are destined ere long to make bright again the earth and sky of the distracted South. Can Kentucky look upon this sublime spectacle of patriotism unmoved, and then say to herself: "I will spend neither blood nor treasure, but I will shrink away while the battle rages, and after it has been fought and won, I will return to the camp, well assured that if I cannot claim the laurels, I will at least enjoy the blessings of the victory?" Is this all that remains of her chivalry—of the chivalry of the land of the

Shelbys, the Johnsons, the Allens, the Clays, the Adairs, and the Davises? Is there a Kentuckian within the sound of my voice to-night, who can hear the anguished cry of his country as she wrestles and writhes in the folds of this gigantic treason, and then lay himself down upon his pillow with this thought of neutrality, without feeling that he has something in his bosom which stings him worse than would an adder? Have we, within the brief period of eighty years, descended so far from the mountain heights on which our fathers stood, that already, in our degeneracy, we proclaim our blood too precious, our treasure too valuable to be devoted to the preservation of such a government as this? They fought through a seven years' war, with the greatest power on earth, for the hope, the bare hope, of being able to found this republic, and now that it is no longer a hope nor an experiment, but a glorious reality, which has excited the admiration and the homage of the nations, and has covered us with blessings as "the waters cover the channels of the sea," have we, their children, no years of toil, of sacrifice, and of battle even, if need be, to give, to save it from absolute destruction at the hands of men who, steeped in guilt, are perpetrating against us and humanity a crime, for which I verily believe the blackest page of the history of the world's darkest period furnishes no parallel? Can it be possible that in the history of the American people we have already reached a point of degeneracy so low, that the work of WASHINGTON and FRANKLIN, of ADAMS and JEFFERSON, of HANCOCK and HENRY, is to be overthrown by the morally begrimed and pigmied conspirators who are now tugging at its foundations? It would be the overturning of the Andes by the miserable reptiles that are crawling in the sands at their base.

The Same Subject Continued.

But our neutral fellow-citizens in the tenderness of their hearts say: "This effusion of blood sickens us." Then do all in your power to bring it to an end. Let the whole strength of this commonwealth be put forth in support of the government, in order that the war may be terminated by the prompt suppression of the rebellion. The longer the struggle continues, the fiercer will be its spirit, and the more fearful the waste of life attending it. You therefore only aggravate the calamity you deplore by standing aloof from the combat. But again they say, "We cannot fight our brethren." Indeed. But your brethren can fight you, and with a good will, too. Wickedly and wantonly have they commenced this war against you and your institutions, and ferociously are they prosecuting it. They take no account of the fact that the massacre with which they hope their swords will, ere long, be clogged, must be the massacre of their brethren. However much we may bow our heads at the confession, it is nevertheless true that every free people that have existed have been obliged, at one period or other of their history, to fight for their liberties against traitors within their own bosoms, and that people who have not the greatness of soul thus to fight, cannot long continue to be free, nor do they deserve to be so.

There is not, and there cannot be, any neutral ground for a loyal people between their own government and those who, at the head of armies, are menacing its destruction. Your inaction is not neutrality, though you may delude yourselves with the belief that it is so. With this rebellion confronting you, when you refuse to co-operate actively with your government in subduing it, you thereby condemn the government, and assume toward it an attitude of antagonism. Your inaction is a virtual indorsement of the rebellion, and if you do not thereby give to the rebels precisely that "aid and comfort" spoken of in the constitution, you certainly afford them a most powerful encouragement and support. That they regard your present position as friendly to them, is proved by the fact that, in a recent enactment of the Confederate Congress confiscating the debts due from their own citizens to those of loyal states, the debts due to the people of Kentucky are expressly excepted. Is not this significant? Does it leave any room for doubt that the Confederate Congress suppose they have discovered, under the guise of your neutrality, a lurking sympathy for their cause which entitles you to be treated as friends, if not as active allies? Patriotic as was the purpose of her apprehensive statesmen in placing her in the anomalous position she now occupies, it cannot be denied that Kentucky by her present attitude is exerting a potent influence in strengthening the rebellion, and is, therefore, false alike to her loyalty and her fame. You may rest well assured that this estimate of your neutrality is entertained by the true men of the country in all the states which are now sustaining the government. Within the last few weeks how many of those gallant volunteers who have left home and kindred and all that is dear to them, and are now under a southern sun, exposing themselves to death from disease and to death from battle, and are accounting their lives as nothing in the effort they are making for the deliverance of your government and theirs; how many of them have said to me in sadness and in longing: "Will not Kentucky help me?" How my soul would have leaped could I have answered promptly, confidently, exultingly: "Yes, she will." But when I thought of this neutrality my heart sank within me, and I did not and I could not look those brave men in the face. And yet I could not answer, "No." I could not crush myself to the earth under the

C*

self-abasement of such a reply. I therefore said—and may my country sustain me—"I hope, I trust, I pray, nay, I believe, Kentucky will yet do her duty."

If this government is to be destroyed, ask yourselves are you willing it shall be recorded in history that Kentucky stood by in the greatness of her strength and lifted not a hand to stay the catastrophe? If it is to be saved, as I verily believe it is, are you willing it shall be written that, in the immeasurable glory which must attend the achievement, Kentucky had no part?

I will only add, if Kentucky wishes the waters of her beautiful Ohio to be dyed in blood—if she wishes her harvest fields, now waving in their abundance, to be trampled beneath the feet of hostile soldiery, as a flower-garden is trampled beneath the threshings of the tempest—if she wishes the homes where her loved ones are now gathered in peace, invaded by the proscriptive fury of a military despotism, sparing neither life nor property—if she wishes the streets of her towns and cities grown with grass, and the steamboats of her rivers to lie rotting at her wharves, then let her join the Southern Confederacy; but if she would have the bright waters of that river flow on in their gladness—if she would have her harvests peacefully gathered to her garners—if she would have the lullabies of her cradles and the songs of her homes uninvaded by the cries and terrors of battle—if she would have the streets of her towns and cities again filled with the hum and throng of busy trade, and her rivers and her shores once more vocal with the steamer's whistle, that anthem of a free and prosperous commerce, then let her stand fast by the stars and stripes, and do her duty and her whole duty as a member of this Union. Let her brave people say to the President of the United States: "You are our chief-magistrate; the government you have in charge, and are striving to save from dishonor and dismemberment, is our government; your cause is indeed our cause; your battles are our battles; make room for us, therefore, in the ranks of your armies, that your triumph may be our triumph also."

Even as with the Father of us all I would plead for salvation, so, my countrymen, as upon my very knees, would I plead with you for the life, aye for the life, of our great and beneficent institutions. But if the traitor's knife, now at the throat of the republic, is to do its work, and this government is fated to add yet another to that long line of sepulchres which whiten the highway of the past, then my heartfelt prayer to God is, that it may be written in history, that the blood of its life was not found upon the skirts of Kentucky.

ITALY.— *William Cullen Bryant.*

  VOICES from the mountains speak;
   Apennines to Alps reply;
  Vale to vale and peak to peak
   Toss an old remembered cry:
    Italy
    Shall be free:
  Such the mighty shout that fills
  All the passes of her hills.

  All the old Italian lakes
   Quiver at that quickening word;
  Como with a thrill awakes;
   Garda to her depths is stirred;
    Mid the steeps
    Where he sleeps,
  Dreaming of the elder years,
  Startled Thrasymenus hears.

  Sweeping Arno, swelling Po,
   Murmur freedom to their meads,
  Tiber swift and Liris slow
   Send strange whispers from their reeds.

Italy
Shall be free,
Sing the glittering brooks that slide,
Toward the sea, from Etna's side.

Long ago was Gracchus slain;
Brutus perished long ago;
Yet the living roots remain
Whence the shoots of greatness grow.
Yet again,
Godlike men,
Sprung from that heroic stem,
Call the land to rise with them.

They who haunt the swarming street,
They who chase the mountain boar,
Or, where cliff and billow meet,
Prune the vine or pull the oar,
With a stroke
Break their yoke;
Slaves but yestereve were they—
Freemen with the dawning day.

Looking in his children's eyes,
While his own with gladness flash,
"Ne'er shall these," the father cries,
"Cringe, like hounds, beneath the lash.
These shall ne'er
Brook to wear
Chains that, thick with sordid rust,
Weigh the spirit to the dust."

Monarchs, ye whose armies stand
Harnessed for the battle-field!
Pause, and from the lifted hand
Drop the bolts of war ye wield.
Stand aloof
While the proof
Of the people's might is given;
Leave their kings to them and heaven.

Stand aloof, and see the oppressed
Chase the oppressor, pale with fear,

As the fresh winds of the west
Blow the misty valleys clear.
Stand and see
Italy
Cast the gyves she wears no more
To the gulfs that steep her shore.

EXTRACTS FROM AN ADDRESS, JULY 4TH, 1861.—
John Jay, Esq.

MY FELLOW-COUNTRYMEN: We have assembled to celebrate the eighty-fifth birthday of American independence, and we come together under circumstances that seem to make us contemporaries and co-actors, as it were, with our fathers of the revolution. The crisis which they met, and which their heroism decided after a seven years' war with Great Britain, again meets us face to face. The early scenes of their struggle for constitutional liberty, have found in our recent experience an historic parallel of even chronological exactness.

The blood of Massachusetts, shed at Lexington on the 19th of April, 1775, was not shed more gloriously than that of the sons of the same old commonwealth, who, marching by our national highway, to the defence of our common capital, were slain at Baltimore on the 19th of April, 1861.

The midnight ride of Paul Revere, famed in history and song, rousing the sleepers as he passed to hasten to defend their country, created no deeper emotion among the colonists of that day, than did our electric wires, flashing far and wide the news of the assault on Sumter and the massacre at Baltimore, and thrilling with a simultaneous burst of sympathy the loyal heart of the American people.

On the 4th of July, 1776, the Congress that met in the state-house at Philadelphia approved the solemn instrument that declared the independence of the American colonies, and announced to the world the birth of a nation. Eighty-five years have rolled by: the actors in that eventful scene have long since gone to their graves: their names belong to history: their sons have grown to manhood and age, and have followed them to the unseen world: and we of the third and fourth generation occupy the stage they trod, and represent the nationality which then was born. Eighty-five years of almost uninterrupted prosperity and unexampled growth! eighty-five years of culture and experience in a century of progress such as the world has never seen before! eighty-five years of thoughtful reflection on the character of the men who laid the foundation of our national glory and of the broad principles of right on which they based the edifice of American freedom!

Those years have passed; their results are written on the map of America, on the page of history, and to-day, the 4th of July, 1861, the American Congress convenes again, at the call of the president, at the capital bearing the name of Washington, to meet the question, whether the republic is to be maintained in its integrity with the constitution proclaimed by Washington, based on the will of the majority, or whether it is to be sundered and shattered by a defeated faction that sets at defiance the will of the people and would trample the constitution in the dust.

If ever the spirits of the departed are permitted to revisit the scenes they loved, and hover like angels around the steps of their successors, we may suppose that Hancock, and the Adamses, Sherman and Wolcott, Carroll and Livingston, Jefferson and Franklin, Robert and Lewis Morris, Wilson and Rush, and all their noble compeers, look down from heaven in this hour upon the

Congress at Washington; and God grant that the sturdy spirit which inspired the first Congress may equally inspire the last!

"Whatever may be our fate," said John Adams, with prophetic vision, after the adoption of the declaration, "be assured that this declaration will stand. It may cost treasure and it may cost blood, but it will richly compensate for both. Through the thick gloom of the present I see the brightness of the future as the sun in heaven. We shall make this a glorious, an immortal day. When we are in our graves our children will honor it. They will celebrate it with thanksgiving, with festivities, with bonfires, with illuminations. On its annual return they will shed tears, not of subjection and slavery, not of agony and distress, but of exultation, of gratitude and of joy. Sir, before God, I believe the hour is come: all that I have, all that I am, all that I hope for in this life, I am now ready here to stake upon it, and I leave off as I began, that, live or die, sink or swim, survive or perish, I am for the declaration. It is my living sentiment, and by the blessing of God it shall be my dying sentiment—independence now, and independence forever!"

The integrity and independence of our country are again in peril, and to-day the issue is with us. We come together now, not, as in past years, to rejoice over a national domain boundless in extent, peopled by countrymen differing, it may be, in their views and institutions, but united in loyalty and affection, at peace in their own borders, and with the great arm of the Union protecting its citizens alike on sea or land, at home or in foreign climes. But we meet in sadness to overlook a divided nation, and to listen to the tramp of martial forces larger than ever before trod the soil of America: the one army bearing proudly aloft the stars and stripes, and keeping step to the music of the Union; the other grasping the banner of rebellion and the black flag of piracy, proclaiming death to the constitution and the Union, and ruin to the commerce of the republic. * * *

To meet the rebel force arrayed against the capital, President Lincoln has called upon the loyal states, and at the word, fresh from the plough, the loom and the workshop, fresh from college seats and the professor's chair, from the bar, the pulpit, and the counting-house, fresh from every department of American industry, the army of the Union is in the field, and the world awaits the impending crisis. Europe looks on with undisguised and wondering interest, and while France and Germany seem instinctively to appreciate our situation, the British cabinet and the British press have strangely blundered, and have muttered something we do not understand, about "rights of belligerents," "a wicked war," and the "bursting of the bubble of democracy."

Such, in brief, is our position at home and abroad, and this day is destined to be memorable—perhaps as memorable in history as that which we have met to celebrate. The action of the Congress now assembled will decide whether the national independence established against the united strength of the British empire in '76 is to fall ignominiously before the attacks of a rebel minority of our own countrymen in '61.

It is to decide the question whether in the next century our descendants shall refer to the fourth of July as the forgotten birthday of an extinct republic, or whether, when we shall sleep with our fathers and our children shall slumber by our side, their grandsons shall meet as we do this day to bless our memories as we bless those of our revolutionary sires: to spread to the breeze, from the Atlantic to the Pacific, on every hill-side and in every valley, the flag of our Union, the stars and stripes that we so proudly love, and join their voices in swelling the cry of Adams: "Independence now, and independence forever!"

While the great issue, the success or failure of the American experiment, the continuance of our Union or its disintegration, rests immediately with the president and with Congress, it rests in an almost equal degree upon each one of us. The American people are at once citizens and sovereigns—the fountain and source of the supreme authority of the land, and to us, the people, will our servants in Congress naturally and properly look for guidance in this extremity. Already have you seen how fairly an honest executive represents the sentiments of the majority of his countrymen, availing himself of their counsels, gathering strength from their energy and determination, and so directing the government that its action keeps time to the beating of the national pulse. Already, in response to the nation's call, has the national government arisen in gigantic strength from the depths of imbecility to which it had fallen, to a position of grandeur, dignity and power, which has silenced the half-uttered sarcasms of European declaimers about the internal weakness of popular institutions.

Most of you—perhaps all of you—have made up your minds deliberately, intelligently and dispassionately in regard to your duty; and it is a general and proper sentiment among us that this is a time for energetic action, not for discussion. But still, as I am here, honored by your appointment, to say something befitting the occasion, I think you will permit me, if indeed you do not regard it as my especial province, to speak frankly of our present duty; to say something of the great theme which engrosses the nation; of which we think when we rise in the morning and when we retire at night, as we go to our work and return to our meals, when we open the morning paper for news and close it for reflection, when we kneel at the family altar and by our own bed-sides, the one great overwhelming subject, the issue of this rebellion, the destiny of our country.   *   *   *

The eyes of the whole world are this day fixed upon you. To Europeans themselves, European questions sink to insignificance compared with the American question now to be decided. Rise, my countrymen, as did our fathers on the day we celebrate, to the majestic grandeur of this question in its twofold aspect, as regards America, and as regards the world. Remember that with the failure of the American republic will fall the wisest system of republican government which the wisdom of man has yet invented, and the hopes of popular freedom cherished throughout the globe.

Let us, standing by our fathers' graves, swear anew, and teach the oath to our children, that, with God's help, the American republic, clasping this continent in its embrace, shall stand unmoved, though all the powers of slavery, piracy, and European jealousy should combine to overthrow it; that we shall have in the future, as we have had in the past, one country, one constitution and one destiny; and that when we shall have passed from earth, and the acts of to-day shall be matter of history, and the dark power now seeking our overthrow shall have been itself overthrown, our sons may gather strength from our example in every contest with despotism that time may have in store to try their virtue, and that they may rally under the stars and stripes to battle for freedom and the rights of man, with our olden war-cry, "Liberty and union, now and forever, one and inseparable."

On the Death of Lieutenant Chas. G. Hunter, U. S. N.—*J. E. Tuel.*

The battle's din, the ocean's roar,
  For thee have ceased their ceaseless strife,
Thy barque hath reached the distant shore,
    Thy freight of life!

No more for thee the vessel's pride,
    No more the curbless sea thy friend,
Thy spirit hard as it to guide,
        As it to bend!

But, chained as was the restless soul
    That filched the lightning fire from high,
Thy rock was proud Ambition's goal,
        Where thou wouldst die!

Thy native element to thee
    Imparted strength and fostered hope,
The warring billow of the sea,
        Thy spirit's scope!

The sudden storm no order knows,
    The cannon's mouth asks not its aim—
Onward the whirlwind missive goes,
        To death or fame!

The storm may scatter hull and deck,
    The cannon gather wounds and death—
Thou wouldst incur like these the wreck,
        Or yield thy breath!

The daring soul no danger knows,
    Its star of glory points the way,
The sun, which bright with halo glows,
        Must blind as sway!

And thou, beneath its dazzling glare,
    Caught from its fire its lurid flame,
And midst its spots of blemish bare
        Wrote bright thy name!

But yet the undimmed stars will tell,
    Whatever clouds obscure the sun,
That when the call of battle fell,
        Thy duty done!

The surging roar, the peoples' wave,
    When thou wast foremost in thy day,
May close its voice above thy grave,
        And pass away!

Thy mem'ry not! so long as deeds
  Which rouse the spirits of the deep,
When for our flag Decatur bleeds,
  And heroes sleep!

Farewell to thee! Life's battle o'er!
  Thy barque hath passed the earthly goal;
No more for thee the ocean's roar,
  Or earth's dark shoal!

Weep! in the hour when glory cries,
  The fame that glistens with her tear,
Then with the passing tribute dries
  Upon her bier!

Farewell to thee! Life's battle o'er!
  Thy barque hath passed the earthly goal;
No more for thee the ocean's roar,
  Or earth's dark shoal!

Republican Government.—*N. Y. Ledger.*

"Republicanism is a failure," say the monarchists of Europe, and now and then a thick-witted, degenerate American echoes the miserable drivel. That crowned heads, and privileged orders that can only exist and flourish in the sunshine of royalty, should view the passing clouds in our political firmament as omens of the speedy and final downfall of republican institutions, is not surprising. The *wish* is father to the *thought*. Neither is it wonderful that peoples who have been taught for ages to believe that the right to govern is transmitted by descent, should place some faith in this hope-engendered notion of their superiors. But that any American should suppose republicanism a failure is monstrous—that he should permit such an absurdity to escape his lips, disgraceful alike to his patriotism and his intelligence.

See what free institutions have done for our country since it cut the ligament that bound it to a throne. Its career has been the miracle of history. It may be said, perhaps, that England, too, has made great progress during the same period. But how? Simply because her government has progressed in liberality—because popular privileges have been extended within her borders—because she has approximated more nearly every year, the institutions and the policy of which some of her wiseacres now predict the overthrow. Our example has given a moral force to the political suggestions and demands of her people, which the crown and the aristocracy have not found it prudent to resist, and to which they have from time to time yielded more and more, as the pressure increased. In all human probability, the rotten borough system would now exist in England if universal suffrage had never been introduced in America.

The ameliorations of despotic rule which have taken place in various parts of Europe during the present century are due to the same cause. They have all been indirect concessions to the republican principle. The "great awakening" of the transatlantic millions commenced with the commencement of our independence, and the roused many have been ever since becoming more formidable to the privileged few. From *us* the former have drunk light, hope and encouragement—from *us* the latter have learned the danger of carrying tyrannt to extremes. If there had been no United States, there had been no United Italy, and millions of Russian serfs would now be grovelling in their chains.

For eighty years a glorious political revolution, sometimes silent, sometimes turbulent, has been going on in all parts of Europe. Its march has been occasionally checked and suspended, but never stopped. What set and kept the ball in motion? The establishment and maintenance of American independence; the example of our success and of our prosperity. "Revolutions," said a profound thinker, "never go backward." This revolution toward the right is as sure to progress as the sun to shine. The hand of God is visible in it, and to doubt it is to doubt Him.

We do not believe that monarchy can survive the universal diffusion of such knowledge as the present systems of public education in enlightened Christian countries are designed to impart. Schoolcraft will ultimately kill kingcraft. When there shall be no ignorance there will be no kings, and royalty of mind will constitute the "right divine" to govern, instead of "royal blood."

It is true that republicanism has its drawbacks. No form of human government can be perfect. But it has this vast advantage over monarchism, that it is not *inherently vicious*, and therefore is not necessarily incapable of securing the "greatest good of the greatest number." On the contrary, the republican system of government is, in *principle* and *theory*, natural, pure and noble, and with the growth of popular intelligence and public virtue, its practical working must continually improve.

Recitative and Song of the Union*—1861.—*Wm. Oland Bourne.*

"To arms! to arms!" they cry,
"Defend that flag, or die!"
"To arms!" amid their tears,
"To arms!" as in the years
When heroes saw the field of battle nigh;
"To arms!" replied the hills;
"To arms!" the mountains grand;
"To arms let him who wills!"
Swept o'er the freeman's land;

*An extract.

It leaped from hill to hill,
.It shook the mountain crag,
For love's electric thrill
Still kept the starry flag;
"To arms!" replied the plains,
The hot blood throbbing through the veins;
For millions rallied with the vow,
"We strike for Freedom surely now,
In heaven's great name the damning wrong shall bow!"

From the steep mountain side,
From the deep flowing tide,
From the green prairies wide,
"Forward!" they cry;
From the far eastern hills,
From the pure flowing rills,
From the great busy mills,
"Onward for aye!"
From the forge, old and grim,
From the mine, dark and dim,
Swelled the bold hero-hymn,
"Onward or die!"
And to their arms they sprung,
Freedom on every tongue,
True to the songs they sung,
Filling the sky:—

"Arm brothers! arm! for the foe is before us,
Filled with deep hate to the Union we love;
Onward we press, with the loud-swelling chorus,
Shaking the earth and the heaven above.
Chorus—Arm, brothers, arm!
For the strife be ye ready!
With an eye ever steady!
Arm, brothers, arm!

"On, brothers, on! for they haste to the battle!
The treason is theirs whom we trusted so long;
For Freedom we fight—not man as a chattel,—
And Union shall triumph—the Right over Wrong.
Chorus—Arm, brothers, arm!

"Haste, brothers, haste! for the moments are flying!
An hour now lost may undo all the past!
And millions of mourners now burdened are sighing,
And terror-struck bow in the force of the blast!
　　　Chorus—Arm, brothers, arm!

"Come, brothers, come! It is time for the starting!
　We pray on the field! At the altar *they* pray
Who mourn for our loss. Up, now, for the parting—
Our children shall bless us for valor to-day!
　　　Chorus—Arm, brothers, arm!

"Swear, brothers, swear! For the Union forever!
Resting not now till each traitor is riven!
God for our land, and of Freedom the Giver,
Onward we haste in the sunshine of heaven.
　　　Chorus—Arm, brothers, arm!"

　　"She lives!" the freeman cried,
　　"She lives!" my heart replied,
　　"She lives!" rolled o'er the plain
　　　And thrilled the waking land
　　That caught it back again
　　　From mountains old and grand;
　　And starry banners waved
　　　From peak, and dome, and spire,
　　The flag of love and peace,
　　　And glory's quenchless fire!

O toiling millions on the old world's shore!
　Look up, rejoicing, for she is not dead!
The soul is living as it lived before,
　When sainted heroes spurned the tyrant's tread;
The strife is earnest and the day wears on,
　And ages tremble with the mighty blow—
Beyond the conflict is a glorious dawn,
　A rapturous birth of Freedom out of woe!
The clouds may gather, and the storm be long,
　And lightnings leap across the darkened sky,
But Freedom lives to triumph over wrong,
　It still will live, for Truth can never die!

Character of Washington.—*Fisher Ames.*

There has scarcely appeared a really great man, whose character has been more admired in his lifetime, or less correctly understood by his admirers. When it is comprehended, it is no easy task to delineate its excellences in such a manner as to give to the portrait both interest and resemblance; for it requires thought and study to understand the true ground of the superiority of his character over many others, whom he resembled in the principles of action, and even in the manner of acting. But perhaps he excels all the great men that ever lived, in the steadiness of his adherence to his maxims of life, and in the uniformity of all his conduct to the same maxims. These maxims, though wise, were yet not so remarkable for their wisdom as for their authority over his life; for, if there were any errors in his judgment (and he discovered as few as any man), we know of no blemishes in his virtue. He was the patriot without reproach; he loved his country well enough to hold his success in serving it an ample recompense. Thus far self-love and love of country coincided; but when his country needed sacrifices that no other man could, or perhaps would, be willing to make, he did not even hesitate. This was virtue in its most exalted character. More than once he put his fame at hazard, when he had reason to think it would be sacrificed, at least in this age. Two instances cannot be denied; when the army was disbanded, and again, when he stood, like Leonidas at the pass of Thermopylæ, to defend our independence against France.

It is, indeed, almost as difficult to draw his character, as the portrait of Virtue. The reasons are similar: our ideas of moral excellence are obscure, because they are complex, and we are obliged to resort to illustrations. Washington's example is the happiest to show what virtue is; and, to delineate his character, we naturally expatiate on the beauty of virtue; much must be felt, and much imagined. His pre-eminence is not so much to be seen in the display of any one virtue, as in the possession of them all, and in the practice of the most difficult. Hereafter, therefore, his character must be studied before it will be striking; and then it will be admitted as a model, a precious one to a free republic.

It is no less difficult to speak of his talents. They were adapted to lead, without dazzling mankind; and to draw forth and employ the talents of others, without being misled by them. In this he was certainly superior, that he neither mistook nor misapplied his own. His great modesty and reserve would have concealed them, if great occasions had not called them forth; and then, as he never spoke from the affectation to shine, nor acted from any sinister motives, it is from their effects only that we are to judge of their greatness and extent. In public trusts, where men, acting conspicuously, are cautious, and in those private concerns where few conceal or resist their weaknesses, Washington was uniformly great, pursuing right conduct from right maxims. His talents were such as assist a sound judgment, and ripen with it. His prudence was consummate, and seemed to take the direction of his powers and passions; for, as a soldier, he was more solicitous to avoid mistakes that might be fatal, than to perform exploits that are brilliant; and, as a statesman, to adhere to just principles, however old, than to pursue novelties; and therefore, in both characters, his qualities were singularly adapted to the interest, and were tried in the greatest perils of the country. His habits of inquiry were so far remarkable, that he was never satisfied with investigating, nor desisted from it, so long as he had less than all the light that he could obtain upon a subject, and then he made his decision without bias.

This command over the partialities that so generally stop men short, or turn them aside in their pursuit of truth, is one of the chief causes of his unvaried course of right conduct in so many difficult scenes, where every human actor must be presumed to err. If he had strong passions, he had learned to subdue them, and to be moderate and mild. If he had weaknesses, he concealed them, which is rare, and excluded them from the government of his temper and conduct, which is still more rare. If he loved fame, he never made improper compliances for what is called popularity. The fame he enjoyed is of the kind that will last forever; yet it was rather the effect than the motive of his conduct. Some future Plutarch will search for a parallel to his character. Epaminondas is perhaps the brightest name of all antiquity. Our Washington resembled him in the purity and ardor of his patriotism; and like him he first exalted the glory of his country. There, it is to be hoped, the parallel ends; for Thebes fell with Epaminondas. But such comparisons cannot be pursued far without departing from the similitude. For we shall find it as difficult to compare great men as great rivers. Some we admire for the length and rapidity of their current, and the grandeur of their cataracts; others for the majestic silence and fulness of their streams: we cannot bring them together to measure the difference of their waters. The unambitious life of Washington, declining fame, yet courted by it, seemed, like the Ohio, to choose its long way through solitudes, diffusing fertility; or, like his own Potomac, widening and deepening his channel as he approaches the sea, and displaying most the usefulness and serenity of his greatness toward the end of his course. Such a citizen would do honor to any country. The constant affection and veneration of his country will show that it was worthy of such a citizen.

However his military fame may excite the wonder of

mankind, it is chiefly by his civil magistracy, that his example will instruct them. Great generals have arisen in all ages of the world, and perhaps most in those of despotism and darkness. In times of violence and convulsion, they rise, by the force of the whirlwind, high enough to ride in it, and direct the storm. Like meteors, they glare on the black clouds with a splendor, that, while it dazzles and terrifies, makes nothing visible but the darkness. The fame of heroes is indeed growing vulgar; they multiply in every long war; they stand in history and thicken in their ranks, almost as undistinguished as their own soldiers.

But such a chief-magistrate as Washington appears, like the pole star in a clear sky, to direct the skilful statesman. His presidency will form an epoch, and be distinguished as the age of Washington. Already it assumes its high place in the political region. Like the milky way, it whitens along its allotted portion of the hemisphere. The latest generations of men will survey, through the telescope of history, the space where so many virtues blend their rays, and delight to separate them into groups and distinct virtues. As the best illustration of them, the living monument to which the first of patriots would have chosen to consign his fame, it is my earnest prayer to Heaven that our country may subsist, even to that late day, in the plenitude of its liberty and happiness, and mingle its mild glory with Washington's.

Sword Chant.— *William Motherwell.*

'Tis not the gray hawk's flight o'er mountain and mere;
'Tis not the fleet hound's course, tracking the deer;
'Tis not the light hoof-print of black steed or gray,
Though sweltering it gallop a long summer's day.

Which mete forth the lordships I challenge as mine:
    Ha! ha! 'tis the good brand
    I clutch in my strong hand,
That can their broad marches and numbers define.
    LAND GIVER! I kiss thee.

Dull builders of houses, base tillers of earth,
Gaping, ask me what lordships I owned at my birth;
But the pale fools wax mute when I point with my sword
East, west, north, and south, shouting, "There am I lord!"
Wold and waste, town and tower, hill, valley, and stream,
    Trembling, bow to my sway,
    In the fierce battle fray,
When the star that rules fate is this falchion's red gleam.
    MIGHT GIVER! I kiss thee.

I've heard great harps sounding in brave bower and hall;
I've drank the sweet music that bright lips let fall;
I've hunted in greenwood, and heard small birds sing;
But away with this idle and cold jargoning!
The music I love is the shout of the brave,
    The yell of the dying,
    The scream of the flying,
When this arm wields death's sickle, and garners the grave.
    JOY GIVER! I kiss thee.

Far isles of the ocean thy lightning hath known,
And wide o'er the mainland thy horrors have shone.
Great sword of my father, stern joy of his hand!
Thou hast carved his name deep on the stranger's red strand,
And won him the glory of undying song.
    Keen cleaver of gay crests,
    Sharp piercer of broad breasts,
Grim slayer of heroes, and scourge of the strong!
    FAME GIVER! I kiss thee.

In a love more abiding than that the heart knows
For maiden more lovely than summer's first rose,
My heart's knit to thine, and lives but for thee;
In dreaming of gladness thou'rt dancing with me,
Brave measures of madness, in some battle-field,
    Where armor is ringing,
    And noble blood springing,

And cloven yarn helmet, stout hauberk, and shield.
DEATH GIVER! I kiss thee.

The smile of a maiden's eye soon may depart;
And light is the faith of fair woman's heart;
Changeful as light clouds, and wayward as wind,
Be the passions that govern weak woman's mind.
But thy metal's as true as its polish is bright:
When ills wax in number,
Thy love will not slumber;
But, starlike, burns fiercer the darker the night.
HEART GLADDENER! I kiss thee.

My kindred have perished by war or by wave;
Now, childless and sireless, I long for the grave.
When the path of our glory is shadowed in death,
With me thou wilt slumber below the brown heath;
Thou wilt rest on my bosom, and with it decay;
While harps shall be ringing,
And scalds shall be singing
The deeds we have done in our old fearless day.
SONG GIVER! I kiss thee.

NATIONAL RECOLLECTIONS THE FOUNDATION OF NATIONAL CHARACTER.—*Hon. Edward Everett.*

AND how is the spirit of a free people to be formed, and animated, and cheered, but out of the storehouse of its historic recollections? Are we to be eternally ringing the changes upon Marathon and Thermopylæ; and going back to read in obscure texts of Greek and Latin of the exemplars of patriotic virtue? I thank God that we can find them nearer home, in our own country, on our own soil; that strains of the noblest sentiment that ever swelled in the breast of man, are breathing to us out of every page of our country's history, in the native eloquence of our mother tongue; that the colonial and provincial councils of America exhibit to us models of the spirit and character which gave Greece and Rome their name and their praise among the nations. Here we ought to go for our instruction; the lesson is plain, it is clear, it is applicable. When we go to ancient history, we are bewildered with the difference of manners and institutions. We are willing to pay our tribute of applause to the memory of Leonidas, who fell nobly for his country in the face of his foe. But when we trace him to his home, we are confounded at the reflection, that the same Spartan heroism, to which he sacrificed himself at Thermopylæ, would have led him to tear his own child, if it had happened to be a sickly babe—the very object for which all that is kind and good in man rises up to plead—from the bosom of its mother, and carry it out to be eaten by the wolves of Taygetus. We feel a glow of admiration at the heroism displayed at Marathon, by the ten thousand champions of invaded Greece; but we cannot forget that the tenth part of the number were slaves, unchained from the workshops and door-posts of their masters, to go and fight the battles of freedom. I do not mean that these examples are to destroy the interest with which we read the history of ancient times; they possibly increase that interest by the very contrasts they exhibit. But they do warn us, if we need the warning, to seek our great practical lessons of patriotism at home; out of the exploits and sacrifices of which our own country is the theatre; out of the characters of our own fathers. Them we know—the high-souled, natural, unaffected, the citizen heroes. We know what happy firesides they left for the cheerless camp. We know with what pacific habits they dared the perils of the field. There is no mystery, no romance, no madness, under the name of chivalry, about them. It is all resolute, manly resistance for conscience's and liberty's sake, not merely of an overwhelming power, but of all the force of long-rooted habits and native love of order and peace.

Above all, their blood calls to us from the soil which we tread; it beats in our veins; it cries to us not merely in the thrilling words of one of the first victims in this cause: "My sons, scorn to be slaves!" but it cries with a still more moving eloquence: "My sons, forget not your fathers!" Fast, oh! too fast, with all our efforts to prevent it, their precious memories are dying away. Notwithstanding our numerous written memorials, much of what is known of those eventful times dwells but in the recollections of a few revered survivors, and with them is rapidly perishing, unrecorded and irretrievable. How many prudent counsels, conceived in perplexed times; how many heart-stirring words, uttered when liberty was treason; how many brave and heroic deeds, performed when the halter, not the laurel, was the promised meed of patriotic daring—are already lost and forgotten in the graves of their authors! How little do we—although we have been permitted to hold converse with the venerable remnants of that day—how little do we know of their dark and anxious hours; of their secret meditations; of the hurried and perilous events of the momentous struggle! And while they are dropping around us like the leaves of autumn, while scarce a week passes that does not call away some member of the veteran ranks, already so sadly thinned, shall we make no effort to hand down the traditions of their day to our children; to pass the torch of liberty—which we received in all the splendor of its first enkindling—bright and flaming, to those who stand next us on the line; so that, when we shall come to be gathered to the dust where our fathers are laid, we may say to our sons and our grandsons: "If we did not amass, we have not squandered your inheritance of glory!"

Not Yet. — *William Cullen Bryant.*

Oh, country, marvel of the earth!
Oh, realm to sudden greatness grown!
The age that gloried in thy birth,
    Shall it behold thee overthrown?
Shall traitors lay that greatness low?
No, Land of Hope and Blessing, No!

And we who wear thy glorious name,
    Shall we, like cravens, stand apart,
When those whom thou hast trusted aim
    The death-blow at thy generous heart?
Forth goes the battle-cry, and lo!
Hosts rise in harness, shouting, No!

And they who founded, in our land,
    The power that rules from sea to sea,
Bled they in vain, or vainly planned
    To leave their country great and free?
Their sleeping ashes, from below,
Send up the thrilling murmur, No!

Knit they the gentle ties which long
    These sister states were proud to wear,
And forged the kindly links so strong
    For idle hands in sport to tear—
For scornful hands aside to throw?
No, by our fathers' memory, No!

Our humming marts, our iron ways,
    Our wind-tossed woods on mountain crest,
The hoarse Atlantic, with his bays,
    The calm, broad Ocean of the West,
And Mississippi's torrent-flow,
And loud Niagara, answer, No!

Not yet the hour is nigh, when they
    Who deep in Eld's dim twilight sit,
Earth's ancient kings, shall rise and say,
    "Proud country, welcome to the pit!
So soon art thou, like us, brought low?"
No, sullen group of shadows, No!

For now, behold, the arm that gave
   The victory in our fathers' day,
Strong, as of old, to guard and save—
   That mighty arm which none can stay
On clouds above and fields below,
Writes, in men's sight, the answer, No!

Tomb of Washington.—*Hon. Joseph W. Savage.**

I EARNESTLY hope that this resolution will be adopted by the house without a dissenting vote. The subject is one of deep interest to every man who first drew his breath on American soil. Sir, it was beautifully said of Washington, that "God made him childless that the nation might call him Father." Mount Vernon was his home; it is now his grave. How fitting, then, sir, it is that we, his children, should be the owners of the homestead, and of our father's sepulchre. No stranger's money should buy it, and no stranger's hand should drive the ploughshare over ashes sacred to every American. No mere individual is worthy to be the owner of a spot enriched with such hallowed memories. The mortal remains of the nation's idol should not be subject to the whim, caprice, or cupidity of any man. These memorials are national, and to the nation they should belong; and it is the duty of every citizen to guard them from violence and dishonor. Sir, no monument has ever been erected over the grave of Washington. He needs none but that which rises in majestic grandeur before the gaze of the world, in the existence of this great republic, with its millions of people rejoicing in the light and liberty of a free government. While the stars and stripes waving above every capital, shall symbolize our national union, will any ask where is

---

* A speech delivered in the Senate of New York, on a resolution calling on Congress to purchase Mount Vernon.

the monument to Washington? I believe, sir, that his name will prove more lasting than marble or brass. When every structure which filial love and gratitude may erect shall have crumbled to dust, the fame of our patriot father will still remain the theme of study and admiration.

There has been but one Washington, and God in His goodness gave him to us. Let us cherish his dust and revere his memory. Let us together own his mansion and tomb. Let the youth of our nation make pilgrimages to the sacred spot, and slake the thirst of unhallowed ambition at the well where Washington was wont to draw; and when patriotism declines, let the vestals of liberty rekindle the flame at the fireside of the nation's sire. Thus, sir, may we do much to keep alive, through successive generations, that patriotic fire which burns in the heart of every true American. Sir, no man can read the life of Washington without rising up from the task a better man: nor can a freeman step within the sacred precincts of Mount Vernon, and not feel the power of those associations which environ him. The troubled sea of passion in his soul subsides, and he seems to hear a voice whispering to his spirit, "Peace, be still, for Washington lies here." Who could visit the farm of Washington and not experience a new thrill of patriotism; or who, without a new incentive to love his country, could ramble through that garden; stand in the hall where heroes of the revolution were welcomed and refreshed; sit down in the library where Washington studied and meditated, and behold the chamber in which he slept and died?

Sir, I am no prophet. But when from such sacred memories as these, I turn to view the opposite picture, the veil of futurity seems to be lifted. I will suppose that this opportunity is unimproved. That cherished inheritance which, with characteristic patriotism, the family of Washington now offer to the country, is forfeited to parsimony. That family pass away, and with it the last hope of securing this peculiar treasure. The heritage enshrined in the hearts of millions is the subject of speculation. Mammon, the earth-ruling demon, flaps his dark wing over the consecrated spot, and dooms it to his most accursed uses. It becomes the resort of the idle, a den of gamblers and inebriates. But I forbear; I can pursue this picture no further. If such desecration is to befall the home and the grave of Washington, then let the curtain fall which hides the future from my view; that day of shame I pray not to see.

It needs no prophet's eye to scan along the line of time, the majestic outline of our nation's destiny, when the fruits of our free government shall be more and more developed, until this vast continent shall be peopled with freemen from sea to sea; when the fame of the nation shall reach the farthest islands and shores—when our star of empire, radiant with the beams of liberty, shall have grown to such magnitude as to attract the eyes and guide the steps of all nations, and when some queen of Sheba shall come over seas and continents to behold our greatness, and see the happy results of the wisdom of Washington—then, sir, will Mount Vernon be sought, and thousands, now unborn, will wish to kiss the earth which cradled, and now covers the Father of his Country. How will we appear in that millennial day of our nation's destiny, if it shall be truly recorded that the most sacred spot which God committed to our custody was thrown away a sacrifice to parsimony, or some fashionable fine-spun theories, with which true patriotism has no fellowship? Will not every American blush with shame, and wish that he could cover from the gaze of nations so dark a blot in the page of our history?

Sir, shall no spot be held sacred by Americans? Have we no reverence for the symbols of departed greatness? True, there are monuments at Bunker Hill and Baltimore

—we have here and there a national memento. The curious can trace the crumbling ramparts, and the remains of hasty breastworks, behind which the stout hearts of our forefathers beat with patriotic zeal, and over which they dealt dismay and death to our enemies. But, sir, as we have been reminded by our governor, these memorials, like ourselves, are fast passing away. Let us, then, secure this honored patrimony. Let Mount Vernon be the perpetual memento of our country's great deliverance, and let the reverence with which it is regarded be the token of our gratitude. And when, in ages hence, the banks of the silvery Potomac shall resound, as now, with the passing vessel, uttering its tribute to the memory of Washington, and the flag at the masthead shall humbly droop, and the mariner stand uncovered, in honor of the sacred spot; let future generations learn the lesson of. gratitude and patriotism, which these tokens shall daily excite at Mount Vernon.

O Land of Happy Hearts and Homes.—*William Allan Butler.*[*]

O LAND of happy hearts and homes!
　Land of the free!
O'er all the earth a welcome comes
　From kindred souls, to thee!
To thee, O land of youth sublime,
Bright jewel on the brow of Time!
　O land of liberty!

Old Ocean clasps thee to his side,
　Land of the free!
And Nature weaves—O beauteous bride!—
　Her richest crown for thee.

---

[*] Mr. Butler, a son of the late Hon. B. F. Butler, is most favorably known as the author of "*Nothing to Wear*," and other humorous and satirical poems: this brilliant lyric gives him high rank as a serious poet.—ED.

For thee, O youthful queen of states,
For thee, the darling of the Fates,
   O land of liberty!

Thy glory brightens as it blooms—
   Land of the free!
Starlike amidst the ancient glooms,
   It wins the world to thee!
To thee, O promised land of rest,
To thee, the Eden of the west!
   O land of liberty!

Far off the golden future gleams,
   Land of the free!
Whose larger light and brighter beams
   Shall flood the years for thee:
For thee, O land of long increase,
For thee, the chosen shrine of peace,
   O land of liberty!

O land of happy hearts and homes,
   Land of the free!
From grateful souls our greeting comes,
   Our song, our pledge to thee!
To thee, O land of hope divine,
Our joys, our loves, our lives are thine,
   O land of liberty!

ADAMS AND JEFFERSON.—*Daniel Webster.*

ADAMS and Jefferson, I have said, are no more. As human beings, indeed, they are no more. They are no more, as in 1776, bold and fearless advocates of independence; no more, as on subsequent periods, the head of the government; no more, as we have recently seen them, aged and venerable objects of admiration and regard. They are no more. They are dead.

But how little is there of the great and good which can die! To their country they yet live, and live forever. They live in all that perpetuates the remembrance of men on earth; in the recorded proofs of their own great actions, in the offspring of their intellect, in the deep engraved lines of public gratitude, and in the respect and homage of mankind. They live in their example; and they live emphatically, and will live, in the influence which their lives and efforts, their principles and opinions, now exercise, and will continue to exercise, on the affairs of men, not only in their own country, but throughout the civilized world.

A superior and commanding human intellect, a truly great man, when Heaven vouchsafes so rare a gift, is not a temporary flame, burning bright for a while, and then expiring, giving place to returning darkness. It is rather a spark of fervent heat, as well as radiant light, with power to enkindle the common mass of human mind; so that, when it glimmers, in its own decay, and finally goes out in death, no night follows; but it leaves the world all light, all on fire, from the potent contact of its own spirit.

Bacon died, but the human understanding, roused by the touch of his miraculous wand to a perception of the true philosophy, and the just mode of inquiring after truth, has kept on its course, successfully and gloriously. Newton died; yet the courses of the spheres are still known, and they yet move on, in the orbits which he saw, and described for them, in the infinity of space.

No two men now live—perhaps it may be doubted whether any two men have ever lived in one age—who, more than those we now commemorate, have impressed their own sentiments, in regard to politics and government, on mankind, infused their own opinions more deeply into the opinions of others, or given a more lasting direction to the current of human thought. Their work doth not perish with them. The tree which they assisted to plant will flourish, although they water it and protect it no longer; for it has struck its roots deep; it has sent them to the very centre; no storm, not of force to burst the orb, can overturn it; its branches spread wide; they stretch their protecting arms broader and broader, and its top is destined to reach the heavens.

We are not deceived. There is no delusion here. No age will come, in which the American revolution will appear less than it is, one of the greatest events in human history. No age will come, in which it will cease to be seen and felt, on either continent, that a mighty step, a great advance, not only in American affairs, but in human affairs, was made on the 4th of July, 1776. And no age will come, we trust, so ignorant, or so unjust, as not to see and acknowledge the efficient agency of these we now honor, in producing that momentous event.

The Tides.—*William Cullen Bryant.*

The moon is at her full, and, riding high,
    Floods the calm fields with light,
The airs that hover in the summer sky
    Are all asleep to-night.

There comes no voice from the great woodlands round
    That murmured all the day;
Beneath the shadow of their boughs, the ground
    Is not more still than they.

But ever heaves and moans the restless Deep;
    His rising tides I hear;
Afar I see the glimmering billows leap:
    I see them breaking near.

Each wave springs upward, climbing toward the fair
    Pure light that sits on high;—
Springs eagerly, and faintly sinks to where
    The mother waters lie.

Upward again it swells; the moonbeams show,
    Again, its glimmering crest;
Again it feels the fatal weight below,
    And sinks, but not to rest.

Again and yet again; until the Deep
    Recalls his brood of waves;
And, with a sullen moan, abashed, they creep
    Back to his inner caves.

Brief respite! they shall rush from that recess
    With noise and tumult soon,
And fling themselves, with unavailing stress,
    Up toward the placid moon.

Oh restless Sea, that in thy prison here
    Dost struggle and complain;
Through the slow centuries yearning to be near
    To that fair orb in vain,

The glorious source of light and heat must warm
    Thy bosom with his glow,
And on those mounting waves a nobler form
    And freer life bestow.

Then only may they leave the watse of brine
    In which they welter here,
And rise above the hills of earth and shine
    In a serener sphere.

Eulogium on a Deceased Patriot.—*Captain T. F. Meagher.*

With beautiful truth the first of English writers in the present century has observed, that, when death strikes down the young, the innocent and brave, for every fragile form from which it lets the parting spirit free, a hundred virtues rise, in shapes of mercy, charity, and love, to walk the world and bless it. What noble conversion of feeling upon this occasion have I not beheld! I see regret where there have been aspersions—tears where there have been taunts—esteem avowed where disdain has been heretofore expressed. No, no; there is not one hand—no, not even the hand clenched against him in his lifetime—there is not one hand that refuses to throw a fond memorial flower upon the grave of the young, the gallant, the generous enlightened patriot. But they who fought in the same ranks as he so bravely did; they who stood beside him, and saw the earnest service he did his country and his country's cause; they in whose young hearts the appeals of his daring soul found quick and truthful echoes, were grieved indeed—grieved to the heart's most inmost depth, when, like some storm-gust, the news of his death swept swiftly by, and crushed the hopes they nourished for him.

But it was so ordained, that in the morning of life he should pass away. He has been called away—called away from his labors and his hopes. He is no more—he is not here. His meteor genius has ceased to burn—his noble heart to beat. But there are thoughts of his, generous sentiments, liberal views, enlightened principles which death could not strike down. These shall dwell amongst us—these will we treasure up as fond memorials, as wakening spells. They will beckon us to the grave, bid us pluck a laurel from the nation's brow, and place it on his tomb.

GEORGE WASHINGTON.—*Charles W. Upham.*

LONG before the war of the American revolution broke out, a leader was raised up and perfectly fitted for the great office. Among the mountain passes of the Blue Ridge and the Alleghanies, a youth is seen employed in the manly and invigorating occupations of a surveyor, and awakening the admiration of the hardy backwoodsmen and savage chieftains by the strength and endurance of his frame, and the resolution and energy of his character. In his stature and conformation he is a noble specimen of a man. In the various exercises of muscular power, on foot and in the saddle, he excels all competitors. His admirable physical traits are in perfect accordance with the properties of his mind and heart; and over all, crowning all, is a beautiful, and, in one so young, a strange dignity of manners and of mien, a calm seriousness, a sublime self-control, which at once compels the veneration, attracts the confidence, and secures the favor of all who behold him. That youth is the leader whom heaven is preparing to conduct America through her approaching trial.

As we see him voluntarily relinquishing the enjoyments, and luxuries, and ease, of the opulent refinement in which he was born and bred, and choosing the perils and hardships of the wilderness; as we follow him, fording swollen streams, climbing rugged mountains, breasting the forest storms, wading through snow-drifts, sleeping in the open air, living upon the coarse food of hunters and of Indians—we trace, with devout admiration, the divinely appointed education he was receiving to enable him to meet and endure the fatigues, exposures, and privations, of the war of independence. Soon he is called to a more public sphere of action, on the same theatre; and again we follow him in his romantic adventures, as he traversed the far-off western wilderness, a special messenger to the French commander on the Ohio, and afterward when he led forth the troops of Virginia in the same direction, or accompanied the ill-starred Braddock to the blood-stained banks of the Monongahela. Everywhere we see the hand of God conducting him into danger, that he might extract from it the wisdom of an experience not otherwise to be attained, and develop those heroic qualities by which alone danger and difficulty can be surmounted—but all the while covering him, as with a shield.

When we think of him, at midnight and in midwinter, thrown from a frail raft into the deep and angry waters of a wide and rushing western river, thus separated from his only companion through the wilderness, with no human aid for miles and leagues around him, buffeting its rapid current, and struggling through driving cakes of ice; when we behold the stealthy savage, whose aim as against all other marks is unerring, pointing his rifle deliberately at him, and firing over and over again; when we see him riding through showers of bullets on Braddock's fatal field, and reflect that never, during his whole life, was he wounded or even touched by a hostile force—do we not feel that he was guarded by an unseen hand? Yes, that sacred person was guarded by an unseen hand, warding off every danger. No peril by flood or by field was permitted to extinguish a life consecrated to the hopes of humanity and to the purposes of heaven. His military preparation was completed by being intrusted with the defence of the frontiers of Virginia and the neighboring colonies—a command which, in the difficulties and embarrassments with which it was crowded, in its general character, and more especially in the widespread and incessant oversight, and forethought, and prudence, and patience it required, most remarkably resembled, was indeed a precise epitome of, the service he afterward discharged as commander-in-chief of the forces of United America.

The warrior is now ready, but the statesman remains to be prepared. He accordingly resigned his commission, and retired to private and civil life. Although not then quite twenty-seven years of age, he had won a splendor of reputation and a completeness of experience, as a military man, such as had never before been acquired in America. For more than sixteen years he rested from his warfare, amid the shades of Mount Vernon, ripening his mind by reading and reflection, increasing his knowledge of practical affairs, entering into the whole experience of a citizen, at home on his farm, and as a delegate to the colonial assembly; and when, at last, the war broke out, and the unanimous voice of the continental congress invested him, as the exigency required, with almost unbounded authority, as their commander-in-chief, he blended, although still in the prime of his life —in the mature bloom of manhood—the attributes of a sage with those of a hero.

A more perfectly fitted and furnished character has never appeared on the theatre of human action, than when, reining up his war-horse beneath the majestic and venerable elm, still standing at the entrance of the old Watertown road upon Cambridge Common, GEORGE WASHINGTON unsheathed his sword, and assumed the command of the gathering armies of American liberty. Those who had despaired, when they beheld their chief despaired no more. The very aspect of his person and countenance concurred with the history of his life in impressing their hearts with a deep conviction that God was with him, in the exercise of a peculiar guardianship, and that in his hands their cause was safe.

Death of Gertrude, and the Lament of Outalissi.
—*Thomas Campbell*

Hushed were his Gertrude's lips; but still their bland
And beautiful expression seemed to melt
With love that could not die; and still his hand
She presses to the heart no more that felt.
Ah heart! where once each fond affection dwelt,
And features yet that spoke a soul more fair.
Mute, gazing, agonizing as he knelt—
Of them that stood encircling his despair,
He heard some friendly words, but knew not what they were.

For now, to mourn their judge and child, arrives
A faithful band. With solemn rites between,
'Twas sung, how they were lovely in their lives,
And in their deaths had not divided been.
Touched by the music, and the melting scene,
Was scarce one tearless eye amidst the crowd:
Stern warriors, resting on their swords, were seen
To veil their eyes, as passed each much-loved shroud—
While woman's softer soul in woe dissolved aloud.

Then mournfully the parting bugle bid
Its farewell, o'er the grave of worth and truth;
Prone to the dust, afflicted Waldegrave hid
His face on earth;—him watched, in gloomy ruth,
His woodland guide; but words had none to soothe
The grief that knew not consolation's name;
Casting his Indian mantle o'er the youth,
He watched, beneath its folds, each burst that came
Convulsive, ague-like, across his shuddering frame.

"And I could weep," th' Oneyda chief
His descant wildly thus begun,
"But that I may not stain with grief
The death-song of my father's son,
Or bow this head in woe;
For by my wrongs, and by my wrath,
To-morrow Areouski's breath
(That fires yon heaven with storms of death)
Shall light us to the foe;

And we shall share, my Christian boy,
The foeman's blood, th' avenger's joy.

"But thee, my flower, whose breath was given
　By milder genii o'er the deep,
The spirits of the white man's heaven
　Forbid not thee to weep;
　　　Nor will the Christian host,
Nor will thy father's spirit, grieve
To see thee, on the battle's eve,
Lamenting, take a mournful leave
　　　Of her who loved thee most:
She was the rainbow to thy sight—
Thy sun—thy heaven of lost delight!

"To-morrow let us do or die!
　But when the bolt of death is hurled,
Ah! whither then with thee to fly,
　Shall Outalissi roam the world?
　　　Seek we thy once-loved home?
The hand is gone that cropped its flowers;
Unheard their clock repeats its hours;
Cold is the hearth within their bowers;
　　　And should we thither roam,
Its echoes and its empty tread
Would sound like voices from the dead.

"Or shall we cross yon mountains blue,
　Whose streams my kindred nation quaffed,
And by my side, in battle true,
　A thousand warriors drew the shaft!
　　　Ah! there, in desolation cold,
The desert serpent dwells alone,
Where grass o'ergrows each mouldering bone,
And stones themselves, to ruin grown,
　　　Like me are death-like old.
Then seek we not their camp; for there
The silence dwells of my despair.

"But hark, the trump!—to-morrow thou
　In glory's fires shalt dry thy tears
Even from the land of shadows now
　My father's awful ghost appears,
　　　Amidst the clouds that round us roll:

> He bids my soul for battle thirst:
> He bids me dry the last—the first—
> The only tears that ever burst
>   From Outalissi's soul;
> Because I may not stain with grief
> The death-song of an Indian chief."

Effects of a Dissolution of the Federal Union.—
Alexander Hamilton.

ASSUMING it, therefore, as an established truth, that, in case of disunion, the several states, or such combinations of them as might happen to be formed out of the wreck of the general confederacy, would be subject to those vicissitudes of peace and war, of friendship and enmity with each other, which have fallen to the lot of all other nations not united under one government, let us enter into a concise detail of some of the consequences that would attend such a situation.

War between the states, in the first periods of their separate existence, would be accompanied with much greater distresses than it commonly is in those countries where regular military establishments have long obtained. The disciplined armies always kept on foot on the continent of Europe, though they bear a malignant aspect to liberty and economy, have, notwithstanding, been productive of the singular advantage of rendering sudden conquests impracticable, and of preventing that rapid desolation, which used to mark the progress of war prior to their introduction. The art of fortification has contributed to the same ends. The nations of Europe are encircled with chains of fortified places, which mutually obstruct invasion. Campaigns are wasted in reducing two or three fortified garrisons, to gain admittance into an enemy's country. Similar impediments occur at every step, to exhaust the strength, and delay the progress, of an invader. Formerly, an invading army would penetrate into the heart of a neighboring country almost as soon as intelligence of its approach could be received; but now, a comparatively small force of disciplined troops, acting on the defensive, with the aid of posts, is able to impede, and finally to frustrate, the purposes of one much more considerable. The history of war in that quarter of the globe is no longer a history of nations subdued, and empires overturned; but of towns taken and retaken, of battles that decide nothing, of retreats more beneficial than victories, of much effort and little acquisition.

In this country the scene would be altogether reversed. The jealousy of military establishments would postpone them as long as possible. The want of fortifications, leaving the frontier of one state open to another, would facilitate inroads. The populous states would with little difficulty overrun their less populous neighbors. Conquests would be as easy to be made as difficult to be retained. War, therefore, would be desultory and predatory. Plunder and devastation ever march in the train of irregulars. The calamities of individuals would ever make the principal figure in events, and would characterize our exploits.

This picture is not too highly wrought; though, I confess, it would not long remain a just one. Safety from external danger is the most powerful director of national conduct. Even the ardent love of liberty will, after a time, give way to its dictates. The violent destruction of life and property incident to war, to continual effort and alarm attendant on a state of continual danger, wil' compel nations the most attached to liberty to resort for repose and security to institutions which have a tendency to destroy their civil and political rights. To be more safe, they at length become willing to run the risk of being less free. The institutions chiefly alluded to are

8

standing armies, and the corresponding appendages of military establishments. Standing armies, it is said, are not provided against in the new constitution; and it is thence inferred that they would exist under it. This inference, from the very form of the proposition, is, at best, problematical and uncertain. But standing armies, it may be replied, must inevitably result from a dissolution of the confederacy. Frequent war and constant apprehension, which require a state of as constant preparation, will infallibly produce them. The weaker states or confederacies would first have recourse to them, to put themselves on an equality with their more potent neighbors. They would endeavor to supply the inferiority of population and resources by a more regular and effective system of defence—by disciplined troops, and by fortifications. They would, at the same time, be obliged to strengthen the executive arm of government; in doing which their constitutions would require a progressive direction toward monarchy. It is the nature of war to increase the executive at the expense of the legislative authority.

The expedients which have been mentioned, would soon give the states, or confederacies, that made use of them, a superiority over their neighbors. Small states, or states of less natural strength, under vigorous governments, and with the assistance of disciplined armies, have often triumphed over large states, or states of greater natural strength, which have been destitute of these advantages. Neither the pride nor the safety of the important states, or confederacies, would permit them long to submit to this mortifying and adventitious superiority. They would quickly resort to means similar to those by which it had been effected, to reinstate themselves in their lost pre-eminence. Thus we should, in a little time, see established in every part of this country the same engines of despotism which have been the scourge of the old world. This, at least, would be the natural course of things; and our reasonings will be likely to be just, in proportion as they are accommodated to this standard. These are not vague inferences, deduced from speculative defects in a constitution, the whole power of which is lodged in the hands of the people, or their representatives and delegates; they are solid conclusions, drawn from the natural and necessary progress of human affairs.

* * * * * * *

If we are wise enough to preserve the Union, we may for ages enjoy an advantage similar to that of an insulated situation. Europe is at a great distance from us. Her colonies in our vicinity will be likely to continue too much disproportioned in strength to be able to give us any dangerous annoyance. Extensive military establishments cannot, in this position, be necessary to our security. But, if we should be disunited, and the integral parts should either remain separated, or, which is most probable, should be thrown together into two or three confederacies, we should be, in a short course of time, in the predicament of the continental powers of Europe. Our liberties would be a prey to the means of defending ourselves against the ambition and jealousy of each other.

This is an idea not superficial or futile, but solid and weighty. It deserves the most serious and mature consideration of every prudent and honest man, of whatever party. If such men will make a firm and solemn pause, and meditate dispassionately on its importance; if they will contemplate it in all its attitudes, and trace it to all its consequences, they will not hesitate to part with trivial objections to a constitution, the rejection of which would, in all probability, put a final period to the Union. The airy phantoms, that now flit before the distempered imaginations of some of its adversaries, would then quickly give place to more substantial prospects of dangers, real, certain, and extremely formidable.

Freedom's Birth.—*M. A. Moses.*

In that dark, gloomy night,
    Ere freedom's bright morn,
When the strong hand of might
    Man's right laughed to scorn—
Through battle and strife,
    Through blood and through death,
Came a glorious life—
    'Twas liberty's birth!
Through the smoke of that conflict pervading the skies,
Behold the day-star of liberty rise!

In the gathering gloom
    Of that perilous hour,
When our fathers o'erturned
    The mad tyrant's power;
Through darkness and storm,
    By night and by day,
The pure light of freedom
    Illumined the way:—
'Twas then, O Columbia, 'mid carnage and war,
First dawned on the world thy bright natal star!

On Lexington's sward,
    Down Bunker's steep side,
From the breasts of the slain
    Ran the crimson life-tide;
Across Delaware's stream,
    Through bleak Valley Forge,
Where blood marked their steps
    In that wild mountain gorge;
Still freedom's blest hope those heroes led on
To battle and death, till triumph was won.

On Camden's hot plains,
    By Brandywine's wave,
The cohorts of foemen
    Found many a grave;
And Yorktown's proud rampart
    In vain raised its side

'Gainst the wild rushing surge
  Of liberty's tide;
In a halo of glory, o'er land and o'er sea,
Now floats in glad triumph the flag of the free!

From hill-top and mountain,
  From valley and plain,
Ring glad shouts from millions
  For liberty's reign;
The forest and prairie,
  The ocean and stream,
In the sunlight of freedom
  With new lustre gleam;
While our bright starry banner, wherever unfurled,
Is humanity's beacon—the hope of the world!

Say, sons of the martyrs
  In freedom's cause slain,
Shall the vilest of traitors
  This land rend in twain?
By the blood of those martyrs
  For you freely given;
By the prayers of the millions
  Ascending to heaven;
Go, kneel at the graves of your fathers, and swear
That our flag shall still float in freedom's pure air!

REFLECTIONS ON THE BATTLE OF LEXINGTON.—*Hon. Edward Everett.*

It was one of those great days, one of those elemental occasions in the world's affairs, when the people rise and act for themselves. Some organization and preparation had been made; but, from the nature of the case, with scarce any effect on the events of that day. It may be doubted, whether there was an efficient order given the whole day to any body of men as large as a regiment. It was the people, in their first capacity, as citizens and as freemen, starting from their beds at midnight, from their firesides and their fields, to take their own cause into their own hands. Such a spectacle is the height of the moral sublime; when the want of every thing is fully made up by the spirit of the cause; and the soul within stands in place of discipline, organization, resources. In the prodigious efforts of a veteran army, beneath the dazzling splendor of their array, there is something revolting to the reflecting mind. The ranks are filled with the desperate, the mercenary, the depraved; an iron slavery, by the name of subordination, merges the free will of one hundred thousand men in the unqualified despotism of one; the humanity, mercy and remorse, which scarce ever desert the individual bosom, are sounds without a meaning to that fearful, ravenous, irrational monster of prey, a mercenary army. It is hard to say who are most to be commiserated, the wretched people on whom it is let loose, or the still more wretched people whose substance has been sucked out, to nourish it into strength and fury. But in the efforts of the people, of the people struggling for their rights, moving not in organized, disciplined masses, but in their spontaneous action, man for man, and heart for heart—though I like not war, nor any of its works—there is something glorious. They can then move forward without orders, act together without combination, and brave the flaming lines of battle, without intrenchments to cover, or walls to shield them. No dissolute camp has worn off from the feelings of the youthful soldier the freshness of that home, where his mother and his sisters sit waiting, with tearful eyes and aching hearts, to hear good news from the wars; no long service in the ranks of the conqueror has turned the veteran's heart into marble; their valor springs not from recklessness, from habit, from indifference to the preservation of a life, knit by no pledges to the life of others; but in the strength and spirit of the cause alone they act, they contend, they bleed. In this they conquer. The people always conquer. They always must conquer. Armies may be defeated; kings may be overthrown, and new dynasties imposed by foreign arms on an ignorant and slavish race, that care not in what language the covenant of their subjection runs, nor in whose name the deed of their barter and sale is made out. But the people never invade; and, when they rise against the invader, are never subdued. If they are driven from the plains, they fly to the mountains. Steep rocks and everlasting hills are their castles; the tangled, pathless thicket their palisado; and nature—God—is their ally. Now he overwhelms the hosts of their enemies, beneath his drifting mountains of sand; now he buries them beneath an atmosphere of falling snows; he lets loose his tempests on their fleets; he puts a folly into their counsels, a madness into the hearts of their leaders; and he never gave, and never will give, a full and final triumph over a virtuous, gallant people, resolved to be free.

Appeal in Favor of the Union.—*James Madison.*

I submit to you, my fellow-citizens, these considerations, in full confidence that the good sense which has so often marked your decisions, will allow them their due weight and effect; and that you will never suffer difficulties, however formidable in appearance, or however fashionable the error on which they may be founded, to drive you into the gloomy and perilous scenes into which the advocates for disunion would conduct you. Hearken not to the unnatural voice, which tells you that the people of America, knit together as they are, by so many cords of affection, can no longer live together as members of the same family; can no longer continue the mutual guardians of their mutual happiness; can no longer be fellow-citizens of one great, respectable and flourishing empire. Hearken not to the voice, which petulantly tells you, that the form of government recommended for your adoption is a novelty in the political world; that it has never yet had a place in the theories of the wildest projectors; that it rashly attempts what it is impossible to accomplish. No, my countrymen; shut your ears against this unhallowed language. Shut your hearts against the poison which it conveys; the kindred blood, which flows in the veins of American citizens, the mingled blood, which they have shed in defence of their sacred rights, consecrate their union, and excite horror at the idea of their becoming aliens, rivals, enemies. And if novelties are to be shunned, believe me, the most alarming of all novelties, the most wild of all projects, the most rash of all attempts, is that of rending us in pieces, in order to preserve our liberties and promote our happiness. But why is the experiment of an extended republic to be rejected, merely because it may comprise what is new? Is it not the glory of the people of America, that, whilst they have paid a decent regard to the opinions of former times and other nations, they have not suffered a blind veneration for antiquity, for custom, or for names, to overrule the suggestions of their own good sense, the knowledge of their own situation, and the lessons of their own experience? To this manly spirit, posterity will be indebted for the possession, and the world for the example, of the numerous innovations displayed on the American theatre, in favor of private rights and public happiness. Had no important step been taken by the leaders of the revolution, for which a precedent could not be discovered; had no government been established, of which an exact model did not present itself—the people of the United States might, at this moment, have been numbered among the melancholy victims of misguided councils; must at best have been laboring under the weight of some of those forms which have crushed the liberties of the rest of mankind. Happily for America, happily, we trust, for the whole human race, they pursued a new and more noble course. They accomplished a revolution which has no parallel in the annals of human society. They reared fabrics of government which have no model on the face of the globe. They formed the design of a great confederacy, which it is incumbent on their successors to improve and perpetuate. If their works betray imperfections, we wonder at the fewness of them. If they erred most in the structure of the Union, this was the work most difficult to be executed; this is the work which has been new-modelled by the act of your convention, and it is that act on which you are now to deliberate and decide.

In Memory of the Heroic Captain Herndon, lost in the Wreck of the Central America.

How soft the murmur of this breeze!
How deep the ocean's purple hue!
How goldenly over all the sun
    Beams in the quiet of the blue!
Ah! who would dream that ought but bliss
And peace could take a sea like this?

Yet but a few brief days ago,
    Death shuddered on the stormy wave,
And Horror shrieked and clasped her hands,
    O'er ocean turning to a grave,
Within whose everlasting deep
Four hundred forms went down to sleep.

O ye so coldly resting here!
    Full many a heart your memory holds;
And many an eye is dim with grief
    In sorrow's pale and silent folds—

But HERNDON, o'er thy glorious shroud
See, a whole nation wails aloud!

Is it not glorious? Honor leans
　　As fondly o'er these burial seas
As e'er she leaned in days of yore
　　Above her own Miltiadés:
No fear with Herndon on the deck,
The last wild crash, the sinking wreck.

And now with all her banners furled,
　　Thy nation in the shadow dim,
Is chanting by the shrouding wave
　　The sad words of a funeral hymn—
What praises through the music swell,
That hero-spirits love so well!

They tell of courage never quelled;
　　Of duty nobly, calmly done;
Of that dark, awful, lonely death;
　　Of everlasting glory won:
And dearer still, a nation's love
For him imparadised above.

Defier of the wrathful wave!
　　Brave warrior with the mighty storm!
Whenever floats the starry flag
　　Where silent lies thy gallant form.
How shall its eagle be unfurled
In broader grandeur to the world!

Then calmly slumber in the sea!
　　Ah, ours the mighty loss, not thine
Whose high, heroic memory gleams
　　Forevermore in glory's shrine!—
He wins a deathless prize whose breath
For man is gladly given to death.

CHARACTER OF HAMILTON.—*Fisher Ames.*

MEN of the most elevated minds have not always the readiest discernment of character. Perhaps he was sometimes too sudden and too lavish in bestowing his confidence: his manly spirit, disdaining artifice, suspected none. But, while the power of his friends over him seemed to have no limits, and really had none, in respect to those things which were of a nature to be yielded, no man, not the Roman Cato himself, was more inflexible on every point that touched, or only seemed to touch, his integrity and honor. With him it was not enough to be unsuspected; his bosom would have glowed like a furnace at its own whispers of reproach. Mere purity would have seemed to him below praise; and such were his habits, and such his nature, that the pecuniary temptations, which many others can only with great exertion and self-denial resist, had no attractions for him. He was very far from obstinate; yet as his friends assailed his opinions with less profound thought than he had devoted to them, they were seldom shaken by discussion. He defended them, however, with as much mildness as force, and evinced that, if he did not yield, it was not for want of gentleness or modesty.

His early life we pass over; though his heroic spirit in the army has furnished a theme that is dear to patriotism, and will be sacred to glory.

In all the different stations in which a life of active usefulness has placed him, we find him not more remarkably distinguished by the extent, than by the variety and versatility, of his talents. In every place, he made it apparent, that no other man could have filled it so well; and in times of critical importance, in which alone he desired employment, his services were justly deemed absolutely indispensable. As secretary of the treasury, his was the powerful spirit that presided over the chaos.

"Confusion heard his voice, and wild uproar
Stood ruled."

Indeed, in organizing the federal government in 1789, every man, of either sense or candor, will allow, the difficulties seemed greater than the first-rate abilities could surmount. The event has shown that his abilities were greater than those difficulties. He surmounted them; and Washington's administration was the most wise and beneficent, the most prosperous, and ought to be the most popular, that ever was intrusted with the affairs of a nation. Great as was Washington's merit, much of it in plan, much in execution, will of course devolve upon his minister.

As a lawyer, his comprehensive genius reached the principles of his profession: he compassed its extent, he fathomed its profound, perhaps, even more familiarly and easily than the rules of its practice. With most men law is a trade; with him it was a science.

As a statesman, he was not more distinguished for the great extent of his views, than by the caution with which he provided against impediments, and the watchfulness of his care over the right and liberty of the subject. In none of the many revenue bills which he framed, though committees reported them, is there to be found a single clause which savors of despotic power; not one that the sagest champions of law and liberty would, on that ground, hesitate to approve and adopt.

It is rare that a man, who owes so much to nature, descends to seek more from industry; but he seemed to depend on industry as if nature had done nothing for him. His habits of investigation were very remarkable; his mind seemed to cling to his subject till he had exhausted it. Hence the uncommon superiority of his reasoning powers—a superiority that seemed to be augmented from

every source, and to be fortified by every auxiliary—
learning, taste, wit, imagination and eloquence. These
were embellished and enforced by his temper and manners, by his fame and his virtues. It is difficult, in the
midst of such various excellence, to say in what particular
the effect of his greatness was most manifest. No man
more promptly discerned truth; no man more clearly
displayed it: it was not merely made visible—it seemed
to come bright with illumination from his lips. But,
prompt and clear as he was—fervid as Demosthenes,
like Cicero full of resource—he was not less remarkable
for the copiousness and completeness of his argument,
that left little for cavil, and nothing for doubt. Some
men take their strongest argument as a weapon, and use
no other; but he left nothing to be inquired for—nothing
to be answered. He not only disarmed his adversaries
of their pretexts and objections, but he stripped them of
all excuse for having urged them; he confounded and
subdued as well as convinced. He indemnified them,
however, by making his discussion a complete map of
his subject; so that his opponents might, indeed, feel
ashamed of their mistakes, but they could not repeat
them. In fact it was no common effort that could preserve a really able antagonist from becoming his convert;
for the truth, which his researches so distinctly presented
to the understanding of others, was rendered almost
irresistibly commanding and impressive by the love and
reverence, which, it was ever apparent, he profoundly
cherished for it in his own. While patriotism glowed
in his heart, wisdom blended in his speech her authority
with her charms.

Unparalleled as were his services, they were nevertheless no otherwise requited than by the applause of all
good men, and by his own enjoyment of the spectacle of
that national prosperity and honor, which was the effect
of them. After facing calumny, and triumphantly sur-

mounting an unrelenting persecution, he retired from office with clean though empty hands, as rich as reputation and an unblemished integrity could make him.

The most substantial glory of a country is in its virtuous great men : its prosperity will depend on its docility to learn from their example. That nation is fated to ignominy and servitude, for which such men have lived in vain. Power may be seized by a nation that is yet barbarous ; and wealth may be enjoyed by one that it finds or renders sordid : the one is the gift and the sport of accident, and the other is the sport of power. Both are mutable, and have passed away without leaving behind them any other memorial than ruins that offend taste, and traditions that baffle conjecture. But the glory of Greece is imperishable, or will last as long as learning itself, which is its monument : it strikes an everlasting root, and bears perennial blossoms on its grave. The name of Hamilton would have honored Greece in the age of Aristides. May Heaven, the guardian of our liberty, grant that our country may be fruitful of Hamiltons, and faithful to their glory!

The Cruel Case of Col. Pegram.—*N. Y. Tribune.*

Who is Pegram? Colonel Pegram? And this is fame! Why, Pegram *was* a colonel of the rebel army in Western Virginia, and Pegram *is* a prisoner, made so, with his tent, epaulettes, sword and general military furniture, by General McClellan. "Well," asks the reader, "what is there extraordinary about that? Are "not colonels of all varieties continually made "prisoners? What is there peculiar about the "case of Pegram?" Why, it is that among other military miscellanies in the pavilion of Pegram the conquering captors found the savagest, most truculent, gunpowdery, give-'em-fits proclamation that ever was issued by any the most phosphorescent general; which, indeed, the reader will readily believe, when we tell him that the said proclamation was the production of Ex-Governor and General Wise's redhot pen. This sultry production, of which we have a copy, is singularly enough headed; "To arms! to arms!" though one cannot understand why "To legs! to legs!" would not have been the kindlier exhortation. We have said that placard was produced by Wise the Wonderful; but, perhaps, considering the thorough and innate modesty of that meek Moses of a man, we should revise our judgment; for we find him spoken of in the body of the document as "the brave, chivalrous, and indomitable General Henry A. Wise;" but then, at the bottom of the same, we find plainly printed: "By order of General Wise," so that we have here the Virginian hero and statesman "ordering" himself to be "proclaimed" at once "brave, chivalrous, and indomitable." This rather than else knocks into the shade of humility the arrogance of oriental monarchs; and, we are afraid, after all, that our Henry is not the modest person that we supposed. Modest generals hardly ever blow their own trumpets after such a *fortissimo* fashion; and great commanders usually leave their "bravery," "chivalry," and "indomitability," to be discovered by the world, without putting them into the orders of the day, and employing a Pegram to puff them. Imagine the Duke of Wellington describing himself as "brave, chivalrous, and indomitable!" Or imagine one of his aids doing it for him! Would there not have been a row, riot, and rumpuss at head-quarters speedily?

But it is in the character of—what shall we say?—thief? Well, thief is a hard word—suppose we say abstractor—abstractions have always been popular in Virginia, and now Floyd has made them really fashionable

—it is as an abstractor that General Wise shines. He who has no sword is advised in the Scriptures to buy one; but this new general says, by way of improvement, let him who has no sword "steal one!" Hear the brave, chivalrous, and indomitable! "Gather," he says, or it is said by his "order," gather every thing in the shape of arms that may be converted into them, and paste the name of the person from whom they are taken upon them, that they may be valued; bring all the powder, every flint, percussion-cap, &c." Floyd has evidently been giving Wise a course of six easy lessons in larceny; and wonderfully has the defender of the oyster-beds improved his precious opportunities. To be sure, he does not call the proposed confiscation stealing—he calls it "gathering" and "taking"—but if we had an uncommonly fine Joe Manton and a small store of ammunition for our private shooting, and Colonel Pegram should carry off the same, we should consider Pegram as a thief and Governor Wise as accessory before the fact. Such "gathering" is especially stealing in Western Virginia, where so many of the inhabitants are loyally and honestly struggling against an oligarchical and military usurpation. Suppose they did paste our name upon the plunder; which we do not believe that they would take much trouble to do; and suppose we did afterward go to Richmond for remuneration! Go to Richmond for a halter! Go to Richmond for tar and feathers! Go to Richmond for further confiscations! These might be secured without the smallest trouble; but that they would be ready to pay Pegram's drafts for property "gathered" is what we are in no hurry to believe. Stealing is altogether too constitutional in that state—it certainly is!

Having arranged these agreeable instructions to Pegram—they remind us of those which Fagin gave to Oliver Twist—General Wise, being done with business, takes to the religion of the occasion: "Be brave," he cries, "and fear not! The God that made the mountains is the God of the lion-hearted and the brave." Very good! very fine, indeed! Only, like other fine things we have heard before, it is egregious nonsense. Why is the God that made the mountains more the God of the lion-hearted and brave than the God that made the valley? This is an interesting point in theology, and we want it settled. Moreover, we insist, for we should be very unwilling to believe otherwise—we insist that the God that made the mountains is also the God of cravens, lily-livered renegades and consummate knaves; and He has a way of showing it, as Pegram has already found to his cost—many of these miraculous mountaineers being now in limbo, with the prospect, if they receive justice, of making one more ascent—and one only!

Another flower from this parterre of a proclamation: "The land of Washington, Henry, Jefferson, and Madison is sacred—it must not, SHALL not, be desecrated." Now, here we agree fully with the ex-governor. Not desecrated—oh, no!—not by wicked rebellion and falsehood to law, and infidelity to the constitution! But this is not what the unwise Wise means. He means, perhaps, that it is "desecration" to send Federal troops into Virginia, and he says that this SHALL not be done. And Pegram, we suppose, all begirt as became a warrior, was reading this very sentence in his tent, and finding his anxious soul much solaced thereby, when along came the ruthless invader and disturbed Pegram's perusal. "He SHALL be expelled," said Pegram, and the next moment he was—ah, well-a-day!—Pegram was a prisoner! This was, to use the language of the proclamation, "a barbarity and atrocity disgraceful to civilization." How Pegram must have tumbled from the seventh heaven of contemplation! Poor Pegram!

EXTRACT FROM A SPEECH DELIVERED IN THE U. S.
SENATE, JULY 27, 1861.—*Hon. Andrew Johnson.*

WE ask the government to come to our aid. We love the constitution as made by our fathers. We have confidence in the integrity and capacity of the people to govern themselves. We have lived entertaining these opinions; we intend to die entertaining them. The battle has commenced. The president has placed it upon the true ground. It is an issue on the one hand for the people's government, and its overthrow on the other. We have commenced the battle of freedom. It is freedom's cause. We are resisting usurpation and oppression. We will triumph; we must triumph. Right is with us. A great and fundamental principle of right, that lies at the foundation of all things, is with us. We may meet with impediments, and may meet with disasters, and here and there a defeat, but ultimately freedom's cause must triumph, for

"Freedom's battle once begun,
Bequeathed from bleeding sire to son,
Though baffled oft, is ever won."

Yes, we must triumph. Though sometimes I cannot see my way clear in matters of this kind, as in matters of religion, when my facts give out, when my reason fails me, I draw largely upon my faith. My faith is strong, based on the eternal principles of right, that a thing so monstrously wrong as this rebellion, cannot triumph. Can we submit to it? Is the senate, are the American people, prepared to give up the graves of Washington and Jackson, to be encircled and governed and controlled by a combination of traitors and rebels? I say let the battle go on—it is freedom's cause—until the stars and stripes (God bless them!) shall again be unfurled upon every cross-road, and from every house-top throughout the confederacy, north and south. Let the Union be reinstated; let the law be enforced; let the constitution be supreme.

If the Congress of the United States were to give up the tombs of Washington and Jackson, we should have rising up in our midst another Peter the Hermit, in a much more righteous cause—for ours is true, while his was a delusion—who would appeal to the American people and point to the tombs of Washington and Jackson, in the possession of those who are worse than the infidel and the Turk who held the Holy Sepulchre. I believe the American people would start of their own accord, when appealed to, to redeem the graves of Washington and Jackson and Jefferson, and all the other patriots who are lying within the limits of the Southern Confederacy. I do not believe they would stop the march, until again the flag of this Union would be placed over the graves of those distinguished men. There will be an uprising. Do not talk about Republicans now; do not talk about Democrats now; do not talk about Whigs or Americans now; talk about your country and the constitution and the Union. Save that; preserve the integrity of the government; once more place it erect among the nations of the earth; and then if we want to divide about questions that may arise in our midst, we have a government to divide in.

I know it has been said that the object of this war is to make war on Southern institutions. I have been in free states and I have been in slave states, and I thank God that, so far as I have been, there has been one universal disclaimer of any such purpose. It is a war upon no section; it is a war upon no peculiar institution; but it is a war for the integrity of the government, for the constitution and the supremacy of the laws. That is what the nation understands by it.

The people whom I represent appeal to the government and to the nation to give us the constitutional protection that we need. I am proud to say that I have met with every manifestation of that kind in the senate, with only a few dissenting voices. I am proud to say, too, that I believe old Kentucky, God bless her! will ultimately rise and shake off the stupor which has been resting upon her; and instead of denying us the privilege of passing through her borders, and taking arms and munitions of war to enable a downtrodden people to defend themselves, will not only give us that privilege, but will join us and help us in the work. The people of Kentucky love the Union; they love the constitution; they have no fault to find with it; but in that state they have a duplicate to the governor of ours. When we look all around, we see how the governors of the different states have been involved in this conspiracy —the most stupendous and gigantic conspiracy that was ever formed, and as corrupt and as foul as that attempted by Catiline in the days of Rome. We know it to be so. Have we not known men to sit at their desks in this chamber, using the government's stationery to write treasonable letters; and while receiving their pay, sworn to support the constitution and sustain the law, engaging in midnight conclaves to devise ways and means by which the government and the constitution should be overthrown? The charge was made and published in the papers. Many things we know that we cannot put our finger upon; but we know from the regular steps that were taken in this work of breaking up the government, or trying to break it up, that there was system, concert of action. It is a scheme more corrupt than the assassination planned and conducted by Catiline in reference to the Roman senate. The time has arrived when we should show to the nations of the earth that we are a nation capable of preserving our existence, and give them evidence that we will do it.

I have already detained the senate much longer than I intended when I rose, and I shall conclude in a few words more. Although the government has met with a little reverse within a short distance of this city, no one should be discouraged and no heart should be dismayed. It ought only to prove the necessity of bringing forth and exerting still more vigorously the power of the government in maintenance of the constitution and the laws. Let the energies of the government be redoubled, and let it go on with this war—not a war upon sections, not a war upon peculiar institutions anywhere; but let the constitution and the Union be its frontispiece, and the supremacy and enforcement of the laws its watchword. Then it can, it will, go on triumphantly. We must succeed. This government must not, cannot fall. Though your flag may have trailed in the dust; though a retrograde movement may have been made; though the banner of our country may have been sullied, let it still be borne onward; and if, for the prosecution of this war in behalf of the government and the constitution, it is necessary to cleanse and purify the banner, I say let it be baptized in fire from the sun and bathed in a nation's blood! The nation must be redeemed; it must be triumphant. The constitution—which is based upon principles immutable, and upon which rest the rights of man and the hopes and expectations of those who love freedom throughout the civilized world—must be maintained.

FREEDOM OF THE ANCIENT ISRAELITES.—*Rev. Dr. Croly.*

THE state of man in the most unfettered republics of the ancient world was slavery, compared with the magnanimous and secure establishment of the Jewish commonwealth. During the three hundred golden years from Moses to Samuel—before, for our sins, we were given over to the madness of innovation and the demand of an earthly diadem—the Jew was free, in the loftiest sense of freedom; free to do all good; restricted only from evil; every man pursuing the unobstructed course pointed out by his genius or his fortune; every man protected by laws inviolable, or whose violation was instantly visited with punishment, by the Eternal Sovereign alike of ruler and people.

Freedom! twin-sister of virtue, thou brightest of all the spirits that descended in the train of religion from the throne of God; thou, that leadest up man again to the early glories of his being: angel, from the circle of whose presence happiness spreads like the sunlight over the darkness of the land! at the waving of whose sceptre, knowledge and peace and fortitude and wisdom, stoop upon the wing; at the voice of whose trumpet the more than grave is broken, and slavery gives up her dead; when shall I see thy coming? When shall I hear thy summons upon the mountains of my country, and rejoice in the regeneration and glory of the sons of Judah!

I have traversed nations; and as I set my foot upon their boundary, I have said, freedom is not here! I saw the naked hill, the morass steaming with death, the field covered with weedy fallow, the silky thicket encumbering the land; I saw the still more infallible signs, the downcast visage, the form degraded at once by loathsome indolence and desperate poverty; the peasant cheerless and feeble in his field, the wolfish robber, the population of the cities crowded into huts and cells, with pestilence for their fellow; I saw the contumely of man to man, the furious vindictiveness of popular rage; and I pronounced at the moment, this people is not free.

In the republics of heathen antiquity, the helot, the client sold for the extortion of the patron, and the born bondmen lingering out life in thankless toil, at once put to flight all conceptions of freedom. In the midst of altars fuming to liberty, of harangues glowing with the most pompous protestations of scorn for servitude, of crowds inflated with the presumption that they disdained a master, the eye was insulted with the perpetual chain. The temple of liberty was built upon the dungeon. Rome came, and unconsciously avenged the insulted name of freedom; the master and the slave were bowed together; the dungeon was made the common dwelling of all.

Resistance to Tyranny.—*Patrick Henry.*

Mr. President: It is natural for man to indulge in the illusions of hope. We are apt to shut our eyes against a painful truth, and listen to the song of that siren till she transforms us into beasts. Is this the part of wise men, engaged in a great and arduous struggle for liberty? Are we disposed to be of the number of those, who, having eyes, see not, and having ears, hear not, the things which so nearly concern their temporal salvation? For my part, whatever anguish of spirit it may cost, I am willing to know the whole truth; to know the worst, and to provide for it.

I have but one lamp, by which my feet are guided; and that is the lamp of experience. I know of no way of judging of the future but by the past. And, judging by the past, I wish to know what there has been in the conduct of the British ministry, for the last ten years, to justify those hopes with which gentlemen have been pleased to solace themselves and the house. Is it that insidious smile, with which our petition has been lately received? Trust it not, sir; it will prove a snare to your feet. Suffer not yourselves to be betrayed with a kiss. Ask yourselves how this gracious reception of our petition comports with those warlike preparations, which cover our waters and darken our land. Are fleets and armies necessary to a work of love and reconciliation? Have we shown ourselves so unwilling to be reconciled, that force must be called in to win back our love? Let us not deceive ourselves, sir. These are the implements of war and subjugation—the last arguments to which kings resort. I ask gentlemen, sir, what means this martial array, if its purpose be not to force us to submission? Can gentlemen assign any other possible motive for it? Has Great Britain any enemy, in this quarter of the world, to call for all this accumulation of navies and armies? No, sir, she has none. They are meant for us: they can be meant for no other. They are sent over to bind and rivet upon us those chains which the British ministry have been so long forging. And what have we to oppose to them? Shall we try argument? Sir, we have been trying that for the last ten years. Have we any thing new to offer upon the subject? Nothing. We have held the subject up in every light of which it is capable; but it has been all in vain. Shall we resort to entreaty and humble supplication? What terms shall we find which have not been already exhausted? Let us not, I beseech you, sir, deceive ourselves longer. Sir, we have done every thing that could be done to avert the storm which is now coming on. We have petitioned; we have remonstrated; we have supplicated; we have prostrated ourselves before the throne, and have implored its interposition to arrest the tyrannical hands of the ministry and parliament. Our petitions have been slighted; our remonstrances have produced additional violence and insult; our supplications have been disregarded; and we have been spurned, with contempt, from the foot of the throne. In vain, after these things, may we indulge the fond hope of peace and reconciliation. There is no longer any room for hope. If we wish to be free;

if we mean to preserve inviolate those inestimable privileges for which we have been so long contending; if we mean not basely to abandon the noble struggle in which we have been so long engaged, and which we have pledged ourselves never to abandon until the glorious object of our contest shall be obtained—we must fight! I repeat it, sir, we must fight! An appeal to arms, and to the God of hosts, is all that is left us. They tell us, sir, that we are weak—unable to cope with so formidable an adversary. But when shall we be stronger? Will it be the next week, or the next year? Will it be when we are totally disarmed, and when a British guard shall be stationed in every house? Shall we gather strength by irresolution and inaction? Shall we acquire the means of effectual resistance by lying supinely on our backs, and hugging the delusive phantom of hope, until our enemies shall have bound us hand and foot? Sir, we are not weak, if we make a proper use of those means which the God of nature hath placed in our power. Three millions of people, armed in the holy cause of liberty, and in such a country as that which we possess, are invincible by any force which our enemy can send against us. Besides, sir, we shall not fight our battles alone. There is a just God, who presides over the destinies of nations, and who will raise up friends to fight our battles for us. The battle, sir, is not to the strong alone; it is to the vigilant, the active, the brave. Besides, sir, we have no election. If we were base enough to desire it, it is now too late to retire from the contest. There is no retreat, but in submission and slavery! Our chains are forged. Their clanking may be heard on the plains of Boston! The war is inevitable—and let it come!—I repeat it, sir, let it come!

It is vain, sir, to extenuate the matter. Gentlemen may cry, peace, peace—but there is no peace. The war is actually begun!

The next gale that sweeps from the north will bring to our ears the clash of resounding arms! Our brethren are already in the field! Why stand we here idle? What is it that gentlemen wish? What would they have? Is life so dear, or peace so sweet, as to be purchased at the price of chains and slavery? Forbid it, Almighty God. I know not what course others may take; but, as for me, give me liberty or give me death!

THE LIBERTY BELL.*— *William Ross Wallace.*

DEDICATED TO ROYAL PHELPS, ESQ.

A sound like the sound of a tempest rolled,
And the heart of a people stirred,
For the bell of freedom at midnight tolled,
Through a fettered land was heard:
    And the chime still rung
    From its iron tongue,
Steadily swaying to and fro;
    And to some it came
    As a breath of flame,
And to some as a sound of woe.

Upon the tall mountain, upon the tost wave,
It was heard by the fettered, and heard by the brave;
It was heard in the cottage, and heard in the hall,
And its chime gave a glorious summons to all.
The old sabre was sharpened, the time-rusted blade
Of the bond started out in the pioneer's glade,
Like a herald of wrath—and the host was arrayed!

Along the tall mountain, along the tost wave,
Swept the ranks of the bond, swept the ranks of the brave;

---

* Rung, in Philadelphia, at the Declaration of Independence. This lyric is from a manuscript national poem. Mr. Gregory will soon issue the lyric in the splendid illustrated style of the "Star Spangled Banner" and Drake's "American Flag."

And a shout as of waters went up to the dome,
    And a sun-drinking banner unfurled,
Like an archangel's pinion flashed out from his home,
    Uttered freedom and hope to the world.
O'er the mountain and tide its magnificent fold,
With a terrible glitter of azure and gold,
In the storm and the sunshine forever unrolled.
It blazed in the valley; it blazed on the mast;
It flew like a comrade abroad with the blast;
And the eyes of whole nations were turned to its light;
    And the hearts of the multitude soon
Were swayed by its stars as they shone through the night,
    Like an ocean when swayed by the moon.

Again through the midnight that bell thunders out;
And banners and torches are hurried about.
A shout as of waters, a long-uttered cry!
How it leaps, how it leaps from the earth to the sky!
From the sky to the earth, from the earth to the sea,
Hear the chorus re-echoed, "*The people are free!*"

That old bell is still seen by the patriot's eye,
And he blesses it ever when journeying by:
Long years have passed over it, and yet every soul
Must thrill in the night to its deep, solemn roll;
For it speaks in its belfry when kissed by the blast,
Like a broad blessing breathed from the lips of the Past.
Long years will roll o'er it, and yet every chime
Must unceasingly tell of an era sublime,
And more splendid, more dear than the rest of all Time.
    O yes! if the flame on our altars should pale,
Let its voice but be heard, and the freeman will start
    To rekindle the fire, while he sees on the gale
All the stars, all the stripes of the flag of his heart

The Solemn Duty of the United States Government.—*The Louisville (Ky.) Journal.*

The present unhappy war was begun by the South, begun for the sake of disunion, and was accepted and is carried on by the United States for the sake of the Union—and not, we hope, in vain. We know from the testimony of numerous southern men, who dare not speak aloud in their own homes, that there are multitudes of men in the South who are at heart for the Union, who, in their secret souls, are praying to the United States for deliverance almost as they pray to heaven for salvation, and who, if ever the power of the United States shall relieve them from the thraldom that now crushes their political lives out of them, will be able to assert and maintain a supremacy in their respective states. We have not an earthly doubt that there is a majority of states whose people, though now apparently unanimous for southern independence, would, if the deadly weight of a relentless despotism were lifted from their minds, hail the restoration of the Union as the ironed prisoner of a dungeon hails the return of God's blessed sunshine, and would greet with exultation even the little privilege of giving free expression to their opinions.

The present positions of several of the southern states were never chosen and have never been indorsed by the citizens of those states. Secession ordinances were passed by legislatures never elected or authorized to act upon the subject; such legislatures placed all the military and pecuniary resources of their states at the disposal of the southern government, and invited the confederate armies to an immediate occupation of their territory; and, after doing all this, they granted to their enslaved and manacled people the empty and miserable mockery of the privilege of deciding whether their states should or should not go into the Southern Confederacy. Of course, where the people would gladly have shouted "no" by tens of thousands, scarcely a solitary "no" was heard. The states, transferred by such monstrous and heaven-defying fraud and violence to the Southern Confederacy, are now subject to its tyrannical laws and requisitions, and their people, who have never been allowed to have a free voice in the fixing of their own destinies, are looking for freedom to a power outside of the dominion of the deadly tyranny under which they draw their breaths. It would be a fearful thing that the loyal millions in the Confederate States should be permanently abandoned by the United States to the miserable doom, to which, through no fault of their own, they have been subjected. Our trust, our conviction is, that, if the mighty armies of the republic, defied as they have been to strife, shall plant the standards of the United States at enough points to guarantee perfect freedom of thought and word and deed to the whole South, a large majority of the people of many, if not all, of the seceding states will declare their loyalty in a thunder-burst of joyous enthusiasm.

The policy of accepting peace on the condition of recognizing the independence of the Southern Confederacy would be a terrible one. Nay, it would be a policy that we but feebly characterize by the word terrible. It would be the death, the everlasting death, of the great and glorious hope that now lives in the hearts of tens of millions upon this continent and hundreds of millions throughout the civilized world. It would be the destruction of the mightiest work that the spirit of freedom has ever done upon the earth. What has been the admiration and the wonder of the nations would be their pity and their scorn. Let no one delude himself with the thought or fancy that a government, a nation, has not a right to defend itself, by all the powers and energies at its command, against disruption and dissolution.

To do this is, as a general truth, among a nation's most
sacred rights and its highest and most solemn duties.
The nation that should not recognize and assert the right
and the duty would be the object of all mankind's con
tempt. Surely no human being supposes that England
or France or Spain or Austria or Russia, if a portion,
even a majority, of a section of either of those kingdoms
or empires should assert the right of erecting their sec-
tion into an independent realm, would permit the right
thus claimed to be practically asserted. It is absurd to
suppose that either of them, upon any claim of a portion
of their people to the right of self-government, would
submit to dismemberment, submit to be divided into
two kingdoms or empires. Sooner would they wage a
war of centuries, a war, as they would justly consider it,
of national life or death.

To submit to the separation of the United States into
two independent powers, would not only be the most
fatal example that we could set for the existing genera-
tion of men, and to all generations that are to come after
us, but would render the whole area of the thirty-four
states one of the feeblest and most wretched portions of
the civilized world. All our old glory would be turned
to midnight darkness. The two republics or two mon-
archies, supposing that to be the number into which our
country should at first be divided, could never remain for
even one year at peace. A thousand causes would render
collisions and wars between them inevitable. Neither
of the two could have the least security against its own
disintegration and dissolution. The United States gov-
ernment at Washington, having established the prece-
dent of permitting eleven or twelve or fifteen states to
go off at pleasure, could not restrain other states from
doing the same thing. Each and every state remaining
even temporarily in the United States would feel that it
had the power to assert and maintain its right of either

seceding into the Southern Confederacy, or of establishing, together with such other states as it might be able to carry with it, an independent sovereignty, and it would exercise this fancied right whenever, for any cause, frivolous or otherwise, it should become dissatisfied with the acts of the government of its section. What is now the United States, as distinguished from the Confederate States, would almost certainly, within half a dozen years, consist of half a dozen petty and jarring powers, with no common head.

The same or even worse would be the condition of the states of the Southern Confederacy, based, as that confederacy avowedly is, and would be, upon the assumption, as a fundamental principle of government, that every state, or every two or three states, must ever be recognized as having the right to establish an independent government or independent governments at will. There would be no government in either section fit to be called one. Our country, that we have been so proud of, would be in a worse condition than the miserable little republics of South America. No pretended sovereignty, north or south, could ever obtain from abroad a loan of even the most inconsiderable amount, for European nations would scorn to intrust their money to governments not even claiming to embody any principle of self-preservation. The powers which have not dared to provoke the warlike energies of earth's great republic would deride us in our helplessness, and, by the presence of even a single man-of-war, compel us to yield obedience to their haughty and tyrannical dictation. Horrible servile insurrections would break out everywhere in the slaveholding region, making fields and firesides desolate.

Masses of slaves, first from the slave states nearest to the free states, and afterward from those more remote, would escape—some by stealth and others openly—till the last vestige of slavery would disappear. All the petty powers, jealous and hostile, would have to keep standing armies, vast in proportion to the means of supporting them, and the consequent taxes would impoverish the people to the point of hopeless and irretrievable ruin. Hundreds and thousands of desperate men, accustomed to blood and violence, and having no means of honest subsistence for themselves and families, would organize gangs of banditti, such as for years have infested Mexico. But this condition of anarchy or half-anarchy could not last forever, or even very long. From the midst of all the confusion and lawlessness and strife, some bold master-spirit would spring up, and, rallying thousands to his standard, pursue his conquering and devastating march until the whole of what has been the United States, would be made a bloody and relentless despotism, as drear and remorseless as any one recorded in history.

And now the question is, whether the United States, through a dread of the inconveniences and even the great sufferings and sacrifices of the war that is upon us, ought to accept this condition of things for the sake of a brief, a hollow, a nominal peace. To our minds it would be a dreadful crime against God and the human race. It would mark the present generation of the people of this country as the guiltiest enemies and murderers of freedom in all the history of the world. Our glorious old fathers of '76 bequeathed not more to us than to the generation that are to come hereafter—their posterity as well as ours—the great and magnificent inheritance of the Union. Our fathers of later periods received, guarded, transmitted, the sacred, the magnificent bequest to us, to be in turn passed down by us to those for whom, as for ourselves, the patriots who won it by their blood ordained it. And now should we, can we, dare we, in the face of heaven and earth, stop the awful bequest in its descent, shiver it into worthless fragments, destroy that which is not our own but mankind's for this and the coming ages, defraud posterity of the richest blessing ordained for them by the sainted and illustrious dead of a dead century, swindle all the human race of this and all the future time of what myriads of millions have contemplated with gratitude and adoration as the mightiest boon of God to his creatures, and leave our names to creak and blacken on the gibbet of infamy as the names of men who cursed their race, and shall be cursed by it as long as there shall be an atmosphere to bear the sound of a curse upon its bosom!

Who is Responsible for the Slavery Agitation?

There are many honest people who honestly believe that the North is responsible for the slavery agitation; and that to Mr. Seward the country is indebted for the irrepressible conflict idea; and that the destruction of our southern trade, and the perilous state of the country, is all owing to northern fanatics; but our political history does not sustain these honest people in their views.

The cunning men in the South, who have for years labored to dissolve the Union, seized upon the slavery question as one on which the southern people were most sensitive, and as best calculated to arouse them to action. Davis, of Massachusetts, remarked in 1833, "that the root of South Carolina's discontent lay deeper than the tariff." Her political economists reasoned that as Charleston had a larger commerce than New York before the adoption of the constitution, and since that time the commerce of New York had grown to be considerably larger than that of Charleston, hence Charleston had suffered for the benefit of New York, and the remedy for this was dissolution of the Union—and when they found the tariff would not unite the southern people, they took hold of the slavery question.

In 1833, Madison writing to Clay; said: "It is painful to see the unceasing efforts to alarm the South by imputations against the North, of unconstitutional designs on the subject of slavery. You are right, I have no doubt, in believing that no such intermeddling disposition exists in the body of our Northern brethren. Their good faith is sufficiently guaranteed by the interest they have as merchants, as ship-owners, and as manufacturers, in preserving a union with the slaveholding states. On the other hand what madness in the South to look for greater safety in disunion. It would be worse than jumping into the fire for fear of the frying-pan. The danger from the alarm is, that the pride and resentment exerted by them may be an overmatch for the dictates of prudence, and favor the projects of a southern convention, insidiously revived, as promising by its councils the best securities against grievances of every sort from the North."

Benton said that "From the beginning of the Missouri controversy up to the year 1835, he looked to the North as the point of danger from the slavery agitation. Since that time he has looked to the South for that danger, as Mr. Madison did two years earlier."

The idea of an irrepressible conflict existing between the interest of the slave and the free states was set forth by Calhoun, in his speech in the senate on the nullification resolutions in 1833. He said: "The contest (between the North and the South) will in fact be a contest between power and liberty, and such he considered the present; a contest in which the weaker section, with its peculiar labor, productions and situation, has at stake all that is dear to freemen."

In commenting on the above, Benton said: "Here is a distinct declaration that there was then a contest between the two sections of the Union, and that that contest was between power and liberty, in which the freedom and the slave property of the South were at stake. This declaration at the time attracted but little attention, there being then no sign of a slavery agitation, but to close observers it was an ominous revelation of something to come, and an apparent laying an anchor to windward for a new agitation on a new subject, after the tariff was done with."

The disunionists have for thirty years been determined to bring about the present state of affairs, and they took hold of the slavery agitation, deeming it the quickest mode of accomplishing their object. They seized upon every thing calculated to inflame the southern mind, but at the same time endeavoring to throw the responsibility of their agitation on the North, in hopes of creating dissension here and forming a party in their favor when the time for action arrived. The fact of the present president and vice-president both coming from the free states, was a great argument with them; they entirely overlooking the fact that Jackson and Calhoun both came from slave states, and both being natives of South Carolina. Yet this was no cause for alarm or agitation among the northern people.

Truth and Freedom.— *Wm. D. Gallagher.*

On the page that is immortal,
  We the brilliant promise see:
"Ye shall know the truth, my people,
  And its might shall make you free!"

For the truth, then, let us battle,
  Whatsoever fate betide!
Long the boast that we are freemen,
  We have made, and published wide.

He who has the truth, and keeps it,
  Keeps what not to him belongs;
But performs a selfish action,
  That his fellow mortal wrongs.

He who seeks the truth, and trembles
  At the dangers he must brave,
Is not fit to be a freeman:
  He, at best, is but a slave.

He who hears the truth, and places
  Its high promptings under ban,
Loud may boast of all that's manly,
  But can never be a man.

Friend, this simple lay who readest,
  Be not thou like either them—
But to truth give utmost freedom,
  And the tide it raises, stem.

Bold in speech, and bold in action,
  Be forever! Time will test,
Of the free-souled and the slavish,
  Which fulfils life's mission best.

Be thou like the noble Ancient—
  Scorn the threat that bids thee fear;
Speak!—no matter what betide thee;
  Let them strike, but make them hear!

Be thou like the first apostles—
  Be thou like heroic Paul;
If a free thought seek expression,
  Speak it boldly! speak it all!

Face thine enemies—accusers;
  Scorn the prison, rack, or rod!
And if thou hast truth to utter,
  Speak! and leave the rest to God.

GEORGE WILKES'S DESCRIPTION OF THE BATTLE OF BULL
RUN.—*New York Ledger.**

THE following extract from one of George Wilkes's letters to his *Spirit of the Times*, gives a vivid picture of the coming up of the rebel reserves at the battle of Bull Run, and shows how utterly impossible it was for our brave men, who had been fighting all day without respite, to hold the ground which they had so heroically won:

THE PAGEANT OF THE ENEMY'S RESERVES.

"Every thing, therefore, indicated another lull, and it could not be made certain to our minds but that we had really won the victory after all, and that the last cannonade was but the angry finish of the enemy. Suddenly a cry broke from the ranks of "Look there! look there!" and, turning their eyes toward Manassas, the whole of our drooping regiments, as well those who were moving to the rear as those who stood, saw a sight which none who gazed upon it will ever forget.

"At a long way off up the rise, and issuing from the enemy's extreme left, appeared, slowly debouching into sight, a dense column of infantry, marching with slow and solid step, and looking, at this noiseless distance, like a *mirage* of ourselves, or the illusion of a panorama. Rod by rod the massive column lengthened, not breaking off at the completion of a regiment, as we had hoped, but still pouring on, and on, and on, till one regiment had lengthened into ten. Even then the stern tide did not pause, for one of its arms turned downward along the far side of the triangle, and, the source of the flood thus relieved, poured forth again, and commenced lining the other in

* This work is not only embellished but strengthened by the extracts from the *New York Ledger*, a great paper owned and edited by a noble and extraordinary man, ROBERT BONNER.—ED.

like manner. Still the solemn picture swelled its volume, till the ten regiments had grown into fifteen, and had taken the formation of three sides of a hollow square. Our awe-struck legions, though beginning to feel the approaches of despair, could not take their eyes from that majestic pageant, and, though experiencing a new necessity, were frozen to the sight. The martial tide flowed on, the lengthening regiments growing into twenty thousand men, with a mass of Black cavalry in its centre, the whole moving toward us, as the sun danced upon its pomp of bayonets, with the solemn step of fate. This was war; compact, well-made, and reasoning war. It was war, too, in all its panoply and glory, as well as in its strength, and we at once comprehended we were beaten."

Competent critics say that Russell, the famous correspondent of the London *Times*, never wrote any thing equal to Wilkes's account of this battle. No father can read with dry eyes the following touching description of the death of a little drummer boy:

"Several fell at this spot, and among others, the favorite drummer boy of the 2d. The poor little fellow was struck by a cannon-ball, which took him just below the arm-pits, and literally cut him in two, his childish shriek of pain mingling with the whistle of the rifled shot as his little life went with it down the wind."

The following is his description of a youthful commander:

"While the 32d was in this position, the 16th and 31st having passed within its range, a youthful orderly rode up to Colonel Matheson to inform him that the Black cavalry, sheltered from his observation by a piece of woods, were coming upon the right, and if he would take a cut with his regiment across the fields, they would be turned back upon their errand.

"The evolution was performed, gave the protection

that was desired, and the Black Horse gave up its purpose in that quarter. While the regiment, however, was adhering to this position, the same youth who had imparted the previous suggestion, rode up to the regiment again, and told Matheson he had better fall back on Centreville, as his duty at that spot had been thoroughly performed. As this was about the first sign of orders (with one single exception) he had received during the entire day, Matheson felt some curiosity to learn who this young lieutenant was, and whence these orders came; he therefore turned sharply on the youth, who, he now perceived, could not be more than twenty-two or twenty-three, and said, 'Young man, I would like to know your name?' The youth replied that he was a son of Quartermaster-General Meigs. 'By whose authority, then, do you deliver me these orders?' was the Californian's next inquiry. The young man smiled, and remarked, 'Well, sir, the truth is, that for the last few hours I have been giving all the orders for this division, and acting as general, too, for there is no general on the field.' This incident is worthy of our notice among the lessons of the day."

THE PIONEERS.—*Charles A. Jones.*

WHERE are the hardy yeomen
Who battled for this land,
And trod these hoar old forests,
A brave and gallant band?
Oh, know ye where they slumber?
No monument appears,
For freedom's pilgrims to draw nigh,
And hallow with their tears?
Or were no works of glory
Done in the olden time?
And has the West no story
Of deathless deeds sublime?

Go ask yon shining river,
    And it will tell a tale
Of deeds of noble daring,
    Will make thy cheek grow pale.
Go ask yon smiling valley,
    Whose harvests bloom so fair,
'Twill tell thee a sad story
    Of the brave who slumber there:
Go ask yon mountain, rearing
    Its forest crest so high;
Each tree upon its summit
    Has seen a warrior die.

They knew no dread of danger,
    When rose the Indian's yell;
Right gallantly they struggled,
    Right gallantly they fell;
From Alleghany's summit,
    To the farthest western shore,
These brave men's bones are lying
    Where they perished in their gore;
And not a single monument
    Is seen in all the land,
In honor of the memory
    Of that heroic band.

Their bones were left to whiten
    The spot where they were slain,
And were ye now to seek them,
    They would be sought in vain.
The mountain cat has feasted
    Upon them as they lay;
Long, long ago they mingled
    Again with other clay:
Their very names are dying,
    Unconsecrate by fame,
In oblivion they slumber,
    Our glory and our shame!

The Men to make a State: their Making and their Marks.*—*Bishop Doane.*

It is only God who sees, and can declare, "the end from the beginning." With him, the end is *in* the beginning: not as the oak is in the acorn; but in its full growth, with all its foliage, and with all its fruits. Shakspeare, that greatest master of humanity, as true in logic, as he is sublime in poetry, has well expressed the nearest that man comes, in this respect, to God; as made with "large discourse, looking before, and after." With God, there is no "after," as there can be no "before." His Past, His Future, is all Present. His name, "I AM."

It is from this aspect of the divine omnipresence, His presence, through all time, as well as in every place—if we may say so, His ubiquitous eternity—that faith derives its confidence, and enterprise its courage. Man is of a day. He plants the acorn; but can hardly hope to sit under the shadow of the oak. He lays the corner-stone; but does not look to see the crowning of the battlement. He nourishes the infant; but counts not upon the comfort of the man. He sows, in hope. Some one, he knows, will reap. He plants, in hope. Some one, he knows, will pluck the fruit. By a beautiful provision—to overcome, to faithful hearts, the curse, that came in with the fall—mortality is thus immortalized. A race, which perishes, is made perpetual. Humanity achieves eternity. Homer felt it, when, to his sightless orbs, were given "the vision and the faculty divine," which, for three thousand years, have been the spell of universal man. Milton owned it, in that modest hope, that he might yet do something which the world would not willingly let die. And that old martyr wrote it in the fire, when, to his brother bishop, he said: "Play the

* A College Address.

man; and we shall light, to-day, a candle, in England, which shall never be put out!"

Neighbors and friends, if there be, anywhere, pre-eminent encouragement for this presentiment of perpetuity, it is here, and in such places as this is. The seed whose life is in these furrows, is the seed of men. The harvest that we hope to ripen, is of hearts. Schools are the seed-plots of the state. An hundred years ago, and they who made this day immortal, were as these are now. In less than half the years that have rolled by since 'seventy-six, these, and their fellows in the colleges which star the land, will sway the state. We link ourselves, through them, with all the future; as they link themselves, through us, with all the past. It is a chain of hearts; and his will bear the recreant's curse who fails the sacred trust. The men who are to mould the nation, must be moulded here. These are the orators, the statesmen, the priests, the patriots, the heroes, of the coming age. Through them, that age will take its mark from us. Their principles, their habits, their characters, will tell, through all the centuries to come, in surges that will roll and swell, forward and onward, till the dreadful day of doom. Can we do better, on the festival which consecrates the memory of the fathers of the state, than to consider how we best shall serve it in the training of its sons? What can be fitter for this, our third anniversary, than the contemplation of its sacred trust toward the commonwealth which shelters it in its broad shadow? *The men to make a state: the making and the marks of men to make a state,* will be appropriate themes to-day.

The men, to make a state, must be intelligent men. I do not mean that they must know that two and two make four; or, that six *per cent.* a year is half *per cent.* a month. I take a wider and a higher range. I limit myself to no mere utilitarian intelligence. This has its place. And this will come almost unsought. The contact of the rough and rugged world will force men to it in self-defence. The lust of worldly gain will drag men to it for self-aggrandizement. But men so made will never make a state. The intelligence which that demands will take a wider and a higher range. Its study will be man. It will make history its cheap experience. It will read hearts. It will know men. It will first know itself. What else can govern men? Who else can know the men to govern men? The right of suffrage is a fearful thing. It calls for wisdom, and discretion, and intelligence, of no ordinary standard. It takes in, at every exercise, the interests of all the nation. Its results reach forward through time into eternity. Its discharge must be accounted for among the dread responsibilities of the great day of judgment. Who will go to it blindly? Who will go to it passionately? Who will go to it as a sycophant, a tool, a slave? How many do! These are not the men to make a state.

The men, to make a state, must be honest men. I do not mean men that would never steal. I do not mean men that would scorn to cheat in making change. I mean men with a single face. I mean men with a single eye. I mean men with a single tongue. I mean men that consider, always, what is right; and do it at whatever cost. I mean men who can dine, like Andrew Marvel, on a neck of mutton; and whom, therefore, no king on earth can buy. Men that are in the market for the highest bidder; men that make politics their trade, and look to office for a living; men that will crawl, where they cannot climb: these are not men to make a state.

The men, to make a state, must be brave men. I do not mean the men that pick a quarrel. I do not mean the men that carry dirks. I do not mean the men that call themselves hard names; as Bouncers, Killers, and the like. I mean the men that walk with open face and unprotected breast. I mean the men that do, but do not talk. I mean the men that dare to stand alone. I mean the men that are to-day where they were yesterday, and will be there to-morrow. I mean the men that can stand still and take the storm. I mean the men that are afraid to kill, but not afraid to die. The man that calls hard names and uses threats; the man that stabs, in secret, with his tongue or with his pen; the man that moves a mob to deeds of violence and self-destruction; the man that freely offers his last drop of blood, but never sheds the first: these are not the men to make a state.

The men, to make a state, must be religious men. States are from God. States are dependent upon God. States are accountable to God. To leave God out of states is to be Atheists. I do not mean that men must cant. I do not mean that men must wear long faces. I do not mean that men must talk of conscience, while they take your spoons. One shrewdly called hypocrisy, the tribute which vice pays to virtue. These masks and vizors, in like manner, are the forced concession which a moral nature makes to him, whom, at the same time, it dishonors. I speak of men who feel and own a God. I speak of men who feel and own their sins. I speak of men who know there is a hell. I speak of men who think the Cross no shame. I speak of men who have it in their heart as well as on their brow. The men that own no future, the men that trample on the Bible, the men that never pray, are not the men to make a state.

The men, to make a state, are made by faith. A man that has no faith is so much flesh. His heart, a muscle; nothing more. He has no past, for reverence; no future, for reliance. He lives. So does a clam. Both die. Such men can never make a state. There must be faith, which furnishes the fulcrum Archimedes could not find, for the long lever that should move the world. There must be faith to look through clouds and storms up to the sun that shines as cheerily on high as on creation's morn. There must be faith that can lay hold on heaven and let the earth swing from beneath it, if God will. There must be faith that can afford to sink the present in the future; and let time go in its strong grasp upon eternity. This is the way that men are made, to make a state.

The men, to make a state, are made by self-denial. The willow dallies with the water, and is fanned forever by its coolest breeze, and draws its waves up in continual pulses of refreshment and delight; and is a willow, after all. An acorn has been loosened, some autumnal morning, by a squirrel's foot. It finds a nest in some rude cleft of an old granite rock, where there is scarcely earth to cover it. It knows no shelter and it feels no shade. It squares itself against the storms. It shoulders through the blast. It asks no favor, and gives none. It grapples with the rock. It crowds up toward the sun. It is an oak. It has been seventy years an oak. It will be an oak for seven times seventy years; unless you need a man-of-war to thunder at the foe that shows a flag upon the shore where freemen dwell: and then you take no willow in its daintiness and gracefulness; but that old, hardy, storm-stayed and storm-strengthened oak. So are the men made that will make a state.

The men, to make a state, are themselves made by obedience. Obedience is the health of human hearts: obedience to God; obedience to father and to mother, who are, to children, in the place of God; obedience to teachers and to masters, who are in the place of father and of mother; obedience to spiritual pastors, who are God's ministers; and to the powers that be, which are ordained of God. Obedience is but self-government in action: and he can never govern men who does not govern first himself. Only such men can make a state.

The Greek Revolution.—*Henry Clay.*

Has it come to this? Are we so humbled, so low, so debased, that we dare not express our sympathy for suffering Greece; that we dare not articulate our detestation of the brutal excesses of which she has been the bleeding victim, lest we might offend some one or more of their imperial and royal majesties? If gentlemen are afraid to act rashly on such a subject, suppose, Mr. Chairman, that we unite in an humble petition, addressed to their majesties, beseeching them, that of their gracious condescension, they would allow us to express our feelings and our sympathies. How shall it run? "We, the representatives of the free people of the United States of America, humbly approach the throne of your imperial and royal majesties, and supplicate that, of your imperial and royal clemency—" I cannot go through the disgusting recital; my lips have not yet learned to pronounce the sycophantic language of a degraded slave! Are we so mean, so base, so despicable, that we may not attempt to express our horror, utter our indignation, at the most brutal and atrocious war that ever stained earth or shocked high heaven? at the ferocious deeds of a savage and infuriated soldiery, stimulated and urged on by the clergy of a fanatical and inimical religion, and rioting in all the excesses of blood and butchery, at the mere details of which the heart sickens and recoils?

If the great body of Christendom can look on calmly and coolly, while all this is perpetrated on a Christian people, in its own immediate vicinity, in its very presence, let us at least evince, that one of its remote extremities is susceptible of sensibility to Christian wrongs, and capable of sympathy for Christian sufferings; that in this remote quarter of the world there are hearts not yet closed against compassion for human woes, that can pour out their indignant feelings at the oppression of a people endeared to us by every ancient recollection, and every modern tie. Sir, attempts have been made to alarm the committee by the dangers to our commerce in the Mediterranean; and a wretched invoice of figs and opium has been spread before us to repress our sensibilities and to eradicate our humanity. Ah! sir, "what shall it profit a man if he gain the whole world and lose his own soul?" or what shall it avail a nation to save the whole of a miserable trade, and lose its liberties?

On the subject of the other independent American states, hitherto it has not been necessary to depart from the rule of our foreign relations, observed in regard to Europe. Whether it will become us to do so or not, will be considered when we take up another resolution, lying on the table. But we may not only adopt this measure: we may go further; we may recognize the government in the Morea, if actually independent, and it will be neither war, nor cause of war, nor any violation of our neutrality. Beside, sir, what is Greece to the allies? A part of the dominions of any of them? By no means. Suppose the people in one of the Philippine Isles, or any other spot still more insulated and remote, in Asia or Africa, were to resist their former rulers, and set up and establish a new government, are we not to recognize them, in dread of the holy allies? If they are going to interfere, from the danger of the contagion of the example, here is the spot, our own favored land, where they must strike. This government, you, Mr. Chairman, and the body over which you preside, are the living and cutting reproach to allied despotism. If we are to offend them, it is not by passing this resolution. We are daily and hourly giving them cause of war. It is here, and in our free institutions, that they will assail us. They will attack us because you sit beneath that canopy, and we are freely debating and deliberating upon the great interests of freemen, and dispensing the blessings of free government. They will strike, because we pass one of those bills on your table. The passage of the least of them, by our free authority, is more galling to despotic powers than would be the adoption of this so much dreaded resolution. Pass it, and what do you do? You exercise an indisputable attribute of sovereignty, for which you are responsible to none of them. You do the same when you perform any other legislative function; no less. If the allies object to this measure, let them forbid us to take a vote in this house; let them strip us of every attribute of independent government; let them disperse us.

Will gentlemen attempt to maintain that, on the principles of the law of nations, those allies would have cause of war? If there be any principle which has been settled for ages, any which is founded in the very nature of things, it is that every independent state has the clear right to judge of the *fact* of the existence of other sovereign powers. I admit that there may be a state of inchoate initiative sovereignty, in which a new government, just struggling into being, cannot be said yet perfectly to exist. But the premature recognition of such new government can give offence justly to no other than its ancient sovereign. The right of recognition comprehends the right to be informed; and the means of information must, of necessity, depend upon the sound discretion of the party seeking it. You may send out a commission of inquiry, and charge it with a provident attention to your own people and your own interests. Such will be the character of the proposed agency. It will not necessarily follow, that any public functionary will be appointed by the president. You merely grant the means by which the executive may act when he thinks proper. What does he tell you in his message? That Greece is contending for her independence: that all sympathize with her; and that no power has declared against her. Pass this resolution, and what is the reply it conveys to him? "You have sent us grateful intelligence; we feel warmly for Greece, and we grant you money that, when you shall think it proper, when the interests of this nation shall not be jeoparded, you may depute a commissioner or public agent to Greece." The whole responsibility is then left where the constitution puts it. A member in his place may make a speech or proposition, the house may even pass a vote, in respect to our foreign affairs, which the president, with the whole field lying before him, would not deem it expedient to effectuate.

But, sir, it is not for Greece alone that I desire to see this measure adopted. It will give to her but little support, and that purely of a moral kind. It is principally for America, for the credit and character of our common country, for our own unsullied name, that I hope to see it pass. Mr. Chairman, what appearance on the page of history would a record like this exhibit? "In the month of January, in the year of our Lord and Saviour, 1824, while all European Christendom beheld, with cold and unfeeling indifference, the unexampled wrongs and inexpressible misery of Christian Greece, a proposition was made in the Congress of the United States, almost the sole, the last, the greatest depository of human hope and human freedom, the representatives of a gallant nation, containing a million of freemen ready to fly to arms, while the people of that nation were spontaneously expressing its deep-toned feeling, and the whole continent, by one simultaneous emotion, was rising, and solemnly and anxiously supplicating and invoking high heaven to spare and succor Greece, and to invigorate her arms in her glorious cause, while temples and senate-houses were alike resounding with one burst of generous and holy sympathy; in the year of our Lord and Saviour, that

Saviour of Greece and of us; a proposition was offered in the American Congress to send a messenger to Greece, to inquire into her state and condition, with a kind expression of our good wishes and our sympathies—and it was rejected!" Go home, if you can; go home if you dare, to your constituents, and tell them that you voted it down; meet, if you can, the appalling countenances of those who sent you here, and tell them that you shrank from the declaration of your own sentiments; that you cannot tell how, but that some unknown dread, some indescribable apprehension, some indefinable danger, drove you from your purpose; that the spectres of scimeters, and crowns, and crescents, gleamed before you and alarmed you; and that you suppressed all the noble feelings prompted by religion, by liberty, by national independence, and by humanity. I cannot bring myself to believe that such will be the feeling of the majority of the committee. But, for myself, though every friend of the cause should desert it, and I be left to stand alone with the gentleman from Massachusetts, I will give to his resolution the poor sanction of my unqualified approbation.

Eulogy on Henry Clay; delivered September, 1852.—*John B. Fry.*

Henry Clay, whose loss a whole nation now mourns, was one of the purest patriots and most sagacious statesmen of this or any other age in the history of the world. In the cause of our common country that wonderful man dedicated the fervor of his brave heart, and the gigantic powers of his extraordinary intellect. Every body concedes this now when he is no more.

And here, fellow-citizens, I crave your indulgence for a brief moment whilst I attempt to respond to the impulses and emotions awakened within me by my allusion to his death. Proudly conspicuous, elevated to the loftiest height, stands his imperishable fame. Yes! so long as civil liberty and constitutional freedom shall retain vitality on the earth—and may they evermore—so long will his fame continue to shed its effulgence over all their pathways—a political sun as inextinguishable as the physical one in the heavens above us. Presidential honors could not have added aught to the brilliancy of his great civic achievements, nor given strength to his ever-glorious example, which, thank God, is already ours, and our country's. Away, away then, all intrusive regrets; for neither the lapse of time, nor revolution, nor change of any sort, can dislodge this Freedom's idol from his secure abode in our warm and grateful hearts.—Noble soul! Years, long years, did he toil for his country's good and glory. And, in many instances, among a large portion of his fellow-citizens, in what manner were his patriotic services requited? Abuse, revilement, opprobrious epithets of every conceivable description, were heaped upon him, causing his generous nature to bleed under accumulated wrongs. And yet, with his path thus hedged in and besieged, how did our hero bear himself?—for there may be heroes as well in senate-houses as on tented fields. Alone intent upon promoting the prosperity, the honor, and the renown of his country, he fixed his steadfast gaze on these, and pursued them with a dauntless intrepidity, and a wonderful energy. Bearing within himself the fullest impress of nature's greatness, he cast his whole weight into the career whence gleam the lights of civilization and republican liberty. In our sadness even, I give you joy; for those calumnies of the past, which, while they pained our hearts and provoked our resentment, because aimed at the "great commoner," yet did not impair our love and confidence toward him, are now hushed into silence, deep and perpetual.

Mr. Clay once said—"Truth is omnipotent, and public justice certain." He lived to witness the triumph of his confiding faith—not, indeed, by presidential honors, but by those higher and more enduring honors which were conferred by his transcendent genius and talent; his exalted patriotism; his accomplished statesmanship; and by a great nation's gratitude and benedictions. Nor shall the American people have the exclusive bestowment of these honors. Wherever and whenever, in other lands, freedom's banner shall float, on it will appear, in letters of gold, the talismanic name of our departed champion—betokening the downfall of despotisms, the political regeneration of the world.

Expiring at peace with his God; his fame monopolizing one of the most resplendent pages in the history of mankind, and embalmed in the purest affection of the devotees of republican institutions everywhere, he needed nothing more. His great reputation, in the absence of his personal presence, still moves onward, and will to the latest generation. The mists of succeeding ages will not obscure its glory; but rather shall they impart to it increasing vividness and splendor. My heart turns instinctively, powerfully, resistlessly, to the tomb where we buried him. There beneath the green sod of his own beloved Kentucky, he sleeps sweetly, gently, peacefully. Thither, for all time, shall repair old men and matrons, young men and maidens, to drop the warm tear of grateful affection on the cherished spot of his calm repose.

What is Life?—*Charles D. Drake.*

An Eagle flew up in his heavenward flight,
Far out of the reach of human sight,
And gazed on the earth from the lordly height
   Of his sweeping and lone career:

"And this is life!" he exulting screams,
"To soar without fear where the lightning gleams,
And look unblenched on the sun's dazzling beams,
　　As they blaze through the upper sphere."

A Lion sprang forth from his bloody bed,
And roared till it seemed he would wake the dead,
And man and beast from him wildly fled,
　　As though there were death in the tone:
"And this is life!" he triumphantly cried,
"To hold my domain in the forest wide,
Imprisoned by naught but the ocean's tide,
　　And the ice of the frozen zone."

"It is life," said a Whale, "to swim the deep;
O'er hills submerged and abysses to sweep,
Where the gods of ocean their vigils keep,
　　In the fathomless gulfs below;
To bask on the bosom of tropical seas,
And inhale the fragrance of Ceylon's breeze,
Or sport where the turbulent waters freeze,
　　In the climes of eternal snow."

"It is life," says a tireless Albatross,
"To skim through the air when the dark waves toss
In the storm that has swept the earth across,
　　And never to wish for rest;
To sleep on the breeze as it softly flies,
My perch in the air, my shelter the skies,
And build my nest on the billows that rise
　　And break with a pearly crest."

"It is life," says a wild Gazelle, "to leap
From crag to crag of the mountainous steep,
Where the cloud's icy tears in purity sleep,
　　Like the marble brow of death;
To stand, unmoved, on the outermost verge
Of the perilous height, and watch the surge
Of the waters beneath, that onward urge,
　　As if sent by a demon's breath."

"It is life," I hear a butterfly say,
"To revel in blooming gardens by day,

And nestle in cups of flowerets gay,
  When the stars the heavens illume;
To steal from the rose its delicate hue,
And sip from the hyacinth glittering dew,
And catch from beds of the violet blue
  The breath of its gentle perfume."

"It is life," a majestic War-horse neighed,
"To prance in the glare of battle and blade,
Where thousands in terrible death are laid,
  And scent of the streaming gore;
To dash, unappalled, through the fiery heat,
And trample the dead beneath my feet,
Mid the trumpet's clang, and the drum's loud beat,
  And the hoarse artillery's roar."

"It is life," said a Savage, with hideous yell,
"To roam unshackled the mountain and dell,
And feel my bosom with majesty swell,
  As the primal monarch of all;
To gaze on the earth, the sky and the sea,
And feel that, like them, I am chainless and free,
And never, while breathing, to bend the knee,
  But at the Manitou's call."

An aged Christian went tottering by,
And white was his hair, and dim was his eye,
And his wasted spirit seemed ready to fly,
  As he said, with faltering breath:
"It is life to move from the heart's first throes,
Through youth and manhood to age's snows,
In a ceaseless circle of joys and woes—
  It is life to prepare for death!"

A Sea Fight.—*J. Fenimore Cooper.*

THE vessel, which appeared so inopportunely for the safety of the ill-manned British cruiser, was, in truth, a ship that had roved from among the islands of the Caribbean sea, in quest of some such adventure as that which now presented itself. She was called La Belle Fontange, and her commander, a youth of two-and-twenty, was already well known in the salons of the Marais, and behind the walls of the Rue Basse des Remparts, as one of the most gay and amiable of those who frequented the former, and one of the most spirited and skilful among the adventurers who sometimes trusted to their address in the latter. Rank, and influence at Versailles, had procured for the young Chevalier Dumont de la Rocheforte a command to which he could lay no claim either by his experience or his services. His mother, a near relative of one of the beauties of the court, had been commanded to use sea-bathing, as a preventive against the consequences of the bite of a rabid lapdog. By way of a suitable episode to the long descriptions she was in the daily habit of writing to those whose knowledge of her new element was limited to the constant view of a few ponds and ditches teeming with carp, or an occasional glimpse of some of the turbid reaches of the Seine, she had vowed to devote her youngest child to Neptune! In due time, that is to say, while the poetic sentiment was at the access, the young chevalier was duly enrolled, and, in a time that greatly anticipated all regular and judicious preferment, he was placed in command of the corvette in question, and sent to the Indies to gain glory for himself and his country.

The Chevalier Dumont de la Rocheforte was brave, but his courage was not the calm and silent self-possession of a seaman. Like himself, it was lively, buoyant, thoughtless, bustling, and full of animal feeling. He had all the pride of a gentleman, and, unfortunately for the duty which he had now for the first time to perform, one of its dictates taught him to despise that species of mechanical knowledge which it was, just at this moment, so important to the commander of La Fontange to possess. He could dance to admiration, did the honors of his cabin with faultless elegance, and had caused the death of an excellent mariner, who had accidentally fallen overboard, by jumping into the sea to aid him, without knowing how to swim a stroke himself—a rashness that had diverted those exertions which might have saved the unfortunate sailor, from the assistance of the subordinate to the safety of his superior. He wrote sonnets prettily, and had some ideas of the new philosophy which was just beginning to dawn upon the world; but the cordage of his ship, and the lines of a mathematical problem, equally presented labyrinths he had never threaded.

It was perhaps fortunate for the safety of all in her, that La Belle Fontange possessed an inferior officer, in the person of a native of Boulogne-sur-Mer, who was quite competent to see that she kept the proper course, and that she displayed none of the top-gallants of her pride, at unpropitious moments. The ship itself was sufficiently and finely moulded, of a light and airy rig, and of established reputation for speed. If it was defective in any thing, it had the fault, in common with its commander, of a want of sufficient solidity to resist the vicissitudes and dangers of the turbulent element on which it was destined to act.

The vessels were now within a mile of each other. The breeze was steady, and sufficiently fresh for all the ordinary evolutions of a naval combat; while the water was just quiet enough to permit the ships to be handled with confidence and accuracy. La Fontange was running with her head to the eastward, and, as she had the advantage of the wind, her tall tracery of spars leaned gently in the direction of her adversary. The Coquette was standing on the other tack, and necessarily inclined from her enemy. Both vessels were stripped to their topsails, spankers, and jibs, though the lofty sails of the Frenchman were fluttering in the breeze, like the graceful folds of some fanciful drapery. No human being was distinctly visible in either fabric, though dark clusters around each mast-head showed that the ready top-men were prepared to discharge their duties, even in the confusion and dangers of the impending contest. Once or twice La Fontange inclined her head more in the direction of her adversary; and then, sweeping up again to the wind, she stood on in stately beauty. The moment was near when the ships were about to cross each other, at a point where a musket would readily send its messenger across the water that lay between them. Ludlow, who closely watched each change of position, and every rise and fall of the breeze, went on the poop and swept the horizon with his glass, for the last time before his ship should be enveloped in smoke. To his surprise, he discovered a pyramid of canvas rising above the sea, in the direction of the wind. The sail was clearly visible to the naked eye, and had only escaped earlier observation in the duties of so urgent a moment. Calling the master to his side, he inquired his opinion concerning the character of the second stranger. But Trysail confessed it exceeded even his long-tried powers of observation to say more than that it was a ship running before the wind, with a cloud of sail spread. After a second and a longer look, however, the experienced master ventured to add, that the stranger had the squareness and symmetry of a cruiser, but of what size he would not yet presume to declare.

"It may be a light ship, under her top-gallant and studding-sails, or it may be that we see only the lofty duck of some heavier vessel, Captain Ludlow;—ha! he has caught the eye of the Frenchman, for the corvette has signals abroad!"

"To your glass!—If the stranger answer, we have no choice but our speed."

There was another keen and anxious examination of the upper spars of the distant ship, but the direction of the wind prevented any signs of her communicating with the corvette from being visible. La Fontange appeared equally uncertain of the character of the stranger, and for a moment there was some evidence of an intention to change her course. But the moment for indecision had passed. The ships were already sweeping up abreast of each other, under the constant pressure of the breeze.

"Be ready, men!" said Ludlow, in a low but firm voice, retaining his elevated post on the poop, while he motioned to his companion to return to the main deck.

"Fire at his flash!"

Intense expectation succeeded. The two graceful fabrics sailed steadily on and came within hail. So profound was the stillness in the Coquette, that the rushing sound of the water she heaped under her bows was distinctly audible to all on board, and might be likened to the deep breathing of some vast animal, that was collecting its physical energies for some unusual exertion. On the other hand, tongues were loud and clamorous among the cordage of La Fontauge. Just as the ships were fairly abeam, the voice of young Dumont was heard, shouting through a trumpet, for his men to fire. Ludlow smiled, in a seaman's scorn. Raising his own trumpet, with a quiet gesture to his attentive and ready crew, the whole discharge of their artillery broke out of the dark side of the ship, as if it had been by the volition of the fabric. The answering broadside was received almost as soon as their own had been given, and the two vessels passed swiftly without the line of shot.

The wind had sent back their own smoke upon the English, and for a time it floated on their decks, wreathed itself in the eddies of the sails, and passed away to leeward, with the breeze that succeeded to the counter-current of the explosions. The whistling of shot and the crash of wood had been heard amid the din of the combat. Giving a glance at his enemy, who still stood on, Ludlow leaned from the poop, and, with all a sailor's anxiety, he endeavored to scan the gear aloft.

"What is gone, sir?" he asked of Trysail, whose earnest face just then became visible through the drifting smoke. "What sail is so heavily flapping?"

"Little harm done, sir—little harm—bear a hand with the tackle on that fore-yard-arm, you lubbers! you move like snails in a minuet! The fellow has shot away the lee fore-top-sail-sheet, sir; but we shall soon get our wings spread again. Lash it down, boys, as if it were butt-bolted;—so; steady out your bowline, forward.— Meet her, you can; meet her you may—meet her!"

The smoke had disappeared, and the eye of the captain rapidly scanned the whole of his ship. Three or four topmen had already caught the flapping canvas, and were seated on the extremity of the fore-yard, busied in securing their prize. A hole or two were visible in the other sails, and here and there an unimportant rope was dangling in a manner to show that it had been cut by shot. Further than this, the damage aloft was not of a nature to attract his attention.

There was a different scene on deck. The feeble crew were earnestly occupied in loading the guns, and rammers and sponges were handled with all the intenseness which men would manifest in a moment so exciting. The Alderman was never more absorbed in his ledger than he now appeared in his duty of a cannoneer; and the youths, to whom the command of the batteries had necessarily been confided, diligently aided him with their greater authority and experience. Trysail stood near the capstan, coolly giving the orders which have been related, and gazing upward with an interest so absorbed as to render him unconscious of all that passed around his person. Ludlow saw, with pain, that blood discolored the deck at his feet, and that a seaman lay dead within reach of his arm. The rent plank and shattered ceiling showed the spot where the destructive missile had entered. Compressing his lips like a man resolved, the commander of the Coquette bent further forward and glanced at the wheel. The quarter-master, who held the spokes, was erect, steady, and kept his eye on the leech of the head-sail, as unerringly as the needle points to the pole.

These were the observations of a single minute. The different circumstances related had been ascertained with so many rapid glances of the eye, and they had even been noted without losing for a moment the knowledge of the precise situation of La Fontange. The latter was already in stays. It became necessary to meet the evolution by another as prompt.

The order was no sooner given, than the Coquette, as if conscious of the hazard she ran of being raked, whirled away from the wind, and, by the time her adversary was ready to deliver her other broadside, she was in a position to receive and to return it. Again the ships approached each other, and once more they exchanged their streams of fire when abeam.

Ludlow now saw, through the smoke, the ponderous yard of La Fontange swinging heavily against the breeze, and the main-topsail come flapping against her mast. Swinging off from the poop by a backstay that had been shot away a moment before, he alighted on the quarter-deck by the side of the master.

"Touch all the braces!" he said, hastily, but still speaking low and clearly; "give a drag upon the bowlines—luff, sir, luff; jam the ship up hard against the wind!"

The clear, steady answer of the quarter-master, and the manner in which the Coquette, still vomiting her sheets of flame, inclined toward the breeze, announced the promptitude of the subordinates. In another minute, the vast volumes of smoke which enveloped the two ships joined, and formed one white and troubled cloud, which was rolling swiftly before the explosions, over the surface of the sea, but which, as it rose higher in the air, sailed gracefully to leeward.

Our young commander passed swiftly through the batteries, spoke encouragingly to his people, and resumed his post on the poop. The stationary position of La Fontange, and his own efforts to get to windward, were already proving advantageous to Queen Anne's cruiser. There was some indecision on the part of the other ship, which instantly caught the eye of one whose readiness in his profession so much resembled instinct.

The Chevalier Dumont had amused his leisure by running his eyes over the records of the naval history of his country, where he had found this and that commander applauded for throwing their topsails to the mast, abreast of their enemies. Ignorant of the difference between a ship in line and one engaged singly, he had determined to prove himself equal to a similar display of spirit. At the moment when Ludlow was standing alone on the poop, watching with vigilant eyes the progress of his own vessel and the position of his enemy, indicating merely by a look or a gesture to the attentive Trysail beneath, what he wished done, there was actually a wordy discussion on the quarter-deck of the latter, between the mariner of Boulogne-sur-Mer, and the gay favorite of the salons. They debated on the expediency of the step which the latter had taken, to prove the existence of a quality that no one doubted. The time lost in this difference of opinion was of the last importance to the British cruiser. Standing gallantly on, she was soon out of the range of her adversary's fire; and, before the Boulognois had succeeded in convincing his superior of his error, their antagonist was on the other tack, and luffing across the wake of La Fontange. The topsail was then tardily filled, but before the latter ship had recovered her motion, the sails of her enemy overshadowed her deck. There was now every prospect of the Coquette passing to windward. At that critical moment, the fair-setting topsail of the British cruiser was nearly rent in two by a shot. The ship fell off, the yards interlocked, and the vessels were foul.

The Coquette had all the advantage of position. Perceiving the important fact at a glance, Ludlow made sure of its continuance by throwing his grapnels. When the two ships were thus firmly lashed together, the young Dumont found himself relieved from a mountain of embarrassment. Sufficiently justified by the fact that not a single gun of his own would bear, while a murderous discharge of grape had just swept along his decks, he issued the order to board. But Ludlow, with his weakened crew, had not decided on so hazardous an evolution as that which brought him in absolute contact with his enemy, without foreseeing the means of avoiding all the consequences. The vessels touched each other only at one point, and this spot was protected by a row of muskets. No sooner, therefore, did the impetuous young Frenchman appear on the taffrail of his own ship, supported by a band of followers, than a close and deadly fire swept them away to a man. Young Dumont alone remained. For a single moment, his eye glared wildly; but the active frame, still obedient to the governing impulse of so impetuous a spirit, leaped onward. He fell, without life, on the deck of his enemy.

Ludlow watched every movement with a calmness that neither personal responsibility, nor the uproar and rapid incidents of the terrible scene could discompose.

"Now is our time to bring the matter hand to hand!" he cried, making a gesture to Trysail to descend from the ladder, in order that he might pass.

His arm was arrested, and the grave old master pointed to windward.

"There is no mistaking the cut of those sails, or the

lofty rise of those spars! The stranger is another Frenchman!"

One glance told Ludlow that his subordinate was right; another sufficed to show what was now necessary.

"Cast loose the forward grapnel—cut it—away with it, clear!" was shouted, through his trumpet, in a voice that rose commanding and clear, amid the roar of the combat.

Released forward, the stern of the Coquette yielded to the pressure of her enemy, whose sails were all drawing, and she was soon in a position to enable her head-yards to be braced sharp aback, in a direction opposite to the one in which she had so lately lain. The whole broadside was then delivered into the stern of La Fontange, the last grapnel was released, and the ships separated.

The single spirit which presided over the evolutions and exertions of the Coquette, still governed her movements. The sails were trimmed, the ship was got in command, and, before the vessels had been asunder five minutes, the duty of the vessel was in its ordinary active, but noiseless train.

Nimble top-men were on the yards, and broad folds of fresh canvas were flapping in the breeze, as the new sails were bent and set. Ropes were spliced, or supplied by new rigging, the spars examined, and, in fine, all that watchfulness and sedulous care were observed, which are so necessary to the efficiency and safety of a ship. Every spar was secured, the pumps were sounded, and the vessel held on her way, as steadily as if she had never fired nor received a shot.

On the other hand La Fontange betrayed the indecision and confusion of a worsted ship. Her torn canvas was blowing about in disorder, many important ropes beat against her masts unheeded, and the vessel itself drove before the breeze in the helplessness of a wreck. For several minutes there seemed no controlling mind in the fabric; and when, after so much distance was lost as to give her enemy all the advantage of the wind, a tardy attempt was made to bring the ship up again, the tallest and most important of her masts was seen tottering, until it finally fell, with all its hamper, into the sea.

God Bless our Stars.—*Benjamin F. Taylor.*

"God bless our stars forever!"
   Thus the angels sang sublime,
When round God's forges fluttered fast,
   The sparks of starry Time!
When they fanned them with their pinions,
   Till they kindled into day,
And revealed creation's bosom,
   Where the infant Eden lay.

"God bless our stars forever!"
   Thus they sang—the seers of old,
When they beckoned to the Morning,
   Through the future's misty fold,
When they waved the wand of wonder—
   When they breathed the magic word,
And the pulses' golden glimmer,
   Showed the waking granite heard.

"God bless our stars forever!"
   'Tis the burden of the song,
Where the sail through hollow midnight
   Is flickering along;
When a ribbon of blue heaven
   Is agleaming through the clouds,
With a star or two upon it,
   For the sailor in the shrouds!

"God bless our stars forever!"
   It is Liberty's refrain,
From the snows of wild Nevada
   To the sounding woods of Maine;

Where the green Multnomah wanders,
    Where the Alabama rests,
Where the thunder shakes his turban
    Over Alleghany's crests;

Where the mountains of New England
    Mock Atlantic's stormy main;
Where God's palm imprints the prairie
    With the type of heaven again—
Where the mirrored morn is dawning,
    Link to link, our lakes along,
And Sacramento's Golden Gate
    Swinging open to the song—

There and there! "Our stars forever!"
    How it echoes! How it thrills!
Blot that banner? Why, they bore it
    When no sunset bathed the hills.
Now over Bunker see it billow,
    Now at Bennington it waves,
Ticonderoga swells beneath,
    And Saratoga's graves!

Oh! long-ago at Lexington,
    And above those minute-men,
The "Old Thirteen" were blazing bright—
    There were only thirteen then!
God's own stars are gleaming through it—
    Stars not woven in its thread;
Unfurl it, and that flag will glitter
    With the heaven overhead.

Oh! it waved above the Pilgrims,
    On the pinions of the prayer;
Oh! it billowed o'er the battle,
    On the surges of the air;
Oh! the stars have risen in it,
    Till the eagle waits the sun,
And Freedom from her mountain watch
    Has counted "thirty-one."

When the weary Years are halting,
    In the mighty march of Time,

And no new ones throng the threshold
  Of its corridors sublime;
When the clarion call, "Close up!"
  Rings along the line no more,
Then adieu, thou blessed banner,
  Then adieu, and not before!

General Lyon.

The funeral honors that have attended General Lyon from the battle-field where he fell, across one half of a continent, taken up from state to state, from city to city, from village to village, and carried forward for near two thousand miles amid the tearful eyes, the bowed heads, and the deepest expressions of personal sorrow of hundreds of thousands of grateful people—such honors never before, perhaps, paid to so young a general—came to their solemn conclusion yesterday in this city. *Dulce et decorum est pro patria mori*, said the Latin poet a great many hundred years ago; and surely, though the sentiment be old and the line as trite as household words, not less true is it now than when Rome sent out her armies to conquer the world, that it is sweet and beautiful to die for one's country. This young soldier, like more than one other, has laid down his life in this war, and has, by his courage, his devotion, and his patriotism, done his country a service by his example, to be preserved ever fresh and green with his memory, that is not often vouchsafed to the wisest and the best of men to do in centuries of time. Not without reason are such noble lives laid upon the altar! We garner up the remembrance of them—how this one saved a state, how that a city, and we crown ourselves with the names of heroes! Not in vain have these young men fallen; for other young men shall reverently lift the crown and remember that such a death as theirs is *dulce et decorum*, if their country needs more lives!

And let us not forget this price which this war has already cost us. The precious blood that has been shed let us weigh, drop by drop, as precious as our private honor and our public name. The cost is not too much for the country's salvation; priceless as it is, it is given freely to purchase the God-given rights of a free people. But the least drop of it all should never have reddened the ground if the sword is sheathed till treason is driven howling from the land, and that peace shall come that shall bid all future generations bless the memory of the men who died for liberty. When Lyon and others are laid with bloody wounds upon the bosom of their mother land, it should be as a pledge that she shall be redeemed from the stain of treason, and made free, and they therein avenged.

Burning of a Ship.—*J. Fenimore Cooper.*

The Skimmer paused, for at that moment a fierce light glared upon the ocean, the ship, and all in it. The two seamen gazed at each other in silence, and both recoiled, as men recede before an unexpected and fearful attack. But a bright and wavering light, which rose out of the forward hatch of the vessel, explained all. At the same moment, the deep stillness which, since the bustle of making sail had ceased, pervaded the ship, was broken by the appalling cry of "Fire!"

The alarm which brings the blood in the swiftest current to a seaman's heart, was now heard in the depths of the vessel. The smothered sounds below, the advancing uproar, and the rush on deck, with the awful summons in the open air, succeeded each other with the rapidity of lightning. A dozen voices repeated the words, "the grenade!" proclaiming in a breath both the danger and the cause. But an instant before, the swelling canvas, the dusky spars, and the faint lines of the cordage, were only to be traced by the glimmering light of the stars; and now the whole hamper of the ship was the more conspicuous, from the obscure background against which it was drawn in distinct lines. The sight was fearfully beautiful; beautiful, for it showed the symmetry and fine outlines of the vessel's rig, resembling the effect of a group of statuary seen by torch-light—and fearful, since the dark void beyond seemed to declare their isolated and helpless state.

There was one breathless, eloquent moment, in which all were seen gazing at the grand spectacle in mute awe, and then a voice rose, clear, distinct, and commanding, above the sullen sound of the torrent of fire, which was roaring among the avenues of the ship:

"Call all hands to extinguish fire! Gentlemen, to your stations. Be cool, men; and be silent!"

There was a calmness and an authority in the tones of the young commander, that curbed the impetuous feelings of the startled crew. Accustomed to obedience and trained to order, each man broke out of his trance, and eagerly commenced the discharge of his allotted duty. At that instant, an erect and unmoved form stood on the combings of the main hatch. A hand was raised in the air, and the call, which came from the deep chest, was like that of one used to speak in the tempest.

"Where are my brigantines?" it said—"Come away there, my sea-dogs; wet the light sails and follow!"

A group of grave and submissive mariners gathered about the "Skimmer of the Seas," at the sound of his voice. Glancing an eye over them, as if to scan their quality and number, he smiled, with a look in which high daring and practised self-command were blended with a constitutional *gaîté de cœur*.

"One deck, or two!"—he added; "what avails a plank, more or less, in an explosion?—Follow!"

The free-trader and his people disappeared in the interior of the ship. An interval of great and resolute exertion succeeded. Blankets, sails, and every thing which offered, and which promised to be of use, were wetted and cast upon the flames. The engine was brought to bear, and the ship was deluged with water. But the confined space, with the heat and smoke, rendered it impossible to penetrate to those parts of the vessel where the conflagration raged. The ardor of the men abated as hope lessened, and after half an hour of fruitless exertion, Ludlow saw, with pain, that his assistants began to yield to the inextinguishable principle of nature. The appearance of the Skimmer on deck, followed by all his people, destroyed hope, and every effort ceased as suddenly as it had commenced.

"Think of your wounded;" whispered the free-trader, with a steadiness no danger could disturb, "we stand on a raging volcano!"

"I have ordered the gunner to drown the magazine."

"He was too late. The hold of the ship is a fiery furnace. I heard him fall among the store-rooms, and it surpassed the power of man to give the wretch succor. The grenade has fallen near some combustibles, and, painful as it is to part with a ship so loved, Ludlow, thou wilt meet the loss like a man! Think of thy wounded; my boats are still hanging at the stern."

Ludlow reluctantly, but firmly, gave the order to bear the wounded to the boats. This was an arduous and delicate duty. The smallest boy in the ship knew the whole extent of the danger, and that a moment, by the explosion of the powder, might precipitate them all into eternity. The deck forward was getting too hot to be endured, and there were places even in which the beams had given symptoms of yielding.

But the poop, elevated still above the fire, offered a momentary refuge. Thither all retired, while the weak and wounded were lowered, with the caution circumstances would permit, into the whale-boats of the smugglers.

Ludlow stood at one ladder and the free-trader at the other, in order to be certain that none proved recreant in so trying a moment. Near them were Alida, Seadrift, and the Alderman, with the attendants of the former.

It seemed an age before this humane and tender duty was performed. At length the cry of "all in!" was uttered, in a manner to betray the extent of the self-command that had been necessary to effect it.

"Now, Alida, we may think of thee!" said Ludlow, turning to the spot occupied by the silent heiress.

"And you!" she said, hesitating to move.

"Duty demands that I should be the last——"

A sharp explosion beneath, and fragments of fire flying upward through a hatch, interrupted his words. Plunges into the sea, and a rush of the people to the boats, followed. All order and authority were completely lost, in the instinct of life. In vain did Ludlow call on his men to be cool, and to wait for those who were still above. His words were lost, in the uproar of clamorous voices. For a moment, it seemed, however, as if the Skimmer of the Seas would overcome the confusion. Throwing himself on a ladder, he glided into the bows of one of the boats, and, holding by the ropes with a vigorous arm, he resisted the efforts of all the oars and boat-hooks, while he denounced destruction on him who dared to quit the ship. Had not the two crews been mingled, the high authority and determined mien of the free-trader would have prevailed; but while some were disposed to obey, others raised the cry of "Throw the dealer in witchcraft into the sea!" Boat-hooks were already pointed at his breast, and the horrors of the fearful moment were about to be increased by the violence of a mutinous contention, when a second explosion nerved the arms of the rowers to madness. With a common and desperate effort, they overcame all resistance. Swinging off upon the ladder, the furious seaman saw the boat glide from his grasp, and depart. The execration that was uttered, beneath the stern of the Coquette, was deep and powerful; but, in another moment, the Skimmer stood on the poop, calm and undejected, in the centre of the deserted group.

"The explosion of a few of the officers' pistols has frightened the miscreants," he said, cheerfully; "but hope is not yet lost!—they linger in the distance and may return!"

The sight of the helpless party on the poop, and the consciousness of being less exposed themselves, had indeed arrested the progress of the fugitives. Still, selfishness predominated; and while most regretted their danger, none but the young and unheeded midshipmen, who were neither of an age nor of a rank to wield sufficient authority, proposed to return. There was little argument necessary to show that the perils increased at each moment; and, finding that no other expedient remained, the gallant youths encouraged the men to pull toward the land; intending themselves to return instantly to the assistance of their commander and his friends. The oars dashed into the water again, and the retiring boats were soon lost to view in the body of darkness.

While the fire had been raging within, another element without had aided to lessen hope for those who were abandoned. The wind from the land had continued to rise, and, during the time lost in useless exertion, the ship had been permitted to run nearly before it. When hope was gone the helm had been deserted, and, as all the lower sails had been hauled up to avoid the flames, the vessel had drifted, many minutes, nearly dead to leeward. The mistaken youths, who had not attended to these circumstances, were already miles from that beach they hoped to reach so soon; and ere the boats had separated from the ship five minutes, they were hopelessly asunder. Ludlow had early thought of the expedient of stranding the vessel, as the means of saving her people; but his better knowledge of their position, soon showed him the utter futility of the attempt.

Of the progress of the flames beneath, the mariners could only judge by circumstances. The Skimmer glanced his eye about him, on regaining the poop, and appeared to scan the amount and quality of the physical force that was still at their disposal. He saw that the Alderman, the faithful François, and two of his own seamen, with four of the petty officers of the ship, remained. The six latter, even in that moment of desperation, had calmly refused to desert their officers.

"The flames are in the state-rooms!" he whispered to Ludlow.

"Not further aft, I think, than the berths of the midshipmen—else we should hear more pistols."

"True—they are fearful signals to let us know the progress of the fire!—our resource is a raft."

Ludlow looked as if he despaired of the means; but, concealing the discouraging fear, he answered cheerfully in the affirmative. The orders were instantly given, and all on board gave themselves to the task, heart and hand. The danger was one that admitted of no ordinary or half-conceived expedients; but, in such an emergency, it required all the readiness of their art, and even the greatness of that conception which is the property of genius. All distinctions of rank and authority had ceased, except as deference was paid to natural qualities and the intelligence of experience. Under such circumstances, the "Skimmer of the Seas" took the lead; and though Ludlow caught his ideas with professional quickness, it was the mind of the free-trader that controlled, throughout, the succeeding exertions of that fearful night.

The cheek of Alida was blanched to a deadly paleness; but there rested about the bright and wild eyes of Seadrift, an expression of supernatural resolution.

When the crew abandoned the hope of extinguishing the flames, they had closed all the hatches, to retard the crisis as much as possible. Here and there, however, little torch-like lights were beginning to show themselves through the planks, and the whole deck, forward of the mainmast was already in a critical and sinking state. One or two of the beams had failed, but, as yet, the form of the construction was preserved. Still the seamen distrusted the treacherous footing, and, had the heat permitted the experiment, they would have shrunk from a risk which, at any unexpected moment, might commit them to the fiery furnace beneath.

The smoke ceased, and a clear, powerful light illuminated the ship to her trucks. In consequence of the care and exertions of her people, the sails and masts were yet untouched; and as the graceful canvas swelled with the breeze, it still urged the blazing hull through the water.

The forms of the Skimmer and his assistants were visible, in the midst of the gallant gear, perched on the giddy yards. Seen by that light, with his peculiar attire, his firm and certain step, and his resolute air, the free-trader resembled some fancied sea-god, who, secure in his immortal immunities, had come to act his part in that awful, but exciting trial of hardihood and skill. Seconded by the common men, he was employed in cutting the canvas from the yards. Sail after sail fell upon the deck, and, in an incredibly short space of time, the whole of the foremast was naked to its spars and rigging.

In the mean time, Ludlow, assisted by the Alderman and François, had not been idle below. Passing forward between the empty ridge-ropes, lanyard after lanyard parted under the blows of their little boarding-axes. The mast now depended on the strength of the wood and the support of a single back-stay.

"Lay down!" shouted Ludlow. "All is gone aft but this stay!"

The Skimmer leaped upon the firm rope, followed by all aloft, and, gliding downward, he was instantly in the hammock-cloths. A crash followed their descent, and an explosion, which caused the whole of the burning fabric to tremble to its centre, seemed to announce the end of all. Even the free-trader recoiled before the horrible din; but when he stood near Seadrift and the heiress again, there was cheerfulness in his tones, and a look of high and even of gay resolution in his firm countenance.

"The deck has failed forward," he said, "and our artillery is beginning to utter fearful signal guns! Be of cheer!—the magazine of a ship lies deep, and many sheathed bulkheads still protect us."

Another discharge from a heated gun, however, proclaimed the rapid progress of the flames. The fire broke out of the interior anew, and the foremast kindled.

"There must be an end of this!" said Alida, clasping her hands in a terror that could not be controlled. "Save yourselves, if possible, you who have strength and courage, and leave us to the mercy of Him whose eye is over all!"

"Go!" added Seadrift, whose sex could no longer be concealed. "Human courage can do no more: leave us to die!"

The looks that were returned to these sad requests were melancholy, but unmoved. The Skimmer caught a rope, and still holding it in his hand, he descended to the quarter-deck, on which he at first trusted his weight with jealous caution. Then looking up, he smiled encouragingly, and said—"Where a gun still stands, there is no danger for the weight of a man!"

"It is our only resource;" cried Ludlow, imitating his example. "On, my men, while the beams will still hold us."

In a moment all were on the quarter-deck, though the excessive heat rendered it impossible to remain stationary an instant. A gun on each side was run in, its tackles loosened, and its muzzle pointed toward the tottering, unsupported, but still upright foremast.

"Aim at the cleets!" said Ludlow to the Skimmer, who pointed one gun, while he did the same office at the other.

"Hold!" cried the latter. "Throw in shot—it is but the chance between a bursting gun and a lighted magazine!"

Additional balls were introduced into each piece, and then, with steady hands, the gallant mariners applied burning brands to the priming. The discharges were simultaneous, and, for an instant, volumes of smoke rolled along the deck and seemed to triumph over the conflagration. The rending of wood was audible. It was followed by a sweeping noise in the air, and the fall of the foremast, with all its burden of spars, into the sea. The motion of the ship was instantly arrested, and, as the heavy timbers were still attached to the bowsprit by the forward stays, her head came to the wind, when the remaining topsails flapped, shivered, and took aback.

The vessel was now, for the first time during the fire, stationary. The common mariners profited by the circumstance, and, darting past the mounting flame along the bulwarks, they gained the top-gallant-forecastle, which, though heated, was yet untouched. The Skimmer glanced an eye about him, and seizing Seadrift by the waist, as if the mimic seaman had been a child, he pushed forward between the ridge-ropes. Ludlow followed with Alida, and the others imitated their example in the best manner they could. All reached the head of the ship in safety, though Ludlow had been driven by the flames into the fore-channels, and thence nearly into the sea.

The petty officers were already on the floating spars, separating them from each other, cutting away the unnecessary weight of rigging, bringing the several parts of the wood in parallel lines, and lashing them anew. Ever and anon, these rapid movements were quickened by one of those fearful signals from the officers' berths, which, by announcing the progress of the flames beneath, betrayed their increasing proximity to the still slumbering volcano. The boats had been gone an hour, and yet it seemed to all in the ship but a minute. The conflagration had, for the last ten minutes, advanced with renewed fury; and the whole of the confined flame, which had been so long pent in the depths of the vessel, now glared high in the open air.

"This heat can no longer be borne," said Ludlow; "we must to our raft, for breath."

"To the raft, then!" returned the cheerful voice of the free-trader. "Haul in upon your fasts, men, and stand by to receive the precious freight."

The seamen obeyed. Alida and her companions were lowered safely to the place prepared for their reception. The foremast had gone over the side, with all its spars aloft; for preparation had been made, before the fire commenced, to carry sail to the utmost, in order to escape the enemy. The skilful and active seamen, directed and aided by Ludlow and the Skimmer, had made a simple, but happy disposition of those buoyant materials on which their all now depended. In settling in the water, the yards, still crossed, had happily fallen uppermost. The booms and all the light spars had been floated near the top, and laid across, reaching from the lower to the topsail-yard. A few light spars, stowed outboard, had been cut away and added to the number, and the whole were secured with the readiness and ingenuity of seamen. On the first alarm of fire, some of the crew had seized a few light articles that would float, and rushed to the head, as the place most remote from the magazine, in the blind hope of saving life by swimming. Most of these articles had been deserted, when the people were rallied to exertion by their officers. A couple of empty shot-boxes and a mess-chest were among them, and on the latter were seated the females, while the former served to keep their feet from the water. As the arrangement of the spars forced the principal mast entirely beneath the element, and the ship was so small as to need little artificial work in her masting, the part around the top, which contained the staging, was scarcely submerged. Although a ton in weight was added to the inherent gravity of the wood, still, as the latter was of the lightest description, and freed as much as possible from every thing that was unnecessary to the safety of those it supported, the spars floated sufficiently buoyant for the temporary security of the fugitives.

"Cut the fast!" said Ludlow, involuntarily starting at several explosions in the interior, which followed each other in quick succession, and which were succeeded by one which sent fragments of burning wood into the air. "Cut, and bear the raft off the ship!—God knows, we have need to be further asunder!"

"Cut not!" cried the half-frantic Seadrift—"My brave!—my devoted!——"

"Is safe;—" calmly said the Skimmer, appearing in the rattlings of the main-rigging, which was still untouched by the fire—"Cut off all! I stay to brace the mizen-topsail more firmly aback."

The duty was done, and for a moment the fine figure of the free-trader was seen standing on the edge of the burning ship, looking with regret at the glowing mass.

"'Tis the end of a lovely craft!" he said, loud enough

to be heard by those beneath. Then he appeared in the air, and sunk into the sea—"The last signal was from the ward-room," added the dauntless and dexterous mariner, as he rose from the water, and, shaking the brine from his head, he took his place on the stage—" Would to God the wind would blow, for we have need of greater distance!"

The precaution the free-trader had taken, in adjusting the sails, was not without its use. Motion the raft had none, but as the topsails of the Coquette were still aback, the flaming mass, no longer arrested by the clogs in the water, began slowly to separate from the floating spars, though the tottering and half-burnt masts threatened, at each moment, to fall.

Never did moments seem so long, as those which succeeded. Even the Skimmer and Ludlow watched in speechless interest, the tardy movements of the ship. By little and little, she receded; and, after ten minutes of intense expectation, the seamen, whose anxiety had increased as their exertions ended, began to breathe more freely. They were still fearfully near the dangerous fabric, but destruction from the explosion was no longer inevitable. The flames began to glide upward, and then the heavens appeared on fire, as one heated sail after another kindled and flared wildly in the breeze.

Still the stern of the vessel was entire. The body of the master was seated against the mizen-mast, and even the stern visage of the old seaman was distinctly visible, under the broad light of the conflagration. Ludlow gazed at it in melancholy, and for a time he ceased to think of his ship, while memory dwelt, in sadness, on those scenes of boyish happiness, and of professional pleasures, in which his ancient shipmate had so largely participated. The roar of a gun, whose stream of fire flashed nearly to their faces, and the sullen whistling of its shot, which crossed the raft, failed to awaken him from his trance.

"Stand firm to the mess-chest!" half-whispered the Skimmer, motioning to his companions to place themselves in attitudes to support the weaker of their party, while, with sedulous care, he braced his own athletic person in a manner to throw all of its weight and strength against the seat. "Stand firm, and be ready!"

Ludlow complied, though his eye scarce changed its direction. He saw the bright flame that was rising above the arm-chest, and he fancied that it came from the funeral pile of the young Dumont, whose fate, at that moment, he was almost disposed to envy. Then his look returned to the grim countenance of Trysail. At moments, it seemed as if the dead master spoke; and so strong did the illusion become, that our young sailor more than once bent forward to listen. While under this delusion, the body rose with the arms stretched upward. The air was filled with a sheet of streaming fire, while the ocean and the heavens glowed with one glare of intense and fiery red. Notwithstanding the precaution of the 'Skimmer of the Seas,' the chest was driven from its place, and those by whom it was held were nearly precipitated into the water. A deep, heavy detonation proceeded as it were from the bosom of the sea, which, while it wounded the ear less than the sharp explosion that had just before issued from the gun, was audible at the distant capes of the Delaware. The body of Trysail sailed upward for fifty fathoms, in the centre of a flood of flame, and, describing a short curve, it came toward the raft, and cut the water within reach of the captain's arm. A sullen plunge of a gun followed, and proclaimed the tremendous power of the explosion; while a ponderous yard fell athwart a part of the raft, sweeping away the four petty officers of Ludlow, as if they had been dust driving before a gale. To increase the wild and fearful grandeur of the dissolution of the royal cruiser, one of the cannon emitted its fiery contents while sailing in the void.

The burning spars, the falling fragments, the blazing and scattered canvas and cordage, the glowing shot, and all the torn particles of the ship, were seen descending. Then followed the gurgling of water, as the ocean swallowed all that remained of the cruiser which had so long been the pride of the American seas. The fiery glow disappeared, and a gloom like that which succeeds the glare of vivid lightning, fell on the scene.

Heroic Speech—1861.—*General B. F. Butler.*

Mr. Mayor and Fellow-Citizens: Your words of welcome are most dear. Home has brought to my mind all those associations of childhood, youth, and manhood that cluster around that sacred name, and in my absence I have known that here at least my motives would not be misunderstood, my acts if worthy would be appreciated, and my reward would be most dear. In the approbation of these my neighbors—if in any thing I have deserved well of my country or have been enabled to render a service to the glorious cause for which we all labor and to the Constitution which we all love—I have received more than my reward to-night. The approbation of my neighbors and townsmen is a fit reward for greater services than mine.

I have endeavored to do my duty, and with the noble Massachusetts soldiers who left this town with me, and so far as action and purpose are concerned, I think we can say you have nothing of which you need be ashamed. Lowell has sent out the best regiment that has left the Commonwealth, and therefore the first in the United

States. The first to be baptized in blood at Baltimore, and the first martyrs in this second revolution, which is greater than the first, was the Sixth—the Lowell regiment.

And when one day the Sixth marched into Baltimore again, about this time in the evening, with the rains of heaven falling upon us, and the lightning of heaven gleaming upon our guns, I saw a spectacle more splendid than I had ever before beheld, or than usually falls to the lot of man to witness—a spectacle of moral sublimity. Treason had done its work and driven the soldiers from the town, but another power had brought them back, and I claim for Massachusetts—for the Sixth —that no man shall say that the soldiers of Lowell are not to have the foremost honors of the war.

More than that, you sent after them other companies, and of one I have the right to speak a word, as it came under my own command. The "Richardson Guard" was better equipped and better cared for than any other company that had marched from Massachusetts or into Virginia, and I am glad to say here publicly that, at the request of the officers of the regular army at Fortress Monroe, that company was made a part of the regular garrison at the Fortress—a compliment that has been paid to no other company by the officers of the regular army. I say again that Lowell has reason to be proud of her soldiers; and have not her soldiers reason to be proud of Lowell?

You say well, sir, there are no parties. We have a country torn at the present hour by intestine war, and until that country is put in peace, in quiet, there must be no party and no thought of party. No compromise, no yielding, nothing but the strong arm, until the glorious flag of the Union floats over every inch of the territory which belongs to the United States of America.

For one, I trust that there may be no attempt at peace, and after remaining a few days here, I am ready to return to my duty, and never return to Lowell until the last time, or until the work is accomplished. We must have peace, but a peace in which the power of the government is acknowledged; it must be a peace which secures the constitutional rights of all men under the Federal government, and no other government. With my fellow-soldiers, whom I have left for the hour, there is no other feeling; and we have heard with pain and regret that there was any other feeling cherished even by a few. Why, sir, let us make a peace for the hour, and it would not be sixty days before we would be involved in war again, if the result of that peace was the separation of this Union into two confederacies. We must have the whole of this country under one government, or else no government at all. There is no middle ground. We must pour out blood and treasure—the first like water, the last like sand—until that is accomplished. If you have no country, what have you left? Nothing! We should be base to give up the rich inheritance bequeathed to us by our fathers, and leave to our children only a broken and ruined country.

Mr. Mayor, I have been led into a digression from the more appropriate duty of the moment, to return to you my sincere thanks for this too great honor. I receive it, not for myself, but for the brave troops under my command, and the gallant navy to whose exertions we are mainly to attribute the recent victory. I receive it for the gallant Commodore Stringham, and I would call your attention to the fact that he is a son of Massachusetts, that a majority of his fleet was fitted out in Massachusetts, so that it was on the whole pretty much a Massachusetts enterprise. When we are abroad we do not echo that prayer with which all our official documents are closed, "God save the Commonwealth of Massachusetts!" but say with fervor everywhere, "God bless the old Commonwealth!"

A War Poem—*George Croly.*

The Turkman lay beside the river;
The wind played loose through bow and quiver;
The charger on the bank fed free,
The shield hung glittering from the tree,
The trumpet, shawm and atabal
Were hid from dew by cloak and pall,
For long and weary was the way
The hordes had marched that burning day.

Above them, on the sky of June,
Broad as a buckler glowed the moon—
Flooding with glory, vale and hill.
In silver sprang the mountain rill,
The shrub in silver bent;
A pile of silver stood the tent;
All soundless, sweet tranquillity—
All beauty, hill, and tent, and tree.

There came a sound—'twas like the gush
When night winds shake the rose's bush!
There came a sound—'twas like the tread
Of wolves along the valley's bed!
There came a sound—'twas like the roar
Of ocean on its wintry shore.

"Death to the Turk!" up rose the yell—
On rolled the charge—a thunder peal?
The Tartar arrows fell like rain—
They clanked on helm, and mail, and chain—
In blood, in hate, in death, were twined
Savage and Greek—mad—bleeding—blind—
And still, on flank, and front, and rear,
Raged, Constantine! thy thirstiest spear!

Brassy and pale—a type of doom—
Labored the moon through deep'ning gloom!
Down plunged her orb—'twas pitchy night!
Now, Turkman, turn thy reins for flight!
On rushed their thousands through the dark!
But in the camp a ruddy spark

Like an uncertain meteor reeled—
Thy hand, brave king, *that* firebrand wheeled!

Wild burst the burning element,
O'er man and courser, flag and tent!
And, through the blaze the Greeks outsprang
Like tigers, bloody—foot and fang!—
With dagger's stab, and falchion's sweep,
Delving the stunned and staggering heap—
Till lay the slave, by chief and khan—
And all was gone that once was man.

A wailing on the Euxine shore—
Her chivalry shall ride no more!
There's wailing on thy hills, Altai!
For chiefs, the Grecian vulture's prey—
But, Bosphorus! thy silver wave
Hears shouts for the returning brave—
The highest of her kingly line—
For there comes glorious Constantine!

THE CONSTITUTION.—*Oliver Bunce.*

By those laws of movement and development, which appertain to all periods, to all men, and to all things, constitutions cannot remain through successive generations the same literal and rigid instruments. There is a necessary progress in intelligence, and an inevitable development of idea and necessity, with whose advancing parallels constitutions must keep pace, if they respond to the needs, represent the liberties, and express the spirit of a people. Around the written form of organic law, history, circumstances, new necessities, associations, precedents, will gather and knit themselves into the very body of the organic word. New ideas will spring up and cling to it. New constructions will arise, be discussed, and eventually become its standard of interpretation. New applications of its laws will occur; and around its simplest provisions will gather precedents and expositions which will give them, under new conditions, new meanings. Hence, in studying our own constitution, we must consider it not only as it was, but as it is. In an age so rapid, and with a people so active in absorbing new ideas and in advancing to new relations, the constitution has, of necessity, taken some color and some meaning from the events in our history. A union like our own cannot stand still, exactly poised between a nationality on one side and a diet of states on the other. It must necessarily move swiftly, where there is an earnest life in the community, either toward a more centralized and compact nationality, or toward a more segregated, divided, and conflicting federation. The march of events has determined which. The full sense and real meaning of the union and the constitution are not what our organic instrument then expressed, but what seventy years of history have made it. However poor or ineffectual may have been the union under the constitution in the beginning, however numerous may have been the checks and limitations proposed by states jealous of an untried and, as yet, unknown authority, the real strength, power, and attitude of the central government are now what events and necessities ordain. The union, indeed, never was a mere faggot of sticks loosely bound together, which any demagogue might untie, or any faction scatter. Or, if only a faggot of sticks, associations, identities of interests, intercommunication arising from commercial and social needs, friendships, family ties, literature, common founts of learning, a common history and common glories, have knit and bound and banded part to part, each putting forth growths that interweave and intertwine among the rest, until the faggot of sticks is so clasped and locked and intergrown together, no one can be wrested away that does not ruthlessly drag with it something rooted in each of the rest, destroying and undoing all. A nation is made not by conventions, but by the operation of principles. A common soil, language, religion, laws, literature, social customs, thoughts and aims, will make a nation without written constitutions; and written instruments that attempt to band together parts not thus naturally wedded, will inevitably fail. We are a nation by the operation of principles that underlie all written law; and we must advance year by year into a more firmly centralized, into a deeper and broader nationality by the vital growth and development of those principles, let the rigid and literal interpretations of any instrument point otherwise or not. But our constitution does not point otherwise. Its framers knew that we were a union already, that we were advancing into a nationality, and thus gave legal form to that which necessities and circumstances were already enacting. There are results that spring with unfailing sequence from antecedents, unshaped and unguided by the will or the conscious aid of men. There are laws operating at the very heart of our civilization which determine nationality, and mark the course of empire. Constitutions must become plastic to the march of events; and we shall not be required in the future of our government to bind ourselves to the rigid framework of a dead letter, which our needs and purposes have outgrown. We must guard, however, between a too rigid formalism on the one hand, and a too free interpretation on the other. The spirit of our constitution points to a nationality, aiming to unite all parts, to secure equality and liberty to all individuals, and to protect section against section. Let us strengthen that nationality by our habits of thought, by breadth of patriotism, by a suppression of local pride and sectional prejudices. Let us look at our banner, not to search out the star which represents the single state to which we belong, but to love and accept the entire galaxy. Let us have done with the narrow claim of state sovereignty, remembering that there is but one flag, which is for the whole; but one constitution which unites us, *e pluribus unum*, not one of many, but all in one; and let our pride, our hopes, our prayers, our sympathies and affections, as well as our ambitions and interests, make us a *nation*.

SANGUINARIA CANADENSIS.—*Joel Benton.*

I.

I KNOW the patch where the waxen milk-white blossoms grow,
   On a pea-green palmate leaf by the woody slope of the hill,
Close to the budding coppice, thick as an army of snow,
   And the May wind drifts their leaves in a heap by the silver rill.

II.

I plucked a flower from its stem, lustrous and fair to see,
   One that had loitered late with a splendor for me to behold;
Saxifrage, coltsfoot, trillium, rue and anemone,
   I bound in a quaint bouquet, with its central nimbus of gold.

III.

Lo, a color of red, of orange, a saffron stain
   Darkens my hand, and clings in a multiplied ragged scar!
"What if I had plucked the flower that was planted in pain,
   And bathed with scarlet blood my country in crimson war?"

IV.

I thought: "O parricide, traitor, perjurer, villain, knave,
   Prince of the rebels, striking at freedom's consummate flower;
You will carry a damning Macbeth stain to your grave
   That shall brighten the name of Arnold to history's latest hour."

EXTRACT FROM A SPEECH ON THE EXTENSION OF SLAVERY.— *William Henry Fry.*

Rome never attained to the solid power assumed for her. She was rotten to the core at the time of Marius and Scylla, and declined thereafter. She lived more and more on the labor of slaves. The food of her people became worse and worse. The standard of wages steadily declined. The quality of agriculture, under slave-labor, regularly withered up as Cincinnati ceased to guide their ploughs. Ancient authors precisely represent the starvation of the slaves. Nero, who, just previous to his death, escaped from Rome and fled ten miles into the country, suffered desperate hunger before he could touch the black bread, the ordinary food of the slaves upon a so-considered magnificent patrician estate. The rabble of Rome were fed on corn gained by annexations in Sicily, Egypt, and the Archipelago. Some two hundred thousand ruffians of this kind, gloating over death-struggles of gladiators in the huge murderings of the Coliseum—in ecstasies as the tragedies in that execrable arena grew thicker, with the map of hell on their faces, as they draggled in filth, gore, and beastliness, at the heels of some patrician annexationist, rich with the plunder of foreign nations—these were fed out of the public purse, the pillaged granaries and general agonies of whole peoples. . . . Leaving aside the ordinary fables of divine origin, which are common to all nations, we find Rome, at the earliest dates, a nation divided into patricians and plebeians, both of the same color, and capable of equal effort in arts and arms, yet the one born to command and the other to obey. This fact, to any mind not necessarily stolid or vicious, would alone shut out all these references to Rome. But there are others which are equally pregnant with meaning to the classical student. Around and about Rome were nations

enjoying what is even now considered no small degree of civilization. Among these stood Etruria, whence Rome derived her softening arts, whose origin is lost in the mazes of antiquity, but whose skill in the pursuits of the beautiful has come down to us in forms which live even in our own day, and are household words. The Pontine Marshes and the circumjacent country, now dealing death in every breeze, were at the time of early Roman history, occupied by forty towns and cities, flourishing and wealthy, according to the standards of those days. The conquest of these places by the Romans, and the centralizing ferocities of Marius and Scylla, and the whole imperial line, blotted them out from the face of the earth, and a materialized jeremiad, a very stench of desolation, only remains to mark where once they stood. . . .
The growth of Rome, which began by the assassination of every country near it, was continued by the same means. Eternally at war, eternally menacing the rest of the world, it was but one great camp. De Lolme characterizes Roman patriotism as the spirit of oppression and murder. Soon a Cincinnatus ceased to own a few acres, and, the fight ended, to return to the plough. The great patrician, with sometimes four hundred slaves under his domestic roof; these four hundred, all white men above caricature in color, form, or brain, were crucified at one time for the single so-called crime of one of them. Such were the inevitable results of the Roman policy.

Revolutionary Story.—*Alice Cary.*

"Good mother, what quaint legend are you reading,
　In that old-fashioned book?
Beside your door I've been this half hour pleading
　All vainly for one look.

"About your chair the little birds fly bolder
    Than in the woods they fly,
With heads dropt slantwise, as if o'er your shoulder
    They read as they went by;

"Each with his glossy collar ruffling double
    Around his neck so slim,
Even as with that atmosphere of trouble,
    Through which our blessings swim.

"Is it that years throw on us chillier shadows,
    The longer time they run,
That, with your sad face fronting yonder meadows,
    You creep into the sun?

"I'll sit upon the ground and hear your story."
    Sadly she shook her head,
And pushing back the thin white veil of glory
    'Twixt her and heaven, she said:

"Ah! wondering child, I know not of your pleading—
    My thoughts were chained, indeed,
Upon my book, and yet what you call reading
    I have no skill to read.

"There was a time once when I had a lover;
    Why look you in such doubt?
True, I am old now—ninety years and over"—
    A crumpled flower fell out

From 'twixt the book-leaves. "Seventy years they've pressed it:
    'Twas like a living flame,
When he that plucked it, by the plucking blessed it."
    I knew the smile that came,

And flickered on her lips in wannish splendor,
    Was lighted at that flower,
For even yet its radiance, faint and tender,
    Reached to its primal hour.

"God bless you! seventy years since it was gathered?"
    "Aye, I remember well;"
And in her old hand, palsy-struck, and withered,
    She held it up to smell.

"And is it true, as poets say, good mother,
    That love can never die?
And that for all it gives unto another
    It grows the richer?" "Aye,

"The homely brier from spring till summer closes,
    All the great world around,
Hangs by its thorny arms to keep its roses
    From off the low, black ground;

"And love is like it—sufferings but try it,
    Death but evokes the might
That, all too mighty to be thwarted by it,
    Breaks through into the light."

"Then frosty age may wrap about its bosom
    The light of fires long dead?"
Kissing the piece of dust she called a blossom,
    She shut the book, and said:

"You see yon ash-tree with its thick leaves, blowing
    The blue side out? (Great Power,
Keep its head green!) My sweetheart, in the mowing,
    Beneath it found my flower.

"A mile off all that day the shots were flying,
    And mothers, from the door,
Looked for the sons, who, on their faces lying,
    Would come home never more.

Across the battle-field the dogs went whining;
    I saw, from where I stood,
Horses with quivering flanks, and strained eyes, shining
    Like thin skins full of blood.

"Brave fellows we had then: there was my neighbor—
    The British lines he saw;
Took his old scythe and ground it to a sabre,
    And mowed them down like straw!

"And there were women then, of giant spirit—
    Nay, though the blushes start,
The garments their degenerate race inherit,
    Hang loose about the heart.

"Where was I, child? how is my story going?"
"Why, where by yonder tree
With leaves so rough, your sweetheart, in the mowing,
    Gathered your flower!" "Ah me!

"My poor lad dreamed not of the red-coat devil
    That just for pastime drew
To his bright epaulet, his musket level,
    And shot him through and through.

"Beside him I was kneeling the next minute—
    From the red grass he took
The shattered hand up, and the flower was in it
    You saw within my book.

"He died." "Then you have seen some stormy weather?"
    "Aye, more of foul than fair;
And all the snows we should have shared together,
    Have fallen on my hair."

"And has your life been worth the living, mother,
    With all its sorrows?" "Aye,
I'd live it o'er again, were there no other,
    For this one memory."

I answered soft—I felt the place was holy—
    One maxim stands approved :
"They know the best of life, however lowly,
    Who ever have been loved."

Voice of the Northern Women.—*Phebe Cary.*

Rouse, freemen, the foemen has risen,
    His hosts are abroad on the plain;
And, under the stars of your banner,
    Swear never to strike it again!

O, fathers, who sit with your children,
    Would you leave them a land that is free?—
Turn now from their tender caresses,
    And put them away from your knee.

O, brothers we played with in childhood
On the hills where the clover bloomed sweet,
See to it, that never a traitor
Shall trample them under his feet.

O, lovers, awake to your duty
From visions that fancy has nursed;
Look not in the eyes that would keep you,
Our country has need of you first.

And we, whom your lives have made blessed,
Will pray for your souls in the fight;
That you may be strong to do battle,
For freedom, for God, and the right.

We are daughters of men who were heroes,
We can smile as we bid you depart;
But never a coward or traitor
Shall have room for a place in our heart.

Then quit you like men, in the conflict,
Who fight for their home and their land;
Smite deep in the name of Jehovah,
And conquer, or die where you stand!

INJUSTICE OF SECESSION.—*President Lincoln.*

WHATEVER concerns the whole should be confined to the whole general government, while whatever concerns only the state should be left exclusively to the state.

This is all there is of original principle about it. Whether the national constitution, in defining boundaries between the two, has applied the principle with exact accuracy, is not to be questioned. We are all bound, by that defining without question. What is now combated is the position that secession is consistent with the constitution—is lawful, is peaceful. It is not contended that there is any express law for it, and nothing should ever be implied as law which leads to unjust or absurd consequences. The nation purchased with money the countries of which several of these states were formed. Is it just they should go off without leave and without refunding? The nation paid very large sums, in the aggregate—I believe nearly a hundred millions—to relieve Florida of the aboriginal tribes. Is it just that she should be off without any return? The nation is now in debt for money applied to the benefit of these so-called seceding states, in common with the rest. Is it just either that creditors shall go unpaid, or the remaining states pay the whole? A part of the present national debt was contracted to pay the old debts of Texas. Is it just that she shall leave and pay no part of this herself? Again, if one state may secede so may another; and when all shall have seceded, none is left to pay the debts. Is this quite just to creditors? Did we notify them of this sage view of ours when we borrowed their money? If we now recognize this doctrine by allowing the seceders to go in peace, it is difficult to see what we can do if others choose to go or to extort terms upon which they will promise to remain.

The seceders insist that our constitution admits of secession. They have assumed to make a national constitution of their own, in which, of necessity, they have either discarded or retained the right of secession, as they insist it exists in ours. If they have discarded it, they thereby admit that, on principle, it ought not to exist in ours; if they have retained it, by their own construction of ours, that shows that, to be consistent, they must secede from one another whenever they shall find it the easiest way of settling their debts, or effecting any other selfish or unjust object.

The principle itself is one of disintegration, and upon which no government can possibly endure.

L'ENVOI.

A Psalm of the Union.* — *William Ross Wallace.*

DEDICATED TO THE HON. HIRAM BARNEY.

I.

God of the Free! upon Thy breath
Our flag is for the Right unrolled
Still broad and brave, as when its stars
    First crowned the hallowed days of old:
For Honor still their folds shall fly,
For Duty still their glories burn,
Where Truth, Religion, Freedom, guard
    The patriot's sword and martyr's urn:

CHORUS—*Then shout beside thine Oak, O North!*
    O South, wave answer with thy Palm!
    And, in our Union's heritage,
    Together lift the Nation's psalm!

II.

How glorious is our mission here!
Heirs of a virgin world are we;
The chartered lords whose lightnings tame
    The rocky mount and roaring sea:
We march—and Nature's giants own
    The fetters of our mighty cars:
We look—and lo, a continent
    Is crouched beneath the Stripes and Stars!

CHORUS—*Then shout beside thine Oak, O North!*
    O South, wave answer with thy Palm!
    And, in our Union's heritage,
    Together lift the Nation's psalm!

* Air—Old Hundred.

III.

No tyrant's impious step is ours;
  No lust of power on nations rolled;
Our Flag—for friends a starry sky,
  For foes, a tempest every fold!
Oh thus we'll keep our Nation's life,
  Nor fear the bolt by despots hurled:
The blood of all the world is here,
  And they who strike us, strike the world!

Chorus—*Then shout beside thine Oak, O North?*
  O South, wave answer with thy Palm!
  And, in our Union's heritage,
  Together lift the Nation's psalm!

IV.

God of the Free! our Nation bless
  In its strong manhood as its birth,
And make its life a star of hope
  For all the struggling of the earth.
Thou gav'st the glorious Past to us;
  Oh let our Present burn as bright,
And o'er the mighty Future cast
  Truth's, Honor's, Freedom's holy light!

Chorus—*Then shout beside thine Oak, O North!*
  O South, wave answer with thy Palm!
  And, in our Union's heritage,
  Together lift the Nation's psalm!

www.ingramcontent.com/pod-product-compliance
Lightning Source LLC
Chambersburg PA
CBHW032144230426
43672CB00011B/2441